The Politics and Anti-Politics of Social Movements

This book explores the nature, significance and consequences of the religious activism surrounding AIDS in Africa. While African religion was relatively marginal in inspiring or contributing to AIDS activism during the early days of the epidemic, this situation has changed dramatically. In order to account for these changes, contributors provide answers to pressing questions. How does the entrance of religion into public debates about AIDS affect policymaking and implementation, church-state relations, and religion itself? How do religious actors draw on and reconfigure forms of transnational connectivity? How do resource flows from development and humanitarian aid that religious actors may access then affect relationships of power and authority in African societies? How does religious mobilization on AIDS reflect contestation over identity, cultural membership, theology, political participation, and citizenship? Addressing these questions, the authors draw on social movement theories to explore the role of religious identities, action frames, political opportunity structures, and resource mobilization in African religions' reactions to the AIDS epidemic. The book's findings are rooted in fieldwork conducted in Tanzania, Uganda, Zambia, Zimbabwe, Ghana, and Mozambique, among a variety of religious organizations.

This book was originally published as a special issue of the *Canadian Journal of African Studies*.

Marian Burchardt is a Sociologist at the Max Planck Institute for the Study of Religious and Ethnic Diversity, Göttingen, Germany. His research explores regimes of religious diversity, secularism, and the politics of urban space. He has published in the *Journal of Religion in Africa*, *Sociology of Religion*, *Comparative Sociology*, and *Oxford Development Studies*.

Amy S. Patterson is Professor of Politics at the University of the South, Sewanee, Tennessee, USA. Her research interests include religion and health in Africa. She has published *The Politics of AIDS in Africa* (2006) and *The Church and AIDS in Africa* (2010), as well as articles in *Africa Today*, *Contemporary Politics*, and the *Journal of Modern African Studies*.

Louise Mubanda Rasmussen is Assistant Professor in the Department of Society and Globalisation at Roskilde University, Denmark. Her research explores the anthropology of development in areas such as AIDS, religion, NGO practice, and celebrity intervention. She has published in *Culture, Health & Sexuality*, *Journal of Progressive Human Services*, and the *Canadian Journal of African Studies*.

The Politics and Anti-Politics of Social Movements

Religion and AIDS in Africa

Edited by

Marian Burchardt, Amy S. Patterson and Louise Mubanda Rasmussen

Routledge
Taylor & Francis Group

LONDON AND NEW YORK

First published 2016
by Routledge
2 Park Square, Milton Park, Abingdon, Oxon, OX14 4RN, UK

and by Routledge
711 Third Avenue, New York, NY 10017, USA

First issued in paperback 2017

Routledge is an imprint of the Taylor & Francis Group, an informa business

British Library Cataloguing in Publication Data
A catalogue record for this book is available from the British Library

ISBN 13: 978-1-138-23737-7 (pbk)
ISBN 13: 978-1-138-93905-9 (hbk)

Typeset in Times
by RefineCatch Limited, Bungay, Suffolk

Publisher's Note
The publisher accepts responsibility for any inconsistencies that may have
arisen during the conversion of this book from journal articles to book chapters,
namely the possible inclusion of journal terminology.

Disclaimer
Every effort has been made to contact copyright holders for their permission to
reprint material in this book. The publishers would be grateful to hear from any
copyright holder who is not here acknowledged and will undertake to rectify
any errors or omissions in future editions of this book.

Contents

Citation Information

The chapters in this book were originally published in the *Canadian Journal of African Studies*, volume 47, issue 2 (August 2013). When citing this material, please use the original page numbering for each article, as follows:

Chapter 1
The politics and anti-politics of social movements: religion and HIV/AIDS in Africa
Marian Burchardt, Amy S. Patterson and Louise Mubanda Rasmussen
Canadian Journal of African Studies, volume 47, issue 2 (August 2013) pp. 171–185

Chapter 2
Can charity and rights-based movements be allies in the fight against HIV/AIDS? Bridging mobilisations in the United States and sub-Saharan Africa
Patricia Siplon
Canadian Journal of African Studies, volume 47, issue 2 (August 2013) pp. 187–205

Chapter 3
Pastors as leaders in Africa's religious AIDS mobilisation: cases from Ghana and Zambia
Amy S. Patterson
Canadian Journal of African Studies, volume 47, issue 2 (August 2013) pp. 207–226

Chapter 4
"To donors, it's a program, but to us it's a ministry": the effects of donor funding on a community-based Catholic HIV/AIDS initiative in Kampala
Louise Mubanda Rasmussen
Canadian Journal of African Studies, volume 47, issue 2 (August 2013) pp. 227–247

Chapter 5
HIV/AIDS activism, framing and identity formation in Mozambique's Equipas de Vida
Rebecca J. Vander Meulen, Amy S. Patterson and Marian Burchardt
Canadian Journal of African Studies, volume 47, issue 2 (August 2013) pp. 249–272

Chapter 6
The abstinence campaign and the construction of the Balokole identity in the Ugandan Pentecostal movement
Alessandro Gusman
Canadian Journal of African Studies, volume 47, issue 2 (August 2013) pp. 273–292

Chapter 7

Yao migrant communities, identity construction and social mobilisation against HIV and AIDS through circumcision schools in Zimbabwe
Anusa Daimon
Canadian Journal of African Studies, volume 47, issue 2 (August 2013) pp. 293–307

For any permission-related enquiries please visit:
http://www.tandfonline.com/page/help/permissions

Notes on Contributors

Marian Burchardt is a Sociologist at the Max Planck Institute for the Study of Religious and Ethnic Diversity, Göttingen, Germany. His research explores regimes of religious diversity, secularism, and the politics of urban space. He has published in the *Journal of Religion in Africa*, *Sociology of Religion*, *Comparative Sociology*, and *Oxford Development Studies*.

Anusa Daimon is a graduate student in the Centre for Africa Studies at the University of the Free State, Bloemfontein, South Africa. His research interests include migration and religion in Africa. He has published in *Africa Insight*, *South African Historical Journal*, and the *Canadian Journal of African Studies*.

Alessandro Gusman is a Postdoctoral Researcher in the Dipartimento di Culture, Politica e Società at the University of Turin, Italy.

Louise Mubanda Rasmussen is Assistant Professor in the Department of Society and Globalisation at Roskilde University, Denmark. Her research explores the anthropology of development in areas such as AIDS, religion, NGO practice, and celebrity intervention. She has published in *Culture, Health & Sexuality*, *Journal of Progressive Human Services*, and the *Canadian Journal of African Studies*.

Amy S. Patterson is Professor of Politics at the University of the South, Sewanee, Tennessee, USA. Her research interests include religion and health in Africa. She has published *The Politics of AIDS in Africa* (2006) and *The Church and AIDS in Africa* (2010), as well as articles in *Africa Today*, *Contemporary Politics*, and the *Journal of Modern African Studies*.

Patricia Siplon is Professor of Political Science at Saint Michael's College, Colchester, Vermont, USA. Her research is based around HIV/AIDS, particularly in East Africa. She is involved with two national AIDS advocacy organizations: Health Gap, based in New York City; and Global Justice, based in Washington, DC.

Rebecca J. Vander Meulen works with the Community Development Department of the Anglican Diocese of Niassa in Mozambique.

The politics and anti-politics of social movements: religion and HIV/AIDS in Africa

Marian Burchardt[a], Amy S. Patterson[b] and Louise Mubanda Rasmussen[c]

[a]Max Planck Institute for the Study of Ethnic and Religious Diversity, Göttingen, Germany; [b]Department of Politics, University of the South, Sewanee, Tennessee, US; [c]Department of Society and Globalisation, Roskilde University, Denmark

Résumé

En 2012, environ vingt-trois millions de personnes en Afrique subsaharienne avaient contracté le VIH, le virus qui cause le sida. Les réponses religieuses à la maladie sont allées de la condamnation des personnes séropositives à la mise au point de services innovants liés au sida. Cet article se sert des idées figurant dans les écrits du mouvement social concernant l'identité collective, l'élaboration de cadres, les ressources et les structures d'opportunités pour interroger la mobilisation religieuse en vue de lutter contre le VIH/le sida. Il démontre que la mobilisation ne peut pas être séparée de facteurs comme les relations entre l'État et la société civile, la dépendance de l'Afrique envers l'aide étrangère, ou la pauvreté qui règne dans le continent. Les activités religieuses de lutte contre le VIH/le sida doivent être analysées dans un espace conceptuel situé entre une approche société civile/politique et un cadre prestataire de services/anti-politique. Autrement dit, la mobilisation religieuse peut parfois chercher à mobiliser le domaine public pour façonner la politique, tout en évitant, à d'autres moments, la politique dans la prestation de services. Des études de cas qui illustrent ces thèmes et mettent en évidence les interactions aux multiples facettes entre la religion et le VIH/le sida sont inclues.

Abstract

In 2012, roughly 23 million people in sub-Saharan Africa were infected with HIV, the virus that causes AIDS. Religious responses to the disease have ranged from condemnation of people with HIV to the development of innovative AIDS-related services. This article utilises insights from the social movement literature about collective identity, framing, resources, and opportunity structures to interrogate religious mobilisation against HIV/AIDS. It demonstrates that mobilisation cannot be divorced from factors such as state–civil society relations, Africa's dependence on foreign aid, or the continent's poverty. Religious HIV/AIDS activities must be analysed in a conceptual space between a civil society/politics approach and a service-provider/anti-politics framework. That is, religious mobilisation may at times seek to engage the public realm to shape policies, while at other times it may shun politics in its provision of services. Case studies that illustrate these themes and demonstrate the multi-faceted interactions between religion and HIV/AIDS are included.

I. Introduction

In 2012, the Joint United Nations Programme on HIV/AIDS (UNAIDS) declared that an estimated 23 million people in sub-Saharan Africa were infected with HIV, the virus that causes AIDS. Two thirds of the people living with HIV globally reside in sub-Saharan

Africa (UNAIDS 2012). The negative effects of the disease on individuals, families, and communities have been well documented (see Barnett and Whiteside 2002). The HIV/ AIDS pandemic is occurring in a context where the vast majority of Africans claim a religious identity, with Islam and Christianity growing rapidly in their number of adherents. Religious individuals and institutions have been crucial in the response to HIV/ AIDS (see Paterson 2001). Yet these responses have not been analysed as a form of social activism. This special issue provides such an analysis. We argue that religious mobilisation occurs in a dynamic space between the realms of explicit political action and depoliticised service delivery.

Based on a workshop we convened on the theme of "Religion, Social Activism, and AIDS" in the Ugandan capital Kampala in 2010, the special issue examines the interface between religious and social movements, using HIV/AIDS as its focal point.[1] Because scholars have tended to view the social movement literature as too rooted in Western experiences or too focused on material resources to apply to the continent, little has been written on social movements in Africa (Ellis and van Kessel 2009). In contrast, this volume demonstrates how social movement concepts provide unique insights into the HIV/AIDS responses of African religious actors and institutions, while situating those activities in Africa's specific political environment. The six articles in this special issue address these themes from a variety of social science perspectives – including political science, anthropology, history, and sociology – and they cover the countries of Tanzania, Mozambique, Ghana, Zambia, Uganda, and Zimbabwe. Additionally, the contributions analyse religious mobilisation by Catholics, mainline Protestants, Pentecostals, and Muslims. This special issue contributes both to our understanding of how social movements operate in Africa and, more specifically, to our analysis of religious responses to HIV/AIDS.

In this introductory article, we first acknowledge the importance of the African political and economic context for understanding the particular manifestations of religious mobilisation on HIV/AIDS. We assert that religious mobilisation on HIV/AIDS cannot be divorced from factors such as state–civil society relations, Africa's dependence on foreign aid, or the continent's poverty. We then outline the ways in which religious responses to HIV/AIDS have been analysed in the social science literature. In so doing, we assert that religious HIV/AIDS activities must be analysed in a conceptual space between a civil society/politics approach and a service-provider/anti-politics framework. Next we examine the ways in which social movement concepts such as identity, framing, resource mobilisation, and opportunity structures elucidate patterns of religious mobilisation in the special issue's case studies. Because we see this special issue as a way to break new ground in the analysis of both African social movements and religious responses to HIV/ AIDS, the final section raises questions for future research.

II.   The African context and social movements

The volume's contributors situate their analyses of religious mobilisation on HIV/AIDS in the context of debates on the nature of the African state and civil society, the intersection of religion and politics, and Africa's place in the global political economy. These debates have tended to downplay (and at times, ignore) the role of social movements in political and social change in Africa. But at the same time, these debates provide important insights about the larger environments in which mobilisation may occur on the continent.

The social science literature has tended to portray African states as neo-patrimonial. In neo-patrimonial states, governance occurs through personalised networks. Reciprocal relations between clients and followers enable clients to access state power, and elites utilise state resources for patronage in order to benefit themselves and their allies. Because politics is not rooted in ideological views or party loyalties, neo-patrimonial alliances can be somewhat fluid (van de Walle 2001). Chabal and Daloz explain:

> The development of political machines and the consolidation of clientelistic networks within the formal political apparatus has been immensely advantageous. It has allowed [political elites] to respond to demands for protection, assistance and aid made by the members of their constituency communities in exchange for the recognition of the political prominence and social status which, as patrons, they crave. (Chabal and Daloz 1999, 14)

The result of these governance patterns is that African states lack the capacity to achieve their developmental goals (Englebert 2000). Corruption, state inefficiency, and mismanagement contribute to Africa's position as the poorest continent on earth. Infrastructure is in disrepair; health systems lack adequate staff, facilities, and medications; and educational institutions are inadequate for the growing number of children in Africa. At the same time, widespread poverty helps to erode state legitimacy, and as citizens have limited loyalty to the state, they tend to evade its policies (Bates 2008). In this context, ethnic groups, clans, and religious factions may manipulate the state for their own objectives (Chabal and Daloz 1999). Thus, while African states have international sovereignty and the legal right to formulate laws, they lack deep roots in society (Englebert 2009).

Weakness leads many states to centralise power, even if those states have aspects of democratic governance. Through the use of repression, cooptation, and patronage, the state limits the space for civil society activity. Classically defined, civil society is the collection of organisations that are autonomous from the state but above the family level (Rothchild and Chazan 1988). In Africa, this conceptualisation is somewhat artificial. Rather than autonomy, civil society groups may cultivate personal linkages to the state, thus hampering their ability to challenge state power. And civil society's effectiveness may be further challenged by its lack of resources and capacity. Rather than being bastions of democracy, civil society organisations may replicate patterns of exclusive, authoritarian governance found in state institutions (Fatton 1995).

The state–civil society nexus is situated in a larger international context in which African political and social actors both influence and are influenced by global resources, norms, and institutions. The continent's reliance on foreign aid is particularly evident in the large amount of donor funding specifically for the HIV/AIDS response. Bilateral and multilateral donors provide at least 80% of the funds for HIV/AIDS prevention, treatment and care programmes in the majority of African countries (UNAIDS 2008). Much of this funding goes to non-governmental organisations (NGOs), faith-based organisations (FBOs), and community-based organisations (CBOs). Rooted in the belief that neo-liberal economic structures and private organisations could best promote Africa's development, this pattern of channelling money to non-state actors has had several unanticipated consequences, many of which are made apparent in the special issue's case studies. First, African civil society groups may become dependent on international donors or transnational NGOs. This reliance influences their accountability and responsiveness to local populations. Second, this massive infusion of donor funds has contributed to the rise of "suitcase NGOs", or local groups without indigenous constituencies that form merely to access funding. In a process that Bayart (1993) terms extraversion, African state and non-state actors stress their poverty, desperation, and deservingness in order to access donor money. In so doing, they rely on well-worn tropes about Africa: its poverty, victimhood, and dependence on the West. As these non-state actors become empowered through external resources, a third consequence may arise: they may directly or indirectly challenge the state and its legitimacy (Rothchild and Chazan 1988; Patterson 2011). NGOs and FBOs may become a substitute for state power, and they may replicate the patterns of neo-patrimonialism, exclusion, and power centralisation evident in the African state (Hearn 2001).

Global norms and institutions are also part of the context in which religious mobilisation on HIV/AIDS occurs. The biomedical approach to HIV/AIDS that focuses on HIV testing, AIDS education, condom distribution, and access to antiretroviral treatment (ART) has overshadowed other approaches such as healing through spiritual means, building communities of care and support, fostering gender equality, and changing social structures. The biomedical approach has become institutionalised in agencies such as UNAIDS, the World Health Organization, and the US Agency for International Development (Youde 2007). As the article by Anusa Daimon illustrates, the biomedical approach may have unanticipated consequences for religious mobilisation. He shows how the scientific finding that male circumcision reduces the rate of HIV infection, and the international health community's acceptance of that finding, created a new opportunity for religious and ethnic mobilisation against HIV/AIDS in Zimbabwe.

As a crucial aspect of the African environment, religion interfaces with both state power and global forces. The articles in the special issue examine religion both as a set of beliefs that influence practices (see the contribution by Alessandro Gusman) and as an institutional structure (see the article by Rebecca Vander Meulen, Amy Patterson, and Marian Burchardt). Religious institutions are some of the most powerful, well-funded organisations within African civil society. Deep belief in spiritual power throughout Africa and the view that religious leaders act as mediators between the physical and spiritual realms mean that African religious leaders tend to have high levels of moral legitimacy (Ellis and Haar 1998). But the relation between religion and the state is not clear cut; religious leaders use their moral authority and voice to shape political processes, while the state may seek to appropriate religious rhetoric, symbols, and spaces for its own ends (Villalón 1995). Networks of state patronage may prevent religious institutions from speaking out against political and social injustices (Longman 2010). On the other hand, transnational linkages may embolden religious actors to become more autonomous from the state (Newell 1995). The fluidity in state–religious relations provides opportunities for religious mobilisation on HIV/AIDS.

Religious HIV/AIDS mobilisation has also benefited from the growth in donor funding for FBOs and the increasingly institutionalised voice these religious actors have in HIV/AIDS policymaking. The passage of the US President's Emergency Plan for AIDS Relief (PEPFAR) in 2003 opened up greater opportunities for FBOs to access funding. Oomman, Bernstein, and Rosenzweig (2008) report that between 2004 and 2006, FBOs in all 15 PEPFAR-focus countries received roughly 10% of all PEPFAR money. This number hides the fact that in several African countries (particularly Kenya and Namibia) the percentage of that country's PEPFAR money which went to FBOs was at least 25%. While many of these FBO recipients were United States (US)-based (e.g., World Vision, Catholic Relief Services), some were major health associations in Africa (e.g., the Churches Health Association of Zambia). Religious institutions also gained representation on AIDS policymaking boards, such as National AIDS Councils. UNAIDS has held special conferences on the important role of FBOs, giving them increased legitimacy in the politics of AIDS.

Religious responses to the pandemic are situated within this context of patronage politics, weak state institutions, and the diffusion of global norms, institutions, and funding for HIV/AIDS. At the local level, civil society groups like religious organisations may be weak, under-resourced, and only somewhat autonomous from either the state or their international benefactors. However, the literature on the African state, civil society, and religion in politics are insufficient for understanding religious responses to HIV/AIDS in Africa. A statist perspective assumes state capture to be the objective of political actors, but religious groups often shun overt political activities. The civil society approach downplays the role of belief and identity in organisational formation and activities. And the literature on the intersection of religion and politics, while stressing belief, ignores questions of institutional dynamics and resources. While these literatures help to explain the context in which religious mobilisation on HIV/AIDS occurs, the social movement literature helps us examine the motivations for activities, the structures whereby such movements emerge and continue, and the ways in which the international arena shapes local-level activities. We now examine the literature on religion and HIV/AIDS in Africa, pointing to ways that our approach sheds new light on this growing field of research.

III. Religious involvement with HIV/AIDS in Africa

Since the onset of the AIDS epidemic in Africa, religion has in various ways been central to the attempts of individuals and groups to make sense of and respond to the disease (Mogensen 1997; Yamba 1997; Dilger 2001; Heald 2002; Becker and Geissler 2007; Burchardt 2011). In many instances, formal religious institutions were initially reluctant to address HIV/AIDS. But since the start of the new millennium, institutional engagement has become prominent throughout Africa (Prince, Denis, and van Dijk 2009). Likewise, academic attention to the relationship between religion and HIV/AIDS was initially limited. But in the last decade, a field of study around HIV/AIDS and religion in Africa has gradually emerged (Dilger, Burchardt, and van Dijk 2010). These studies have generally moved away from the instrumental approach to religion found in the public health and policy literature (which focuses on whether religion is useful or detrimental to the goals of HIV prevention) towards an emphasis on "the way people rely on shared religious practice and personal faith in order to conceptualise, explain and thereby act upon the epidemic" (Becker and Geissler 2007, 2). The first studies in this field tended to emphasise how religion was harnessed to respond to the crises of health, morality, sexuality, and gender relations that HIV/AIDS had engendered (see Smith 2004; Becker 2007; Behrend 2007; Dilger 2007; Prince 2007; Burchardt 2010). More recent studies have focused on the large-scale introduction of ART in Africa since 2004, highlighting the complicated interplay between religious and biomedical practices that characterise this new situation (Burchardt 2009; Kwansa 2010; Tocco 2010; Togarasei 2010; Rasmussen 2011).

Following the work of Prince, Denis, and van Dijk (2009), we can group these studies of religious involvement with HIV/AIDS into three main categories. One area of study concerns the role of religion in how people deal with illness and death, treatment and care for the sick, and the questions around morality, sexuality, and kinship that the epidemic engenders. A second area of study concerns how the epidemic has transformed religious practices and theologies in Africa. A third area concerns the place of religion in the public sphere, both in relation to civil society and government and in the realm of development and public health. Until now, most studies have primarily been situated in the first area, with some theological works in the second (see Dube 2002; Haddad 2005; Togarasei 2010). While a few recent contributions have focused on the third area of study (see Joshua 2010; Leusenkamp 2010; Patterson 2010), this special issue will bring this area of study to the forefront through its emphasis on how religious actors have mobilised around HIV/

AIDS. We bring a new angle to these debates by using the social movement literature to emphasise the multifarious nature of religious engagements with HIV/AIDS in the public realm. We situate this religious mobilisation in a conceptual space between two theoretical poles: the politics of AIDS and the anti-politics of AIDS.

The politics of AIDS perspective focuses on the ways in which religious groups operate as civil society actors engaged in a political struggle over how to address this public health crisis. This view directs our attention to how religious actors mobilise in order to interact with, seek influence on, or challenge the HIV/AIDS policies of states and powerful international health institutions. It helps us to pay attention to how HIV/AIDS is politicised in the national arena and how religious groups attempt to influence the fight against HIV/AIDS. It elucidates how religious groups frame and address the disease through both formal political bodies and other forms of collective action, and through the creation of particular collective identities in the public sphere. This religious activism can also be analysed in the context of transnational advocacy networks that help local groups project and amplify concerns suppressed in the national arena into an international arena (Keck and Sikkink 1998). However, the contributions in this special issue do not view these transnational linkages to be a central phenomenon when it comes to religious actors. In fact, Patricia Siplon's article outlines some of the obstacles that religious actors may face in becoming part of transnational advocacy networks around HIV/AIDS.

The anti-politics perspective highlights the role of religious institutions in what Ferguson (1994) terms the anti-politics machine of development. Ferguson argues that development discourse depoliticises poverty by turning the issue into a technical matter of development assistance. With regards to HIV/AIDS, problems of unequal gender relations, orphan care, and limited access to health care have become technical matters of development and public health projects. In contrast to Ferguson's original analysis, in recent decades, the depoliticising effects of development have not been coupled with an expansion of bureaucratic state power, but rather with an expansion of "transnational governmentality" networks (Ferguson and Gupta 2002). The considerable HIV/AIDS funding that Africa has received has been channelled to non-state actors, in effect placing much of the service delivery in the hands of transnational networks of private voluntary organisations rather than the African state (Ferguson 2006). Local NGOs become drawn into these anti-politics webs of development as they implement the programmes of Western donors. This view challenges a simplistic understanding of social movements as mobilising the grass roots against a more powerful state.

The anti-politics perspective helps us to pay attention to the conditions under which social movements in Africa operate. In particular, it cautions us that local groups are not necessarily autonomous entities that represent the needs of local people and that the involvement of religious groups in development efforts may help to maintain the status quo, rather than to challenge state power (Hearn 2001; Kelsall and Mercer 2003). As Dilger (2010) illustrated in his presentation at our workshop on religion and AIDS activism, the anti-politics view makes us sensitive to the kinds of collective action that are possible in national and transnational political spaces that are shaped by neo-patrimonialism, semi-authoritarian regimes, weak states, and transnational governmen-tality networks.

The process of extraversion provides an example of how anti-political and political forces may be connected. Through extraversion religious leaders may gain political and social power by successfully playing the game of depoliticised development, as illustrated in Patterson's contribution in this special issue (see also Englund 2003; Burchardt 2013). Vander Meulen and colleagues also highlight the fact that it is not only religious leaders but also rank-and-file members of religious groups who may use the opportunities provided by transnational governmentality networks to pursue their own social agendas of everyday survival or upward social mobility. We now turn to the ways in which the social movement literature helps us to better analyse the multiple and often contradictory ways in which religious actors engage in collective HIV/AIDS activities in the space between the politics and anti-politics of AIDS.

IV. Moving religion

From the start of the pandemic, social movements have been part of the very broad spectrum of social actors that emerged in response to HIV/AIDS in Africa. Activist networks, often consisting of globally interconnected advocacy groups, engaged in variegated campaigns that aimed to mobilise material resources for prevention, support for HIV-positive people, and medical treatment. These networks often took the shape of NGOs aimed at bringing together wide-ranging constituencies with a view towards wielding greater representation in policymaking. They urged African states to recognise the severity of HIV/AIDS as a political problem, and they attempted to hold governments accountable. In this context, the most visible forms of activism were probably those that mobilised around access to ART, which many African governments – in ironic agreement with some Western public health sceptics – initially saw as a solution unfeasible for African contexts.

Social science research that employed social movement concepts was largely limited to treatment campaigns and to investigations of the South African Treatment Action Campaign (TAC). Most studies focused on the multiple entanglements of local NGOs, African states and governments, and their external counterparts (such as Western governments, multilateral organisations, or private philanthropic initiatives). Such a focus is justified because these entanglements, and the ways they play out on transnational, national, and local levels, are crucial for understanding HIV/AIDS responses. But this focus also conceals wide-ranging forms of collective action, without which many AIDS responses (such as social support networks or local AIDS councils) would be impossible. Therefore, our understanding of the production of AIDS institutions remains incomplete without analysing how social movements have contributed to building these institutions.

The limitations of existing research are also a consequence of the narrow focus of social-movement scholars on forms of progressive activism such as mobilisation around human rights, gender equality, environmental protection, or democracy. What remains out of sight is that in Africa these agendas are often pursued in religious arenas. Moreover, religious innovation quite often emerges through religious movements, which need to be addressed in terms of social-movement research even if their goals and agendas do not conform to modernist or progressive ideas (see Ellis and van Kessel 2009). Against this backdrop, this special issue explores how social movement theory illuminates the dynamic aspects of religious mobilisation around HIV/AIDS and the production and ongoing transformation of AIDS institutions in Africa.

We consider these conceptual perspectives to be organised along two analytical axes. The first concerns the mobilisation of resources that collective actors need to achieve their goals (Edwards and McCarthy 2004), and the ways in which mobilisation processes are set within specific political opportunity structures that open and circumscribe spaces for contestation, claims-making, and success (Tarrow 1989). The second axis relates to people's motivations for engagement in collective action. Here, we posit that collective action is both premised on and creates collective identities (Melucci 1996); these identities are closely aligned with shared interpretations of the social world and the problems that need to be tackled through collective action. In other words, shared frames largely enable social movements because they provide a common perception of a series of events or specific social developments (Snow et al. 1986).

Resources, especially the lack thereof, are one of the key factors associated with the lack of progress and failure to combat the pandemic in Africa. In this regard, one can look at the analytical purchase of the resource mobilisation perspective from a dual angle. On the one hand, social movements engaging with HIV/AIDS need to mobilise resources to successfully organise and carry out their struggles. On the other hand, these very campaigns may also be directed at forcing African states and Western donors to provide more resources to the fight against HIV/AIDS. Edwards and McCarthy note that:

> The assumption that resource availability enhances the likelihood of collective action is generally taken for granted by contemporary analysts of social movements. Human time and effort along with money are the most widely appreciated kinds of resources that are more or less available to collective actors. But the simple availability of resources is not sufficient; coordination and strategic effort is typically required in order to convert available pools of individually held resources into collective resources and to utilise those resources in collective action. (Edwards and McCarthy 2004, 116)

As the articles by Vander Meulen and colleagues, Louise Rasmussen, and Patterson show, resources and their coordination can take a variety of forms and functions. Because many Africans lack sufficient material resources to meet their daily needs, time, labour, and collective solidarity are among the most important resources local populations supply in mobilisation. These are usually pooled and organised through voluntary engagement, as Vander Meulen and colleagues' account of the Anglican Church *Equipas da vida* in Mozambique illustrates. While researchers have often pointed to the crucial role of volunteerism in initiating and sustaining HIV/AIDS projects, the contradictions entailed in volunteerism have sometimes escaped their attention. Time for volunteering can be limited in rural areas, particularly during the harvest season, and people's need to pursue erratic income-generating opportunities may curtail their ability to regularly volunteer. This inconsistency can negatively affect the work of activist groups. Because HIV-positive volunteers often initiate and sustain many collective activities, these volunteers' changing health conditions can contribute to the unstable nature of collective action on HIV/AIDS. Beyond these practical problems, volunteering itself may be contested if participants feel that resources, which may possibly accrue from their engagement, should be redistributed on a personalised basis, for example through payments for their labour.

There is a need to analytically distinguish between indigenous and external resources and to question the different ways in which the interplay between the two affects forms of and motivations for participation, organisational dynamics, and the outcomes of collective mobilisation. Indigenous resources are crucial for developing support networks and solving practical problems related to HIV/AIDS, but their effects may remain limited unless indigenous efforts lead to broad-based consensus about fundamental injustices in society (for the case of TAC, see Friedman and Mottiar [2006]). In many cases, collective action involves claims to resources on states and international actors using discourses of either rights or needs and deservingness, and religious groups are found to employ both strategies.

During the last twenty years, Christian initiatives and FBOs have been particularly active and successful in lobbying for AIDS resources. One of their major moral resources has been their extremely wide reach and the fact that they felt entitled to represent huge numbers of people. As a consequence of Christian activism, a large amount of resources have been channelled through FBOs, churches, Christian health facilities, and communities in Africa to carry out biomedical HIV/AIDS interventions. These external resources illustrate the success of past mobilisation, but they also enable religious groups to further engage in future activism.

As argued above, access to donor resources may have multiple and contradictory effects. Funding agencies may require religious groups to organise HIV/AIDS-related practices according to an NGO model of public action with administrative rules of accountability and transparency. As Rasmussen demonstrates in her analysis of a Catholic FBO based in Kampala, complying with these rules allowed this Christian community to access funds in order to provide efficient services to many HIV-positive people, but also led to the bureaucratisation of the charismatic and spiritual sources that had fuelled initial engagement. As with many other social movements across the world, mobilisation can result in a process of professionalisation, which for some threatens to dry out the spiritual and religious terrain on which participation has flourished.

Resource mobilisation strategies both shape and are shaped by transnational configurations of power, technology, and values – what may be termed political opportunity structures. They are also structured by the national and local landscape of political opportunities and the aforementioned neo-patrimonial forms of governance in African society. Chabal and Daloz (1999, 29) explain: "Whether rooted in primordial or clientelistic ties, social relations are inevitably based on personalized bonds of mutually beneficial reciprocity". It is these ties of reciprocity that condition religious mobilisation on HIV/AIDS. Burchardt (2013) argues that what social movement research calls resource mobilisation must be conceptualised in terms of patronage. This perspective allows us to see that activism often entails skilful performances of need and deservingness that are projected onto donor audiences, and that the resources accruing from such strategies and performances often work to nurture networks of patronage. Within these neo-patrimonial networks, individual leaders act as brokers and intermediaries in extended patron–client chains, offering target groups and aid recipients in exchange for material resources, which they administer with a view towards structuring power relationships within these chains. Simultaneously, these target groups double as activist groups that mobilise both in the interest of HIV-positive people and in the name of human rights and shared religious sentiments.

Political opportunities for successful HIV/AIDS mobilisation also depend on African governments' willingness to prioritise the epidemic on national policy agendas. This prioritisation may be associated with prevalence rates and the ways in which HIV/AIDS statistics circulate in political discourses. This "politics of numbers" may generate political legitimacy for action or inaction, a point that Patterson's comparative analysis on church activism on AIDS in Ghana and Zambia elucidates. In addition, these dynamics heighten the crucial ways that leadership can shape political opportunities. Importantly, Patterson also notes that demobilisation occurs if leadership is not continuously refreshed and reinvigorated. In contrast, Dilger (2010) argues that a lack of leadership among Tanzania's religious groups was reflected in the absence of common goals on the basis of which government might have been challenged. He also argues that the civil society response in Tanzania has been determined by a high degree of extraversion, and that activists' engagements were constrained by the mutual dependence between NGO workers and clients.

The complexities of religious leadership as a resource were also revealed in a roundtable discussion that involved Ugandan religious leaders that we organised as a part of the workshop in Kampala. Religious leaders were outspoken about the political limitations of their HIV/AIDS activities. They emphasised the need to keep good working relationships with political elites and to operate within a pragmatic political calculus in which each step requires a careful weighing of costs, possible outcomes, and religious ethics. In light of research findings, the discussion also revealed that religious leaders' discourses and ideas about the status quo depend on the audiences into which the meaning of religious leadership on HIV/AIDS is projected and the diverging expectations confronting these leaders. The panel illustrated how religious leaders are both constrained and motivated by the political opportunity structures they encounter.

In their critical reassessment of the political opportunity structures perspective, Armstrong and Bernstein (2008) contend that the approach is based too strongly on the idea of contestation around the state as a singular source of power, and they suggest a multi-institutional politics approach instead. We claim that because social and religious mobilisation around HIV/AIDS in Africa involves a variety of transnational actors, religious communities in Western countries, and states and national governments, it offers important evidence that such a multi-institutional approach is needed.

While theories addressing the role of resource mobilisation and political opportunity structures help to explain African religious mobilisation on HIV/AIDS, they sometimes fall short of speaking to the cultural and cognitive dimensions of social movements. Focusing on structural shifts, these approaches inevitably struggle with questions of why specific groups of actors define certain areas of social life to be problematic, how shared interpretations of events emerge through negotiations, and how these interpretations and the collective strategies they enable are both based on and generate collective identities. To address these limitations, we turn to our second axis of investigation: collective identities and framing (Snow et al. 1986; Melucci 1996). Polletta and Jasper raise crucial questions about collective identities and mobilisation:

> To what extent are collective identities constructed in and through protest rather than preceding it? Is the identity a group projects publicly the same one that its members experience? Are collective identities imposed on groups or invented by them? Do individuals choose collective identities to maximise their self-interest or do interests flow from identities? How is collective identity different from ideology? From interest? From solidarity? (Polletta and Jasper 2001, 285)

Gusman, Daimon, Patterson and Rasmussen grapple with these questions as they investigate the ways in which religious communities are able to mobilise discourses of compassion and shared humanity to motivate people to participate. However, collective action frames and collective identities are also highly relevant in that they allow for the demarcating of religious and cultural boundaries in Africa's shifting landscape of religious diversity. In this context of diversity, shared religious identities produce shared understandings of HIV/AIDS and of the position of one's religious community within the complex moral territories of blame and stigma or respectability and moral selfhood associated with the disease.

In his analysis of born-again Christian identities and the sexual abstinence campaign in Uganda, Gusman shows that the relationship between HIV/AIDS campaigns and the collective identities of religious movements is reciprocal. In the mid-1980s, the presence of AIDS fostered the development of a collective born-again identity among Pentecostals. In turn, Pentecostals came to wield a great deal of power in framing the country's HIV/AIDS discourse in the new millennium. Similarly, in his presentation at the Uganda workshop, van Dijk (2010) noted the curious simultaneity of the emergence in Malawi of Pentecostal activism and AIDS. He demonstrated that the fashioning of the Pentecostal collective identity served as the cultural platform from which young Pentecostal preachers began to challenge existing notions of gerontocratic authority. Through their forms of preaching they increasingly claimed authority for themselves based on the notion of "having matured in the faith".

The collective identities approach and framing theory are conceptually linked in that they both question the very concepts of interests and actors that other theories take for granted. Both are constructivist in orientation and take a rigorous interest in processes of communication and the resulting discourses and structures of meaning in the public sphere. While identity theory focuses more on what these aspects tell us about agency, framing theory is more concerned with perception and meaning. Snow et al. (1986, 464) claim that "by rendering events or occurrences meaningful, frames function to organize experience and guide action, whether individual or collective. So conceptualized, it follows that frame alignment is a necessary condition for movement participation, whatever its nature or intensity."

The contributions of Daimon and Siplon are most explicitly inspired by the framing concept. In her comparison of AIDS activism in the US and Tanzania, Siplon explains the power of global "master frames" of AIDS mobilisation, namely rights-based and charity-based approaches (see Snow and Benford 1992). As she argues, the charity-based approach that many faith-based groups espouse is rooted in the idea of a hierarchy of deservedness, a concept which suggests that certain groups are more deserving of aid than others because of their innocence, vulnerability, or motivations. Rights-based approaches, by contrast, reject such ideas and claim a universality of deservedness. However, she also shows how "frame extension", through a focus on uncontroversial issues of access to facilities that promote basic human needs, can help to bridge these divides. In his account of Malawian Muslim communities in Zimbabwe, Daimon demonstrates how biomedical findings regarding the beneficial impact of male circumcision for HIV prevention have affected collective identities in these communities. While previously understood primarily in primordial terms, the inherited practice of male circumcision has been reframed in a way that highlights precisely these health-related aspects and their importance for constructing a new identity around being a "modern" Malawian Muslim in Zimbabwe.

V.   Open questions

This special issue engages the theme of religious mobilisation on HIV/AIDS from multiple perspectives, situating religious activities in the space between overt political activities and anti-political development efforts. To do this, the contributors capitalise on the insights of the social movement literature, such as its emphasis on resources, political opportunities, identities, and framing, in order to better assess religious responses to the disease. In the process, though, these articles do not ignore the larger African political and economic context – an arena in which patronage politics, poverty, and international donors and funding are prominent.

Because we view this special issue as a first step in the further exploration of the intersections between social movements, religion, and HIV/AIDS in Africa, we conclude the introduction with questions for future inquiry. The first relates to the emergence of new religious movements in response to disease. Historians such as Ranger (1996) have shown that throughout the twentieth century epidemics often went hand in hand with the emergence of new religious, particularly prophetic, movements. The attraction of these movements seemed to lie in specific forms of representing hardship, misfortune, blame, and redemption. The dramatic rise of neo-Pentecostalism in Africa over the last twenty years raises the question of how (or if) such processes of religious change are related to the

AIDS pandemic. While it is too early to answer such a question, we can say that HIV/AIDS has had discernible effects on religious landscapes and that the Pentecostal belief in spiritual salvation and its emphasis on moralism are closely linked to anxieties around HIV/AIDS. Additionally, the rise of Pentecostalism is set within a context where the idiom of witchcraft first helped African inhabitants make sense of HIV infection (Mogensen 1997; Yamba 1997; Ashforth 2010). In societies greatly affected by HIV/AIDS, what is the relationship between the Pentecostal promise of spiritual protection and increased accusations of witchcraft? In terms of broader societal responses to the disease, how might the answer to this question inform opportunities for inter-religious collaboration, and particularly work with African Traditional Religious leaders, to address HIV/AIDS?

A second arena of research arises from the Gusman contribution to this special issue. He points out that through their mobilising strategies, Pentecostal leaders also have excluded and demobilised others. He demonstrates the ways that an emphasis on sexual morality among some Pentecostals excluded some HIV-positive Ugandans from the religious community, including fellow Pentecostals. The engagement of some religious actors may be particularistic. If religious mobilisation on HIV/AIDS excludes religious minorities or downplays the rights of women or other marginalised groups, how does this affect its contribution to the public good of fighting HIV/AIDS? Future research should examine the conditions under which mobilisation may be exclusive or inclusive or may negatively or positively affect Africa's broader development and democratisation processes.

Finally, as Siplon's article illustrates, the engagement of African religious actors in the global AIDS advocacy network can be somewhat problematic. Yet, at times religious actors have participated in this movement, particularly on the issue of universal access to antiretroviral treatment. How might the social movement literature help us better understand such dynamics? What types of new religious or secular identities or national and global political opportunity structures might create patterns of collaboration? Part of the challenge in answering these questions is methodological: disentangling the causal relations within transnational networks requires multi-levelled analysis. Yet, the long-term ability of religious and non-religious actors to sustain mobilisation to address the scourge of HIV/AIDS in Africa necessitates such methodological creativity and greater research into these questions.

Note

1. The workshop was funded by the Calvin Center for Christian Scholarship at Calvin College in Grand Rapids, Michigan. It was supported by the International Research Network on AIDS and Religion in Africa and hosted by the Working Group on the Social and Political Aspects of AIDS in Uganda, Child Health and Development Centre, Makerere University, Kampala.

Bibliography

Armstrong, Elizabeth A., and Mary Bernstein. 2008. "Culture, Power, and Institutions: A Multi-institutional Politics Approach to Social Movements." *Sociological Theory* 26 (1): 74–99.
Ashforth, Adam. 2010. "Spiritual Insecurity and AIDS in South Africa." In *Morality, Hope and Grief. Anthropologies of AIDS in Africa*, edited by Hansjörg Dilger and Ute Luig, 43–60. Oxford: Berghahn Books.
Barnett, Tony, and Alan Whiteside. 2002. *AIDS in the Twenty-first Century: Disease and Globalisation*. New York: Palgrave MacMillan.
Bates, Robert. 2008. *When Things Fell Apart: State Failure in Late-century Africa*. New York: Cambridge University Press.

Bayart, Jean-François. 1993. *The State in Africa: The Politics of the Belly*. London: Longman.

Becker, Felicitas. 2007. "The Virus and the Scriptures: Muslims and AIDS in Tanzania." *Journal of Religion in Africa* 37 (1): 16–40.

Becker, Felicitas, and P. Wenzel Geissler. 2007. "Introduction: Searching for Pathways in a Landscape of Death: Religion and AIDS in East Africa." *Journal of Religion in Africa* 37 (1): 1–15.

Behrend, Heike. 2007. "The Rise of Occult Powers, AIDS and the Roman Catholic Church in Western Uganda." *Journal of Religion in Africa* 37 (1): 41–58.

Burchardt, Marian. 2009. "Subjects of Counselling: HIV/AIDS, Religion and the Management of Everyday Life in South Africa." In *AIDS and Religious Practice in Africa*, edited by P. Wenzel Geissler and Felicitas Becker, 335–358. Leiden: Brill.

Burchardt, Marian. 2010. "Ironies of Subordination: Ambivalences of Gender in Religious AIDS Interventions in South Africa." *Oxford Development Studies* 38 (1): 63–82.

Burchardt, Marian. 2011. "Missionaries and Social Workers: Visions of Sexuality in Religious Discourse." In *Religion and Social Problems*, edited by Titus Hjelm, 142–156. London: Routledge.

Burchardt, Marian. 2013. "Faith-based Humanitarianism: Organizational Change and Everyday Meanings in South Africa." *Sociology of Religion* 74 (1): 30–55.

Chabal, Patrick, and Jean Paul Daloz. 1999. *Africa Works: Disorder as Political Instrument*. Bloomington: Indiana University Press.

Dilger, Hansjörg. 2001. "'Living PositHIVely in Tanzania'- The Global Dynamics of AIDS and the Meaning of Religion for International and Local AIDS Work." *Afrika Spectrum* 36: 73–90.

Dilger, Hansjörg. 2007. "Healing the Wounds of Modernity: Salvation, Community and Care in a Neo-Pentecostal Church in Dar es Salaam, Tanzania." *Journal of Religion in Africa* 37 (1): 59–83.

Dilger, Hansjörg. 2010. "Heavenly Action: Religion, Class and the 'Failures' of AIDS Activism in Urban Tanzania." Paper presented at the workshop 'AIDS, Religion and Social Activism in Africa,' Kampala, Uganda, July 5–9.

Dilger, Hansjörg, Marian Burchardt, and Rijk van Dijk. 2010. "Introduction—The Redemptive Moment: HIV Treatments and the Production of New Religious Spaces." *African Journal of AIDS Research* 9 (4): 373–383.

Dube, Musa. 2002. "Fighting with God: Children and HIV/AIDS in Botswana." *Journal of Theology for Southern Africa* 114: 31–42.

Edwards, Bob, and John D. McCarthy. 2004. "Resources and Social Movement Mobilization." In *The Blackwell Companion to Social Movements*, edited by David A. Snow, Sarah A. Soule and Hanspeter Kriesi, 116–151. Malden, MA: Blackwell Publishing.

Ellis, Stephen, and Gerrie ter Haar. 1998. "Religion and Politics in Sub-Saharan Africa." *The Journal of Modern African Studies* 36 (2): 175–201.

Ellis, Stephen, and Ineke van Kessel, eds. 2009. *Movers and Shakers. Social Movements in Africa*. Leiden: Brill.

Englebert, Pierre. 2000. *State Legitimacy and Development in Africa*. Boulder, CO: Lynne Rienner Publishers.

Englebert, Pierre. 2009. *Africa: Unity, Sovereignty and Sorrow*. Boulder, CO: Lynne Rienner Publishers.

Englund, Harri. 2003. "Christian Independency and Global Membership: Pentecostal Extraversions in Malawi." *Journal of Religion in Africa* 33 (1): 83–111.

Fatton, Robert. 1995. "Africa in the Age of Democratization: The Civic Limitations of Civil Society." *African Studies Review* 38 (2): 67–110.

Ferguson, James. 1994 [1990]. *The Anti-politics Machine: 'Development,' Depoliticization, and Bureaucratic Power in Lesotho*. Minneapolis: University of Minnesota Press.

Ferguson, James. 2006. *Global Shadows - Africa in the Neoliberal World Order*. Durham, NC: Duke University Press.

Ferguson, James, and Akhil Gupta. 2002. "Spatializing States: Toward an Ethnography of Neoliberal Governmentality." *American Ethnologist* 29 (4): 981–1002.

Friedman, Steven, and Shauna Mottiar. 2006. "Seeking the High Ground: The Treatment Action Campaign and the Politics of Morality." In *Voices of Protest. Social Movements in Post-Apartheid South Africa*, edited by Richard Ballard, Adam Habib and Imraan Valodia, 23–44. Scottsville: University of KwaZulu Natal Press.

Haddad, Beverely. 2005. "Reflections on the Church and HIV/AIDS: South Africa." *Theology Today* 62 (1): 29–37.

Heald, Suzette. 2002. "It's Never as Easy as ABC: Understandings of AIDS in Botswana." *African Journal of AIDS Research* 1 (1): 1–10.

Hearn, Julie. 2001. "The 'Uses and Abuses' of Civil Society in Africa." *Review of African Political Economy* 28 (87): 43–53.

Joshua, Stephen Muoki. 2010. "A Critical Historical Analysis of the South African Catholic Church's HIV/AIDS Response between 2000 and 2005." *African Journal of AIDS Research* 9 (4): 437–447.

Keck, Margaret, and Kathryn Sikkink. 1998. *Activists Beyond Borders: Advocacy Networks in International Politics*. Ithaca, NY: Cornell University Press.

Kelsall, Tim, and Claire Mercer. 2003. "Empowering People? World Vision & 'Transformatory Development' in Tanzania." *Review of African Political Economy* 30 (96): 293–304.

Kwansa, Benjamin Kobina. 2010. "Complex Negotiations: 'Spiritual' Therapy and Living with HIV in Ghana." *African Journal of AIDS Research* 9 (4): 449–458.

Leusenkamp, Alexander M. J. 2010. "Religion, Authority and Their Interplay in the Shaping of Antiretroviral treatment in Western Uganda." *African Journal of AIDS Research* 9 (4): 419–427.

Longman, Timothy. 2010. *Christianity and Genocide in Rwanda*. New York: Cambridge University Press.

Melucci, Alberto. 1996. *Challenging Codes. Collective Action in the Information Age*. Cambridge: Cambridge University Press.

Mogensen, Hanne Overgaard. 1997. "The Narrative of AIDS among the Tonga of Zambia." *Social Science & Medicine* 44 (4): 431–439.

Newell, Jonathan. 1995. "'A Moment of Truth'? The Church and Political Change in Malawi, 1992." *The Journal of Modern African Studies* 33 (2): 243–262.

Oomman, Nandini, Michael Bernstein, and Steven Rosenzweig. 2008. "The Numbers Behind the Stories." Report for Center for Global Development. Accessed October 9, 2011. http://www.cgdev.org/files/15799_file_theNumbersBehindTheStories.PDF

Paterson, Gillian. 2001. *AIDS and African Churches: Exploring the Challenges*. London: Christian Aid.

Patterson, Amy S. 2010. "Church Mobilisation and HIV/AIDS Treatment in Ghana and Zambia: A Comparative Analysis." *African Journal of AIDS Research* 9 (4): 407–418.

Patterson, Amy S. 2011. *The Church and AIDS in Africa: The Politics of Ambiguity*. Boulder, CO: First Forum Press.

Polletta, Francesca, and James M. Jasper. 2001. "Collective Identity and Social Movements." *Annual Review of Sociology* 27 (1): 283–305.

Prince, Ruth. 2007. "Salvation and Tradition: Configurations of Faith in a Time of Death." *Journal of Religion in Africa* 37 (1): 84–115.

Prince, Ruth, Philippe Denis, and Rijk van Dijk. 2009. "Introduction to Special Issue: Engaging Christianities: Negotiating HIV/AIDS, Health, and Social Relations in East and Southern Africa." *Africa Today* 56 (1): v–xviii.

Ranger, Terence. 1996. "Plagues of Beasts and Men: Prophetic Responses to Epidemic in Eastern and Southern Africa." In *Epidemics and Ideas: Essays on the Historical Perception of Pestilence*, edited by Terence Ranger and Paul Slack, 241–268. New York: Cambridge University Press.

Rasmussen, Louise Mubanda. 2011. "From Dying with Dignity to Living with Rules: AIDS Treatment and 'Holistic Care' in Catholic Organisations in Uganda." PhD thesis, Centre of African Studies, University of Copenhagen.

Rothchild, Donald, and Naomi Chazan, eds. 1988. *The Precarious Balance: State and Society in Africa*. Boulder, CO: Westview Press.

Smith, D. J. 2004. "Youth, Sin and Sex in Nigeria: Christianity and HIV/AIDS-related Beliefs and Behaviour among Rural–Urban Migrants." *Culture, Health and Sexuality* 6 (5): 425–437.

Snow, David A., and Robert D. Benford. 1992. "Master Frames and Cycles of Protest." In *Frontiers in Social Movement Theory*, edited by Aldon D. Morris and Carol McClurg Mueller, 133–155. New Haven, CT: Yale University Press.

Snow, David A., E. Burke Rochford Jr, Steven K. Worden, and Robert D. Benford. 1986. "Frame Alignment Processes, Micromobilization, and Movement Participation." *American Sociological Review* 51 (4): 464–503.

Tarrow, Sidney. 1989. *Democracy and Disorder: Protest and Politics in Italy 1965–1975*. Oxford: Clarendon Press.

Tocco, Jack Ume. 2010. "'Every Disease Has Its Cure': Faith and HIV Therapies in Islamic Northern Nigeria." *African Journal of AIDS Research* 9 (4): 385–395.

Togarasai, Lovemore. 2010. "Christian Theology of Life, Death and Healing in an Era of Antiretroviral therapy: Reflections on the Responses of Some Botswana Churches." *African Journal of AIDS Research* 9 (4): 429–435.

UNAIDS (Joint United Nations Programme on HIV/AIDS). 2008. "Domestic and International AIDS Spending." *Global AIDS Report 2008*. Accessed October 1, 2011. http://www.unaids.org/en/ourwork/managementandexternalrelationsbranch/partnershipsdepartment/resource mobilizationdivision

UNAIDS (Joint United Nations Programme on HIV/AIDS). 2012. *2012 UNAIDS World AIDS Day Report-Results*. Accessed February 7, 2013. http://www.unaids.org/en/media/u naids/contentassets/documents/epidemiology/2012/gr2012/JC2434_WorldAIDSday_results_ en.pdf

van de Walle, Nicolas. 2001. *African Economies and the Politics of Permanent Crisis*. New York: Cambridge University Press.

van Dijk, Rijk. 2010. "Self-framing and Self-mobilisation: Pentecostal Faith, Agency and Activism in Africa." Paper presented at the workshop 'AIDS, Religion and Social Activism in Africa,' Kampala, Uganda, July 5–9.

Villalón, Leonardo. 1995. *Islamic Society and State Power in Senegal*. New York: Cambridge University Press.

Yamba, C. Bawa. 1997. "Cosmologies in Turmoil: Witchfinding and AIDS in Chiawa, Zambia." *Africa: Journal of the International African Institute* 67 (2): 200–223.

Youde, Jeremy. 2007. *AIDS, South Africa and the Politics of Knowledge*. Aldershot: Ashgate Publishers.

Can charity and rights-based movements be allies in the fight against HIV/AIDS? Bridging mobilisations in the United States and sub-Saharan Africa

Patricia Siplon

Department of Political Science, Saint Michael's College, Colchester, VT, USA

Résumé

Les interventions de lutte contre le VIH/le sida impulsées par les activistes, et ce de par le monde, ont abouti à des changements sans précédent dans la manière dont les maladies infectieuses sont définies et dans la mobilisation des ressources pour leur traitement dans les pays en développement, en particulier en Afrique subsaharienne. Cependant, les communautés qui ont constitué des sources cruciales d'interventions sont très divergentes. Aux États-Unis, où l'épidémie a été identifiée pour la première fois, la riposte la plus robuste a émané de la communauté homosexuelle, avec son orientation associée liée aux droits. En Afrique subsaharienne, les communautés de base religieuse ont été des acteurs cruciaux et ont généralement adopté une approche basée sur la charité pour leur travail. Tandis que la globalisation et les succès du mouvement mondial de lutte contre le sida mettent ces groupes en contact plus étroit, la question de savoir si ces approches divergentes peuvent fonctionner devient de plus en plus importante. Dans cet article, j'ai recours aux concepts de l'identité collective et de l'élaboration de cadres pour examiner le développement des deux approches et pour suggérer que l'activité d'extension des cadres pourrait constituer un outil utile au moment de relier des approches divergentes.

Abstract

The activist-fuelled responses to HIV/AIDS around the world have resulted in unprecedented changes to the way infectious disease is defined and treated and in the mobilisation of resources for treatment in developing countries, particularly in sub-Saharan Africa. However, the communities that have been critical sources of response are widely divergent. In the United States, where the epidemic was first identified, the strongest response was within the gay community, with its attendant rights-based orientation. In sub-Saharan Africa, faith-based communities have been critical actors, and have generally taken a charity-based approach to their work. As globalisation and the successes of the global AIDS movement draw these groups into closer contact, the question of whether these divergent approaches can work in alliance becomes ever more important. In this paper I use the concepts of collective identity and framing to examine the development of both approaches and to suggest that the activity of frame extension may be a helpful tool in bridging divergent approaches.

I. Introduction

The response to HIV/AIDS, fuelled by various forms of activism throughout the world, has been remarkable. The first mobilisation occurred in the United States (US), in recognition of a new disease that appeared to be endangering the lives of individuals within several socially-marginalised groups. This mobilisation eventually connected with other responses, particularly in sub-Saharan Africa, to the death and destruction caused there by HIV/AIDS. The ultimate aim of these mobilisations is the same: to provide medical care and support for individuals and communities already affected, and to prevent future infection. But the major frameworks of the mobilised communities – largely rights-based in the US, primarily charity-based in sub-Saharan Africa – differ in very important ways. This article seeks to examine whether and how these differences may be bridged.

The selection of cases in this paper is dictated largely by the historical circumstances of the AIDS pandemic. The US is important for several reasons. It is the country where AIDS was first officially identified, and was home to the earliest organised political mobilisations in response to the disease. Most of the antiretrovirals (ARVs) used to treat the disease were first patented and marketed in the US, and it was the birthplace of the first formal political statement of rights, the Denver Principles, on HIV/AIDS. It later became the leading donor of funding to sub-Saharan African nations responding to HIV/AIDS through multilateral programmes such as the Global Fund to Fight AIDS, Tuberculosis and Malaria (GFATM) and through the bilateral President's Emergency Plan for AIDS Relief (PEPFAR).

As a region, sub-Saharan Africa has suffered proportionally the most devastation from HIV/AIDS, with the largest total numbers of deaths, infections and children orphaned by AIDS. Tanzania is an East African country with a population of approximately 42 million and an adult HIV prevalence rate of 6%. It has benefitted from the boost in global funding on HIV/AIDS, and 95% of its budget for HIV/AIDS comes from external funding, with PEPFAR accounting for 58% of all spending, and the GFATM 22% (Aasen and Hellevik 2010). Although no single country can be completely representative of AIDS in sub-Saharan Africa, Tanzania's sizable population and HIV prevalence and its significant experience as the recipient of donor funds mobilised by the global AIDS activist movement make it a case suggestive of larger mobilising trends.

The article briefly outlines two key theoretical concepts from the social movement literature: collective identity formation and framing. These tools help make sense of the responses to and mobilisations against HIV/AIDS in different contexts. Because conceptual differences between rights and charity as bases for mobilisation are central to this discussion, the next section defines and explains these concepts and then contrasts the approaches. The paper then turns to an examination of each approach in context, beginning with the mobilisation of a rights-based AIDS activist movement in the US and then turning to the mobilisations in Tanzania around the challenges wrought by AIDS. The next section describes the ways in which these mobilisations and others have come into contact through the globalisation of the AIDS pandemic and responses to it. The concluding section returns to the central question of the paper – namely whether two movements with strongly divergent collective identities and frames can be allies in the struggle against HIV/AIDS – to suggest that frame extension may be the most effective way of bridging differences between approaches.

II. Methodology

This article is based on intermittent fieldwork begun in 1994 in the US and in 2002 in Tanzania. Using participant observation and unstructured interviews, I have worked with activists in the US on treatment access, needle exchange, compensation issues for people with haemophilia, and social service support for people living with HIV/AIDS (PWAs). In Tanzania, I worked with PWAs and non-governmental organisations (NGOs), including

AIDS Widows in Tanzania (AWITA), the Zanzibar Association of People Living with HIV/AIDS (ZAPHA +), the Lutheran Health Center (now Hospital) and the Ilula Orphan Program (IOP), doing research and mobilisation support on issues of stigma, treatment access, orphan support and water scarcity. This paper attempts to draw on the breadth of these experiences, as well as on the literature that has emerged over the past decade, to retrace key developments in the emergence of activist responses in both countries, describe the frameworks which animate these developments, and examine the points of current and potential alliance between the mobilisations.

III.   Frames and identity formation

Two key theoretical concepts that can help to examine this question of alliances are the notions of *framing* and *identity formation.* Although there are many organisations and individuals who have responded to the US and global AIDS pandemic, two groupings are particularly relevant. In the first case, this is the gay community, which was the most visible and vocal source of activism around HIV/AIDS first as an emerging issue in the US, and later as a global, and particularly African, health issue. The second is faith-based communities. Although they were present and responded to AIDS in some places in the US, in Africa they have had a proportionally stronger presence. This includes both local African congregations and religious leaders in places heavily AIDS-affected, and the Western churches and missionary organisations that helped to provide much of the medical treatment and social support services in these same places. The gay and faith-based communities had starkly different means of framing issues, challenges and solutions, as well as highly divergent self-identities.

Identity formation has been simply defined as "the construction of a 'we'" and posited as "a strong and preliminary condition for collective action" (Melucci 1996, 8). The collective actor formed through the collective identity process develops the capacity to resolve problems and in the process becomes increasingly autonomous within its network of relationships with other actors. As it develops this capacity it also controls its membership, by defining the criteria for joining, and the ways that members may recognise one another and are recognised (Melucci 1996, 75). Van Steklenburg and Klandermans (2009, 32) suggest that group identity itself becomes the motivation for individual participation: "Collective action participation is seen as a way to show who 'we' are and what 'we' stand for, and people experience commitment and solidarity with the group".

A key activity of collective actors is the development of frameworks through which events and goals may be discussed within the group and shared with outsiders. Frames are shared interpretations, and in the context of activism, refer to shared visions of events and changes and perceptions of what should be done in response to them. Frame alignment occurs when groups and individuals have "congruent and complementary" values, goals and activities, and occurs through four basic processes: frame bridging, frame amplification, frame extension and frame transformation (Snow et al. 1986, 467). Bridging is outreach to individuals or groups to create linkages based on congruent values, or what activists often refer to as "movement building". In 1987 Larry Kramer made a historical speech at the Gay and Lesbian Community Services Center in New York City, challenging his audience to organise politically after decrying the apathy of government in the face of a new and deadly disease (Smith and Siplon 2006, 23). This event, often credited with providing the initial spark for the formation of the leading AIDS activist organisation in the US, the AIDS Coalition to Unleash Power (ACT UP), exemplifies this outreach.

Frame amplification is the reinforcement, deepening and clarification of the shared interpretive framework, and occurs in two ways: values amplification (such as repeated emphasis on individual rights, including rights to privacy, free expression and health by US AIDS activists) and belief amplification (such as activist insistence that pharmaceutical companies have a moral obligation to make drugs affordable or that the state's indifference to the suffering of PWAs constituted criminal neglect).

While frame bridging and amplification are processes of formation and growth, frame extension and transformation are processes of change and adaptation. In frame extension, a movement or organisation extends its scope of activity to incorporate new demands, campaigns and/or goals, thereby creating new mobilisation and outreach opportunities (Snow et al. 1986). This was arguably the process that the US-based AIDS activist movement underwent when it extended its treatment goals beyond Americans who were HIV-positive and demanded global universal treatment access. Finally, frame transformation involves, as the term implies, the deepest level of change for collective actors. In cases where causes and values may not be congruent with, or are ideologically at odds with, potential adherents, drastic measures may be in order: "New values may have to be planted and nurtured, old meanings or understandings jettisoned and erroneous beliefs ...reframed" (Snow et al. 1986, 473). Such transformations may be domain-specific, for example when a previously accepted social practice is framed as unacceptable or inexcusable. When AIDS activists reframed the profit-seeking behaviour of the pharmaceutical industry from normal corporate action to deadly and exploitative profiteering off the potential deaths of its HIV-positive customers, a domain-specific transformation occurred among bystanders who adopted the new frame. Most sweeping are the transformations of global interpretive frames, when a new framework is adopted and becomes a master lens which allows interpretation of experiences and events in completely different ways. In the US, some HIV-positive haemophiliacs underwent such a global transformation when they joined the gay-community-based part of the AIDS activist movement and accepted the underlying rights-based vision as a way to define the ideal relationship of the state to its citizens.

IV. Rights-and charity-based approaches: what is the difference?

What does it mean to be rights-or charity-based? Both rights-and charity-based mobilisations can be seen as collective actions that seek to transfer resources to individuals or groups who are suffering in their absence. They differ, however, in at least three important ways. First, there is the issue of the hierarchies of deservedness; second, the role of the state; and finally, equalisation of power.

The term "hierarchies of deservedness" refers to the notion held by charity-based groups that certain groups or individuals are more deserving of aid than others, because of their innocence, their vulnerability, their motivations or other reasons. Charity-based organisations may adopt these differing categories of deservedness for ideological or pragmatic reasons (or a combination of both). Ideologically, they may embrace the idea that providing equal levels of a good or service across all categories of recipients rewards bad behaviour and decisions, or equally values all recipient groups. Thus, for example, a charity-based group may focus more on provision of HIV prevention services for preventing mother-to-child transmission over services to prevent transmission among injection drug users and prisoners. Pragmatically, charity-based groups may see a focus on certain categories of recipients, especially in the face of highly limited resources, as the most successful way to effect policy change (which may or may not be expanded at a later point). Thus, some early American charity-based advocates for AIDS medical treatment focused on providing AIDS drugs to HIV-positive mothers, knowing that it would be easier to convince American policymakers to provide benefits to mothers and babies than to the entire population. A final practical advantage of the charity-based approach is that it often can be effectively employed as a narrative demonstrating the helplessness of certain categories of recipients (e.g., with "poster children"), and thus an effective mobiliser or fundraiser among sympathetic audiences.

Human-rights-based groups reject such classifications, arguing that rights are absolute, interdependent and indivisible (Schmidt-Traub 2009, 74). Braveman and Gruskin (2003, 540) define human rights as "internationally recognised norms applying equally to all people everywhere in the world". Such a definition foreshadows the tension between, for example, rights-based campaigns for universal treatment access (as an operationalisation of the human right to health) and charity-based campaigns designed to support HIV-positive children in need of treatment.

Rights-based campaigners lay the main responsibility for achievement of these rights at the door of the state. In regard to the right to health, Braveman and Gruskin (2003, 540) argue that "governments are responsible for prevention, treatment and control of disease and the creation of conditions to ensure access to health facilities, goods and services" as well as "related rights to education, information, privacy, decent living and working conditions, participation and freedom from discrimination". The obligations of states in a rights-based perspective extend not only to the governments of the citizenry but to the governments of powerful and wealthy donor nations. These states have legal (as well as moral) obligations to provide international aid (Yamin 2010, 4). Additionally, they are required to refrain from actions that would not respect the rights of citizens of recipient countries and to protect the rights of these citizens from the actions of third parties (such as international corporations) (Mok 2010; Yamin 2010).

Finally, rights-based and charity-based activists diverge on the question of agency or power among those who are the perceived beneficiaries of the activism. For charity-based activists the deservedness of the beneficiaries often becomes a key rallying point in mobilising additional adherents to the cause: the greater the victimhood of the beneficiaries, the more compelling the case. Yet, there is a cost, which has been demonstrated, for example in the case of haemophiliacs in the US, many of whom dissociated themselves from the larger rights-based AIDS activist movement to pursue compensation from the US government for their infections. They ultimately received some compensation (as a "compassionate relief fund") but not the political power to affect future regulatory decisions (Siplon 2007, 24). For rights-based activists, conversely, the empowerment of the affected is just as important as the transfer of resources. This empowerment allows them to have a voice, not only in decisions about resource transfers and policy but also in defining the problem itself, including the structural issues that contribute to it.

How have these differences played out in the mobilisation and activism of both rights- and charity-based groups in the US and sub-Saharan Africa? The next section examines the development of the rights-based activist movement that has had a critical role in defining and responding to HIV/AIDS first in the US.

V. The emergence of a rights-based response in the US

Although the human immune deficiency virus (HIV) had almost certainly been killing people worldwide for decades, official recognition came in 1981 when the US government agency responsible for tracking disease, the Centers for Disease Control and Prevention (CDC), ran a short article entitled simply "Pneumocystis Pneumonia – Los Angeles" in its *Morbidity and Mortality Weekly Report* (MMWR). The article noted cases of the rare form of pneumonia in five young men in the Los Angeles area (CDC 1981).

Almost two years later, after studying the new infectious disease and releasing several more reports in the *MMWR*, the CDC made a pronouncement with important political consequences. On 3 March 1983, the CDC claimed it had found four groups at heightened risk of infection: homosexual men with multiple sexual partners; intravenous heroin injectors; recent Haitian immigrants; and haemophiliacs. While these four groups were quickly lumped together and dubbed the "AIDS 4-H club", their responses to this identification with the new disease were highly disparate.

Within and around each group, the dimensions of group identity and issue framing played major roles. Of the four groups, it was the Haitians who most strongly mobilised to dissociate themselves from identification with HIV/AIDS. Already struggling against xenophobic attitudes towards legal and especially undocumented Haitian immigrants, the last thing the Haitian community needed was another source of suspicion. The community mobilised two waves of protest. In 1985 they successfully demanded that the CDC remove Haitians from its "at-risk" list. In a second wave of protests that climaxed in 1990, the Haitian community targeted the Food and Drug Administration (FDA) and again successfully advocated for the removal of the ban on blood donations by Haitians (Siplon 2002, 7).

The reaction of the second group, heroin users, was deeply complicated by the politics of race and religion in the urban areas where at-risk users were concentrated. Given the criminalisation of drug use in the US, heroin users had a strong incentive not to publicly associate, and thus, not to organise. But others organised on their behalf, particularly within African-American communities. In many African-American communities there was deep suspicion among local civic and religious leaders of public health and activist voices advocating for a "harm reduction" approach to HIV prevention. Harm reduction takes a non-judgemental approach to risk behaviours such as drug use and sex, and seeks to minimise any possible negative repercussions from these behaviours. Examples include condom distribution and syringe (or needle) exchange. Abstinence, on the other hand, is predicated on the idea that the behaviours themselves are root problems and that consequences such as disease transmission are predictable outcomes of these problems. Abstinence approaches require the total suspension of risk behaviours. In drug use policy, abstinence proponents advocate for total cessation of drug using behaviours while harm reductionists see a continuum of policies – from syringe exchange to methadone maintenance to drug treatment – as options for reducing the risks associated with drug use. In urban communities with large African-American communities, leaders of these communities viewed outsiders advocating harm reduction as promoting a cheap form of containment policy. They feared that needle exchange would continue to concentrate drug use and the drug trade within minority urban communities but provide no new resources for reducing drug use within these communities.

Although public health officials associated haemophilia with HIV early in their analysis of the new disease, political organising within the haemophilia community came much later and was marked by a divisive split in terms of both identity formation and framing. Unlike the other three communities, which tended to be geographically concentrated in coastal cities, individuals within the haemophilia community tended to be distributed randomly. In the 1980s pre-Internet world, the group was held together by communications and information provided by the National Hemophilia Foundation (NHF) and regional Hemophilia Treatment Centers. Initially, haemophiliacs failed to organise because they were misinformed about the level of HIV infection within their community and then because the NHF and other advocacy groups encouraged them to prioritise the confidentiality of their HIV status over political demands (Siplon 2002, 54). Later, a significant segment of the haemophilia community split and joined ranks with the activist movement centred within the gay community, and much of the remaining haemophilia community mobilised as well. But the split widened over two issues. First, there was the question of identity, with more conservative elements of the haemophilia community resisting identification with the gay community. There was also the question of framing, with the more conservative part of the haemophilia community favouring a hierarchy of deservedness focusing on the "innocence" and victimhood of its membership in contrast to the rights-based frame employed by AIDS activists coming from the gay community.

Of the four groups identified within the original AIDS 4-H "club", it is homosexual men, as part of a larger gay and lesbian community, who are identified most strongly with AIDS. The gay community came to be associated with AIDS not only because homosexual men were identified early as infected by and at-risk for the new syndrome, but equally importantly, because the gay community explicitly decided to become actively involved in the response to the emerging disease threat. This decision stemmed from several concerns. First, and most obviously, a new and deadly disease was striking down men in the prime of their lives with no known treatment, or initially, even tests for early detection. The gay community wanted the government to take on the same sense of urgency it was experiencing. Equally importantly, however, the community saw the question of how the disease should be framed as paramount. This was partly in response to conservative religious and political leaders who presented the new disease as a supposed consequence of homosexuality and homosexual behaviour.

A number of those who mobilised early around HIV/AIDS were veterans of earlier activism around anti-discrimination and sexual freedom for sexual minorities. In addition to fighting for protection from discrimination in the workplace and other social spheres, many had been part of the struggle to create gay-positive spaces and institutions. The framing of the new disease as an outcome of homosexual activity jeopardised the outcomes of many of these hard-earned struggles. Thus, lesbians experienced this same threat to the gay community, and constituted an important segment of the activist cadres who came forward as activists, or people associated with HIV/AIDS.

One of the difficult challenges which the gay community faced was in addressing two threats simultaneously. On the individual level, people needed to be protected from HIV transmission. But on a societal level, the gay community needed to be protected from those who sought to stigmatise or even criminalise gay sexual behaviour. In finessing this tricky situation, the gay community developed the concept of "safer sex" and endorsed the harm reduction approach that underlined the strategy. Instead of judging an act as morally good or bad, harm reduction, and in this particular case, safer sex suggested that an act could be evaluated based on the level of risk of negative consequences. The act of sex between (any) two people could be made safer by performing it with a physical barrier to prevent the exchange of bodily fluids. Calls for protected sex could be gay-positive, but at the same time address the real threat of HIV transmission.

The identification of the gay *and* lesbian community with AIDS had other important ramifications. A number of the activist lesbians were also veterans of the feminist movement, and in particular political advocacy around women's health (Stoller 1995; Wolf 1990). This movement had operated on several levels. In addition to making demands on health providers and the state, it was also inwardly directed. That is, it stressed personal transformation and public advocacy as equally important. This tenet was emphasised in the widely quoted but anonymously-attributed slogan: "the personal is political". The key to this personal transformation is self-empowerment – seizing authority over one's own body, personal relationships and, in this case, medical treatment.

Self-empowerment does not preclude activism that targets change in the policies and attitudes of the state and larger society. In the case of AIDS activism, the two have gone hand in hand, allowing activists to seek change on levels from the individual to the society. Two key developments of these individual and societal approaches illustrate their complementary nature. The first occurred in 1983 at the second national AIDS Forum held in Denver, Colorado. About a dozen people who had been diagnosed with AIDS were invited to the Forum. However, once they arrived they were relegated to a hospitality suite while doctors and researchers conferred with one another about their findings. The group selected two leaders, Michael Callen and Bobbi Campbell, who helped the group give voice to their collective frustrations through the creation of a manifesto listing a set of guidelines for themselves, health-care practitioners and the public at large. The first point was a rejection of the terms "victim" and "patient" in favour of "people with AIDS" (PWAs). The recommendations included ideas equalising power relations between PWAs and their health-care providers. There was also a list of the rights of PWAs, including the rights to as "full and satisfying sexual and emotional lives as anyone else", "quality medical treatment and social service provision without discrimination of any form", and the representation of PWAs on boards and within organisations that claim to address AIDS issues and services (The Denver Principles 1983). The group dubbed their work the Denver Principles and unveiled them by storming the closing session and unfurling the sheet on which they had written them from a balcony.

The Denver Principles were a critical moment in making self-empowerment, a defining part of both the identity of people with and at risk for HIV infection and the framework that they used for discussing HIV with broader audiences. A second game-changing event occurred in March 1987. The drug company Burroughs-Wellcome (now part of Glaxo SmithKline) had just set the price of the first licensed anti-HIV drug, azidothymidine (AZT) at $10,000 per year. People who had been waiting for the drug were incensed by its high price tag. Over 250 members of the new activist organisation ACT UP demonstrated against Burroughs-Wellcome on Wall Street, where they managed to hold up traffic and gain national news coverage. Using flashy props (including an effigy of FDA Commissioner Frank Young) and fact sheets, ACT UP clearly articulated its anger at a number of other targets, which included President Reagan, the FDA, the National Institutes of Health (NIH), and the insurance industry.

Together, the Denver Principles and the ACT UP protests helped to establish and exemplify a new form of disease-based advocacy within the US. Earlier models of organising around diseases were implicitly or explicitly charity-based. Relying on the compassion of others, fundraising drives like the March of Dimes and Muscular Dystrophy Telethons served up stories of deserving "innocent victims" needing the intercession of medical science or kind philanthropists to save them from death or lives filled with tragedy. Although these traditional approaches had been successful in garnering funds and services, from the perspective of the AIDS movement, this model was not only undesirable but antithetical to the goals of the movement. From a self-empowerment perspective, the charity model moved in exactly the opposite direction. Patients and those affected by diseases were purposely framed as victims, with extremely limited agency to solve their own problems. The more helpless and vulnerable the victim, the more likely that the public and the state would be moved to help.

Victims were also desirable from this model in that they were viewed as "innocent" and therefore deserving of state and societal aid. But the construction of such an identity also implies a hierarchy of deservedness. Instead of seeking to achieve the "most deserving" status, AIDS activists embraced an approach predicated on health as a human right. All human beings, they argued, deserved access to the highest possible standard of care, regardless of the cause of their illness or their status in society. It was only by embracing these two new standards of self-empowerment and fundamental rights that it was possible to create a successful social movement that was, for the first time, based on a stigmatised sexually transmitted disease.

ACT UP explicitly combined self-empowerment and rights-based demands as it grew, and chapters mushroomed around North America and Europe. Established as all-volunteer, consensus-driven organisations, chapters held open meetings to make decisions about actions and activities. Using an array of tactics, including non-violent civil disobedience, vivid props and imagery to attract coverage from mainstream media, the chapters levelled demands at local, state and national government, as well as at private entities such as pharmaceutical corporations. Activists usually showed up dressed in signature black T-shirts bearing an inverted neon pink triangle reminiscent of those that gay men were forced to wear in Nazi concentration camps: these shirts bore the logo "Silence = Death".

All of these elements proved to be a highly successful combination. The movement targeted multiple actors, including government (national and local) and private entities such as the pharmaceutical industry. In his book *Impure Science*, Steven Epstein (1996) documents that these actions resulted in substantive policy changes and power changes, including the processes of clinical trials and bureaucratic approvals and the balance of power between doctors and patients.

ACT UP and its allies also took on a powerful religious institution, the Catholic Church, in a controversial "Stop the Church" action inside Saint Patrick's Cathedral, which targeted the Church's stances on condoms and safer sex education. The controversy of the action came from its tactics, which included the interruption of a mass, distribution of condoms within the church and – most upsetting to the congregants – the desecration of a communion wafer (Smith and Siplon 2006, 32–33). These actions, and particularly the Stop the Church protest, illustrate important points of both the identity of AIDS rights-based activists and their framing activities. From an identity perspective, in order to conduct a protest that was symbolically so antithetical to devout Catholics, activists would have to see themselves as having no common identity with the religious adherents. As a framing event, it is again clear that the movement did not see people with strong religious leanings as potential targets for outreach, since "Stop the Church" would not demonstrate congruent values. It might, however, appeal to potential activists who felt that the Church disregarded the rights of PWAs or others. As a form of frame amplification, the publicity that the protest garnered helped to emphasise the willingness of the movement's members to take on any target it viewed as failing to respect the rights of PWAs or persons at risk of infection. And as a frame extension, it clearly demonstrated that issues of transmission for the at-risk were as important as those of treatment and care for PWAs.

Needle exchange: the flashpoint between rights- and faith-based NGOs

Although ACT UP and allied activist groups were wildly successful with demands related to care, treatment and the mobilisation of state resources, with prevention they faced serious counter-mobilisations that involved direct clashes of values. For ACT UP and others favouring the rights-based ideas embodied in the harm reduction approach, their work was meant to directly benefit injection drug users at risk for HIV transmission. For faith-based groups and their allies, the goal was to protect the larger community from the perceived negative moral and health impacts of drug users and their using activity, such as crime and prostitution.

As noted above, in the realm of sexual activity, the concept of safer sex was the activist answer to the potentially contradictory goals of reducing the risk of HIV transmission while affirming the sexual and relational rights of everyone. It was not a big jump to apply the same harm reduction mindset to people with a different risk behaviour – drug use – through the intervention of needle exchange.

Activist groups pressured both the federal government – which was holding fast to the just-say-no policies articulated by the Reagan administration – and the state and especially local governments to at least decriminalise the possession of syringes and ideally provide needle exchange groups. And while they applied this pressure, they often took matters into their hands and – sometimes legally, more often not – ran their own needle exchanges. The programmes often operated in low-income urban minority neighbourhoods, and were staffed by white activist volunteers who did not live in the communities where they did the exchanges.

The federal government has been remarkably consistent in maintaining the anti-harm reduction stance it first articulated in 1985. The line in the sand was drawn by the National Institute of Drug Abuse (NIDA), which categorically announced that "NIDA does not feel comfortable telling drug users not to use dirty needles or share needles. NIDA's position is based on [the clear] message, 'Do not use drugs'" (Bayer 1989, 220). The announcement was given teeth with a formal ban on federal funding for needle exchange and for studies of the effectiveness of such programmes.

But for city governments and local health departments dealing with the on-the-ground realities of AIDS and drug use, the story has been different. It is here that the struggles have been largely waged, and often the debate has directly pitted harm reduction advocates from the rights-based AIDS activist movement against formal and informal leaders of minority communities directly or indirectly representing faith-based communities. New York City became the epicentre of a high-profile battle waged from pulpits, in newspapers and during City Council meetings in the late 1980s. When Mayor Koch agreed, after much debate, to a pilot needle exchange programme, the largest newspaper serving the African-American community, the *Amsterdam News,* ran a front page editorial calling for Koch's resignation and saying in part:

> What Koch is saying is this: Your clergy doesn't matter. Your politicians don't matter. Your medical community sucks wind. Your community leaders are cowards, and you Blacks and Latinos are dumb as hell. I will do precisely what I want 'cause I am the mayor. (Cohen 1999, 206)

When African-American mayor David Dinkins succeeded Koch, he lost no time in making good on a campaign promise to shut down the controversial programme.

Although the struggles over needle exchange were often fought along racial and ideological lines, one of the notable exceptions occurred in Philadelphia, which hosts the largest still-existing ACT UP chapter in the US. As with other US-based ACT UP chapters, it began with a largely white gay activist base, but it is unique in having made the demographic shift by successfully growing its membership and leadership with the active participation of individuals from inner city communities of colour. This ability to transition its demographic base may be attributed in large part to a deliberate focus by a few core members on the often-unarticulated needs of low-income people of colour with AIDS (Smith and Siplon 2006, 61–62). A significant number of these members have histories of drug use and/or incarceration, and many are involved in religious communities.

In addition to pursuing many of the same treatment and support service policies that other ACT UP chapters have fought for, ACT UP Philadelphia has parlayed the experiences and understanding of its membership into highly effective policy advocacy in additional realms, most notably concerning the needs of the currently or formerly incarcerated. As a result, Philadelphia prisons have condom distribution, unlike prisons around the country, and the city has a noteworthy programme designed to ensure the successful re-entry of formerly-incarcerated HIV-positive individuals into the general community.

The simultaneous experience of much of ACT UP Philadelphia's membership with both drug use and religious communities has also led to other innovative and unique solutions to AIDS policy questions. One of ACT UP Philadelphia's sustained campaigns is aimed at lifting the ban on federally funded needle exchange. In the face of pressure from activists and public health figures, President Clinton directed his Secretary of Health and Human Services, Donna Shalala, to conduct a study on the evidence on needle exchange and report a final recommendation to him. When news leaked that Secretary Shalala would be in Philadelphia the Sunday before the recommendation was to be made, the organisation had to contend with the competing identities of its membership – as harm reduction advocates but also religious individuals not willing to offend abstinence-based faith leaders. A 1999 article written by long-time ACT UP members Julie Davids and Asia Russell recounts the group's resolution of the conflict:

> Long-time ACT UPers, remembering earlier actions with different constituencies, imagined a loud confrontation inside the church. But newer members noted that many people we work with would be outraged by raising hell inside a church. The outcome? Inside the packed sanctuary, hundreds turned their backs on Shalala while whispering in unison: "Donna Shalala, you killed my sister, you killed my brother." The eerie reproach emboldened participants without violating their beliefs. (Russell and Davids 1999)

In keeping with a maxim of ACT UP activists, ACT UP Philadelphia had managed to conduct an action that was within the comfort zone of its activist membership and outside that of its target. Shalala publicly announced her endorsement of needle exchange as a policy that would enhance public health, although her boss, President Clinton, ultimately shrank from lifting the ban, like his predecessors. From an identity perspective, the organisation had managed to honour the competing identity bases of the activists. As a framing issue, the activists were also successful in creating a message that interpreted Secretary Shalala's obligation as one of saving lives – a frame that at least temporarily transcended the abstinence versus harm reduction frames over which the sides had been fighting.

VI. Responses to AIDS in the African context

Although the impact of AIDS in sub-Saharan Africa was far deadlier than in the US, responses were severely hampered by the hugely disproportionate lack of resources in the region. The continent lacked well-resourced health systems and surveillance of new illnesses, let alone treatment for them. Yet, as communities watched more and more men and women in the prime of life suffer the painful deaths of "slim disease", awareness of the disease was unavoidable. But unlike the US, where a rights-based AIDS activist movement was clearly in ascendancy, responses in sub-Saharan Africa spanned the spectrum. In some places, most notably South Africa, veterans of other rights-based struggles took up AIDS and levelled treatment- and prevention-based demands that were highly congruent with the values of their allies in North America.

The most notable example of this approach was the Treatment Action Campaign (TAC) of South Africa. The organisation was "born" on International Human Rights Day (10 December) 1998 when people gathered in Cape Town under the auspices of the National Association of People Living with AIDS (NAPWA) to initiate a new campaign to demand treatment for PWAs. TAC eventually became an autonomous organisation and by 2004 boasted 150 chapters around the country, all run by an elected executive committee. Its most famous leader, Zackie Achmat, is perhaps the most well-known HIV-positive activist in the world. Known as the "Gandhi of the AIDS movement", he refused to access antiretroviral therapy through private channels, publicly pledging to continue his "drug fast" until the government of South Africa provided these drugs for his fellow HIV-positive citizens. He put aside the pledge on 4 August 2003, when the South African government announced it planned to begin distributing ARVs in public clinics (Smith and Siplon 2006, 85–88).

Since its inception, TAC has pushed the government of South Africa to, among other things, provide treatment for its citizens and drug therapy to prevent mother-to-child transmission, and it has forced the international pharmaceutical industry to abandon a lawsuit against the South African government for pursuing generic medications. It mobilised thousands of citizens in marches and acts of non-violent civil disobedience, pursued lawsuits and showed its ability to work in coalition with other powerful South African civil society forces, including the Congress of South African Trade Unions (COSATU) and numerous national and local faith-based communities. And TAC has helped to organise other smaller AIDS activist groups across sub-Saharan Africa.

Yet, despite the very significant voices of TAC and organisations like it, faith-based responses to HIV/AIDS in sub-Saharan Africa have played a proportionally larger role than in the US for several reasons. First and most obviously is the sheer magnitude of the role of religion generally in sub-Saharan Africa. Africans are much more likely to be active members of a faith community than North Americans, and the size of religious populations – particularly Christians – is growing quickly (Patterson 2011). Religious institutions play important roles not only in shaping norms and values of their memberships but also in providing vital services in countries with limited state capacity. In fact, UNAIDS noted in 2009 that an estimated 30 to 70% of health care in sub-Saharan Africa is provided by faith-based organisations, and that facilities operated by these groups are the only ones that exist in many areas (UNAIDS 2009, 10). In her 2011 study, Amy Patterson provides a fivefold typology of church responses to AIDS based on two criteria: early (pre-2001) or late response and broad or narrow focus of activities (the fifth category is churches that have taken no action). In rejecting a typology based on the substance of church activities, she offers several justifications, including the fact that "there is not enough variation among African churches on these controversial topics [e.g., condom distribution, prevention programmes for sexual minorities, gender empowerment] for developing a typology because most African Christians are conservative on these issues" (Patterson 2011, 38–39). Although this offers good justification for her typology, it is also a salient point for the larger question on the values clash between rights- and charity-based AIDS organising that is the subject of this article.

In Tanzania, by the early 2000s a plethora of PWA organisations had sprung up to deal with HIV/AIDS. The earliest was Service, Health and Development for People Living with HIV and AIDS (SHEDEPHA), the first registered PWA organisation in the country. SHEDEPHA was rapidly joined by other PWA organisations including the Tanzania Network of People Living with HIV/AIDS (TANEPHA) and the Zanzibar Association of People Living with HIV/AIDS (ZAPHA +). But there was no single secular actor analogous to ACT UP in the US, and resources, particularly for treatment and social services, tended to be concentrated within the faith-based communities, often connected with local or missionary faith-based health and educational institutions. A particular set of features have made the emergence of a single secular organisation or coalition of such groups problematic. First is the problem of poverty. Unlike in the US where many of the initial members of ACT UP were middle-class college graduates, most of the early founders of PWA organisations were poor, with low education levels, and many were unemployed or working in the informal economy. In front of the goal of AIDS advocacy was the goal for day-to-day economic survival. When money began to come into the country through PEPFAR, the GFATM and other external sources, PWA groups and service organisations began to compete fiercely for it (Boesten 2011; Beckman and Bujra 2010). Unlike in the US, where activist leaders were able to fall back on their jobs, or at least some social safety net, PWA leaders in Tanzania often saw the PWA organisations themselves as potential employment opportunities. The result, according to Beckman and Bujra (2010, 1060), is that "Few leaders are wedded to a politics of social transformation or prioritizing the very poorest – they benefit by working within the system rather than challenging it".

Because of these competitive forces, and the de-politicising role that they play, PWA and local secular AIDS service organisations have been relegated to a much smaller advocacy role than activist organisations in the US. But the importance of faith-based organisations, which as noted above, play a major role in civil society in sub-Saharan Africa generally, is heightened. For illustrative purposes I have chosen to focus on two faith-based organisations in the rural Iringa region of Tanzania, a region where I have conducted research since 2005. These organisations – the Ilula Orphan Program (IOP) and the Lutheran Health Center (now Hospital) – both operate with significant support from the local communities and congregations (Lutheran and Methodist respectively), as well as from faith communities in the US and Europe. Iringa is the most heavily AIDS-impacted region within Tanzania, and Ilula is believed to be one of the most, if not the most, heavily-impacted ward within the region. The impact has been seen not only in the number of people who are sick or have died, but in the number of orphans, which is extremely high.

The IOP began in 1998 as a sponsorship programme when Norwegian-American missionary Berit Skaare agreed to find Western sponsors who would pay the school fees of local children and help with the costs of attendance. Since its founding, the programme has helped over one thousand children to attend and/or graduate from school, including about a dozen university graduates. In addition, the IOP has added numerous other programmes, including a pre-school, foster family programme, orphan centre for girls, and community HIV/AIDS prevention seminars and education.

The Lutheran Health Center officially changed its status to a hospital in 2008, when the Kilolo District split and it became the official District Hospital for the new Kilolo Rural District. It also became the site of one of the first rurally-based ART centres in the country in 2007, and now operates a mobile HIV/AIDS treatment and testing clinic on Saturdays.

Although both organisations are heavily engaged in the care and support of people living with AIDS and their families, they operate from a very different frame than that embraced by American activists. First and most obviously, in contrast to the consciously secular activities of rights-based activists, religion is infused into the daily activities of both organisations. Both the hospital and the orphan centre begin with morning prayers and the singing of hymns for everyone working at the facilities. Second, in selecting both their activities and those who will be eligible for their services, both organisations employ hierarchical systems of "deservedness", which is antithetical to rights-based advocates. Obviously some of these decisions are forced by the need to do triage within a heavily overtaxed system where the material needs of the community are enormous and growing, but neither organisation denies that perceived moral deservedness plays an important role. For example, although both organisations are heavily involved in prevention activities, their message is abstinence and faithfulness within relationships, and neither organisation will engage in condom distribution. These decisions on which services to provide privilege people who are sexually abstinent or monogamous over those who are not, although there is evidence that the latter type of services are desired by potential recipients. Four of seven girls interviewed about their unwanted pregnancies in 2008 fieldwork identified actual information about condoms and family planning as critical deficiencies in the HIV and pregnancy prevention seminars they had attended at the IOP before becoming pregnant. In the words of one informant: "The only way to not get pregnant is to not have sex so we don't get HIV, but if the IOP conducted meetings about this and how to train us about sex, maybe less girls would be pregnant" (Mooney 2008, 13). Both organisations are very aware of the existence of a burgeoning sex trade between very poor young women and the truck drivers who use the main road that bisects the ward, but neither organisation believes that it can or should conduct safer sex education, condom distribution or an alternative income generation intervention among the sex workers. Such interventions would cast the organisations themselves in a morally suspect light.[1]

Views on these issues are not entirely monolithic however. In a 2007 interview, the nurse who runs the HIV treatment centre at the Lutheran Hospital noted that the hospital had an obligation to provide condoms to unmarried young women who sought them. When challenged by her husband, an elder in the local Lutheran Church, she retorted that if the hospital was not willing to provide this service then it should support the creation of an independent youth centre where peer educators could do the education and distribution. She further noted that she has multiple identities as a strong Lutheran and as an HIV nurse, but that her professional obligations outweigh her personal moral beliefs.[2]

Additionally, a number of leaders of both organisations have found a third response to the morally-fraught issue of risk behaviour through the process of frame extension. In Ilula, local leaders have long noted that a major underlying cause of transactional sexual activity is water scarcity. The extreme scarcity and poor quality of water in the area has turned it into a commodified resource which men and boys control and sell, and women are responsible for procuring for household needs. Where women have no money to buy this commodity, they may engage in transactional sex for money or directly for access to water. Girls who are living on their own while attending secondary school encounter the same problem. The problem is so common that informants consistently mentioned the same "rate" in the area: one 40 litre bucket of water per (unprotected) sex act.[3] Once HIV enters a household, the situation further deteriorates as the water needs of the household go up and the capacity to get it further declines. The answer to this problem, then, is neither abstinence- nor harm-reduction-based interventions (neither of which will help a woman who is not in a position to negotiate sex with her partner), but greater access to water. Only by adding water to the "AIDS agenda" will the local problem be effectively addressed.

VII. AIDS activism goes global

In an earlier era, it might have been possible for these two divergent perspectives to coexist because they might not have had much contact with one another. But in the era of globalisation, it is increasingly common for social movements to form connections transnationally (Keck and Sikkink 1998), and that has certainly happened in the realm of HIV/AIDS.

By the late 1990s the situation around HIV/AIDS had shifted dramatically in the US. Most notably, the use of antiretroviral drugs (ARVs) in combination – known as triple therapy or the "cocktail" – transformed AIDS from a fatal to a chronic disease. Largely as a result of the policy advocacy of AIDS activism, a variety of policies had been implemented to protect the rights of PWAs, and the passage and reauthorisation of the Ryan White CARE Act helped states and cities pay for treatment and services for people infected with and affected by HIV. With many key aspects of the epidemic at least controlled in the Western world, some AIDS activists began to shift their gaze to the 95% of the world's cases that lay in the Global South. Western HIV-positive activists and their allies, including medical-care professionals and rights-based organisations increasingly recognised the gap between the access to medication and prevention and support services enjoyed by most people living with AIDS in the Western world, and the stark unmet need in developing – particularly African – countries. Three critical factors came together to help the new focus on global AIDS mobilisation. First, there was the fact that there were strong AIDS activist organisations with very different stories of their creation, but similar frame orientations, already existing in a number of crucial countries, most notably South Africa (with TAC) and Brazil (where PWAs and their allies had used the Brazilian constitutional right to health to successfully advocate for universal treatment). Second, by the late 1990s, the anti-globalisation movement was gathering steam, and had significant shared goals and targets with the emerging global AIDS movement. Finally, the dispersion of new technologies, first in the form of email, the Internet and mobile phones, later with the widespread use of social media sites, though disproportionately available in the West made instant and near-constant communication among advocates and activists around the world immeasurably easier.

There was enormous activity in the first few years of the new millennium that accelerated the campaigns of the global AIDS movement. One of the major obstacles to treatment was that effective interventions, and particularly treatment, were simply unaffordable in developing countries. With price tags for annual supplies of ARVs in the US averaging over $10,000 per year, AIDS activists looked to Brazil. Forced by its activists to provide universal ARV therapy, Brazil had turned to its generic industry to supply the medication, and was providing its citizenry ARVs at a cost of around $700 per year. Armed with this information that generic ARVs and other programmes could be made available to at least tens of thousands of people at a cost of a few billion dollars per year, activists had the frame they needed to put forward a new set of global demands. They also had the events to showcase their actions, first in the 2000 International AIDS Conference which was held in an African country for the first time. With activists flocking to South Africa, working with TAC and marching arm in arm in massive street demonstrations, the theme of the conference quickly became treatment access. In 2001 the Indian generic drug company Cipla announced that it would make a $350 version of the cocktail available, and for the first time the United Nations (UN) held a general assembly meeting (UNGASS) on AIDS in New York City in June 2001, which became another major media event for activists to press their cases for the rights of people with AIDS to care, lack of stigma and discrimination, and especially, treatment.

The outcome of this activity has been several ambitious and far-reaching programmes to do exactly what activists had been calling for. On the international level, the UN began a new fund: the Global Fund to Fight AIDS, Tuberculosis and Malaria (GFATM). Pooling billions in contributions from the developed countries, the GFATM evaluates proposals from developing countries and awards multi-year grants to successful proposals. In addition, in 2003 President George W. Bush launched the largest bilateral public health programme ever, the President's Emergency Plan for AIDS Relief (PEPFAR) – a five year 15 billion dollar initiative targeting fifteen countries, most of them in sub-Saharan Africa. Even more remarkable, five years later after strong activist pressure, PEPFAR was re-authorised at more than triple the spending levels for the next five years. Given the prevalence of faith-based organisations as treatment and care providers and critical community institutions, these groups were often tapped as local and national partners for the implementation of PEPFAR programmes.

VIII.   Conclusion: can charity-and rights-based movements be allies?

Throughout the history of AIDS activism within and between countries, the rights-based ethos of Western activists has played a critical role. The advocacy work of rights-based activists in the US and their allies in Brazil, South Africa and elsewhere defined the campaign for generic medications that have made treatment affordable, and fought to mobilise the resources for new programmes to pay for them. But charity-based organisations also lobbied for the money from Western donors, and without the work of FBOs animated largely with charity-based frameworks, there would be precious few local institutions on which to build a response, and even less health-care infrastructure (particularly in rural areas) from which to provide treatment, support and prevention services. Given the critical nature of both collective actors, the question becomes all the more pressing: can they be allies in the fight against AIDS?

On one level, the answer is obvious. When it comes to treatment issues, they can and they have. The rights-based activist perspective suggests that all people deserve the most effective treatment available because health is a human right. The charity perspective may be slightly different, positing that we have an obligation to help relieve the suffering of others because we must show them compassion, but the effective result is the same: both groups will work hard to see that suffering patients are offered life-saving therapies.

The tougher questions come with respect to prevention, and to anti-stigma and discrimination work. Here, the frames of the two groups are much harder to align, and the collective identities of the groups make the task more challenging still. The rights-based perspective is that inherent within the rights to privacy and free expression are the rights to make personal decisions about sexual and other behaviour, and that prevention work should not infringe on these rights. The faith-based perspective sees sexual and other risk behaviours as moral or immoral and discourages behaviours it deems immoral. By definition, these two views are antithetical. In addition, the AIDS activist collective identity remains firmly entrenched in the gay-based identity politics from which it came. Not only do openly gay, lesbian, bisexual and transgender activists continue to be crucial leaders and participants in the movement they founded, but an important part of the collective identity of the whole movement is that all of its participants – of whatever sexual identity – are gay-positive and affirming of the rights of people of all sexual orientations. Again, this represents an extreme challenge to charity-based organisations of Africa, particularly if they have a faith-based orientation which suggests that homosexuality constitutes deviancy and creates a category of people unworthy of assistance, let alone empowerment.

The theoretical notions of collective identity and framing offer two tools that may at least partially bridge the impasse. Within the realm of collective identity is a lesson that comes from the PWA movement. There is a cross-cutting identity which links activism in the US and in Africa, and that is the identity of those who are actually HIV-positive. Whether a white gay man living in New York City or a young heterosexual mother living in East Africa, a positive HIV test binds the two individuals together with a shared identity that neither may have wanted, but which both must confront. It is in the interest of all PWAs to continue to advocate for the principles of fair treatment and representation opportunities espoused within the Denver Principles, and if they do, they will also be able to construct a shared identity that at least partially cuts through race, class, sexual orientation and religious affiliation. And if that collective identity can be forged, the allies of those people will share a commonality in their support for people living with AIDS, and have a common basis for activities. One example of such a bridging embodied in a single person is Canon Gideon Byamugisha, who went public as an HIV-positive Anglican priest in Uganda in the early 1990s. With funds from a Christian aid agency in 2002, he established the continent-wide African Network of Religious Leaders Living with or Personally Affected by HIV/AIDS (ANERELA) (Nolen 2007). Through ANERELA he is effectively creating an identity – for the group's membership and for the wider community which the religious leaders serve – to suggest that HIV status should not create hierarchies of deservedness.

The process of framing, and particularly of frame extension, is another potential tool for bridging divides. Many of the major policy battles between rights- and faith-based activists have been waged on what may be termed downstream interventions. They occur at the point of individual behaviours, whether they are focused on convincing people to abstain from behaviours outright or to modify the behaviour for better outcomes. But there may be points of agreement in the idea that it is often structural determinants, particularly in resource-constrained settings, that drive people to risk behaviours in the first place. A focus on access, for example, to basic human needs including food, water and education is non-controversial precisely because almost all of us can understand and agree that they lead to less human suffering and to a greater ability of humans to avoid having to make decisions that may have negative long-term consequences. Such a focus will require some adjustments by both rights- and charity-based activists. Although rights-based activists agree in principle on the indivisibility and interdependence of rights, there is sometimes a tendency to become overly focused on narrower areas, often for the practical reason of creating winnable campaigns. Charity-based activists, on the other hand, will need to recognise the critical long-term role of the state, in terms of both resource mobilisation and sustainability. But whether we define them as rights or acts of religious charity, it is in the interests of everyone to extend our framing of AIDS to incorporate goals of sustainably providing for the basic necessities of everyone.

Notes

1. Interview with IOP Officer, by author. Ilula, Tanzania, 30 June 2008.
2. Interview with HIV nurse, by author. Ilula, Tanzania. 10 June 2007.
3. Interviews with community members, by author. Ilula, Tanzania. 4 and 5 June 2009.

Bibliography

Aasen, Berit, and Siri B. Hellevik. 2010. "Local Level Implementation of Global HIV/AIDS Programmes in Ilala Municipality, Dar es Salaam, Tanzania." Presented at AIDS 2010. Vienna, Austria.

Bayer, Ronald. 1989. *Private Acts, Social Consequences: AIDS and the Politics of Public Health.* New Brunswick, NJ: Rutgers University Press.

Beckman, Nadine, and Janet Bujra. 2010. "The 'Politics of the Queue': The Politicization of People Living with HIV/AIDS in Tanzania." *Development and Change* 41 (6): 1041–1064.

Boesten, Jelke. 2011. "Navigating the AIDS Industry: Being Poor and Positive in Tanzania." *International Institute of Social Studies* 42: 781–803.

Braveman, Paula, and Sofia Gruskin. 2003. "Poverty, Equity, Human Rights and Health." *Bulletin of the World Health Organization* 81: 539–545.

Centers for Disease Control. 1981. "Pneumocystic Pneumonia – Los Angeles." *Morbidity and Mortality Weekly Report* 30: 250–252.

Cohen, Cathy. 1999. *The Boundaries of Blackness: AIDS and the Breakdown of Black Politics.* Chicago, IL: University of Chicago Press.

"The Denver Principles". 1983. www.actupny.org/documents/Denver.html

Epstein, Steven. 1996. *Impure Science: AIDS, Activism and the Politics of Knowledge.* Berkeley, CA: University of California Press.

Keck, Margaret E., and Kathryn Sikkink. 1998. *Activists Beyond Borders.* Ithaca, NY: Cornell University Press.

Melucci, Alberto. 1996. *Challenging Codes: Collective Action in the Information Age.* New York: Cambridge University Press.

Mok, EmilyA. 2010. "International Assistance and Cooperation for Access to Essential Medicines." *Health and Human Rights* 12: 73–81.

Mooney, Kate. 2008. "When Empowerment Fails: Understanding the Problems of Sexual Pressure on Young Women in Tanzania: The Case of Unwanted Pregnancies." Unpublished research paper. Saint Michael's College: Colchester, VT.

Nolen, Stephanie. 2007. *28: Stories of AIDS in Africa.* New York: Walker & Company.

Patterson, Amy. 2011. *The Church and AIDS in Africa: The Politics of Ambiguity.* Boulder, CO: First Forum Press.

Russell, Asia, and Julie Davids. 1999. "The Way We Live Now: ACT UP Philadelphia." *POZ Magazine* 47. http://www.poz.com/articles/214_1519.shtml

Schmidt-Traub, Guido. 2009. "The Millennium Development Goals and Human Rights-Based Approaches: Moving Towards a Shared Approach." *The International Journal of Human Rights* 13 (1): 72–85.

Siplon, Patricia. 2002. *AIDS and the Policy Struggle in the United States.* Washington, DC: Georgetown University Press.

Siplon, Patricia. 2007. "Power and the Politics of HIV/AIDS." In *The Global Politics of AIDS*, edited by Paul Harris and Patricia Siplon, 17–34. Boulder, CO: Lynne Rienner.

Smith, Raymond, and Patricia Siplon. 2006. *Drugs into Bodies: Global AIDS Treatment Activism.* Westport, CT: Praeger Publishers.

Snow, David, E. Burke Rochford Jr, Steven K. Worden, and Robert D. Benford. 1986. "Frame Alignment Processes, Micromobilization, and Movement Participation." *American Sociological Review* 51 (4): 464–481.

Stoller, Nancy. 1995. "Lesbian Involvement in the AIDS Epidemic: Changing Roles and Generational Differences." In *Women Resisting AIDS: Feminist Strategies of Empowerment*, edited by Beth E. Schneider and Nancy E. Stoller, 270–285. Philadelphia, PA: Temple University Press.

UNAIDS. 2009. "Partnership with Faith-based Organizations: UNAIDS Strategic Framework." http ://data.unaids.org/pub/Report/2010/jc1786_fbo_en.pdf

Van Steklenburg, Jacquelien, and Bert Klandermans. 2009. "Social Movement Theory: Past, Present and Prospects." In *Movers and Shakers: Social Movements in Africa*, edited by Stephen Ellis and Ineke van Kessel, 17–44. Leiden: Brill.

Wolf, Maxine. 1990. "AIDS and Politics: Transformation of our Movement." In *Women, AIDS and Activism*, edited by ACT UP/NY Women and AIDS Book Group, 233–237. Boston, MA: South End Press.

Yamin, Alicia Ely. 2010. "Our Place in the World: Conceptualizing Obligation Beyond Borders in Human Rights-Based Approaches to Health." *Health and Human Rights* 12: 3–14.

Pastors as leaders in Africa's religious AIDS mobilisation: cases from Ghana and Zambia

Amy S. Patterson

Department of Politics, University of the South, Sewanee, USA

Résumé

Cet article examine la manière dont les pasteurs ont mobilisé leurs disciples religieux pour aborder la question du VIH et du sida au Ghana et en Zambie. Il soutient que les pasteurs qui ont obtenu de bons résultats ont eu recours aux structures organisationnelles de l'Église pour soutenir et renforcer leurs activités, ont formulé les messages de mobilisation autour du VIH et du sida d'une manière acceptable pour leurs fidèles et leurs sociétés dans leur ensemble, et ont tiré parti des opportunités politiques en évolution, en particulier les opportunités de collaboration avec des acteurs externes comme les bailleurs de fonds et les Églises occidentales. Cet article positionne l'analyse en Zambie et au Ghana, deux pays qui forment un contraste sur le plan de leurs taux de prévalence du VIH et du degré d'attention de la part des bailleurs de fonds qu'ils ont reçu pour lutter contre le VIH et le sida. Cet article affirme que, si les pasteurs ont une mesure de libre arbitre dans le processus de mobilisation sociale, ils sont aussi influencés par les contextes sociaux et culturels plus larges dans lesquels ils évoluent.

Abstract

This article examines the ways that pastors have mobilised their religious followers to address the issue of HIV and AIDS in Ghana and Zambia. The work argues that successful pastors have utilised church organisational structures to support and empower their activities, they have framed HIV and AIDS mobilisation messages in a way that is acceptable to their congregants and to their broader societies, and they have capitalised on changing political opportunities, particularly those opportunities for collaboration with external actors such as donors and Western churches. The work situates the analysis in Zambia and Ghana, two countries that contrast in their HIV prevalence rates and the amount of donor attention and funding they have received for combating HIV and AIDS. The article asserts that while pastors have agency in the social mobilisation process, they are also affected by the broader social and cultural contexts in which they operate.

I. Introduction

In its 2001 Declaration of Commitment on HIV/AIDS, the United Nations General Assembly stated that "strong leadership at all levels of society is essential for an effective response to the epidemic" (UN 2001, 15). The Joint United Nations Programme on HIV/ AIDS (UNAIDS) has explicitly called for heightened political commitment to the pandemic from leaders in civil society, business, and academic and religious organisations (Piot 2006). Despite these actions, scholars have provided limited analysis of the ways that individual leaders in either state or non-state institutions have mobilised in response to HIV and AIDS. This article fills this gap, with its analysis of leadership by pastors in

Zambia and Ghana. In doing so, it straddles the divide between the political process theorists who argue that mobilisation results from resources, political opportunities, and organisational structures (see Tarrow 1989; McAdam, McCarthy, and Zald 1996), and the constructionists who maintain that collective identity and framing lead to mobilisation (see Goodwin and Jasper 2004; Snow et al. 1986). This work argues that pastors who have successfully mobilised their religious followers to address the disease have capitalised on existing church organisational structures, used frames that resonate with their religious adherents, and embraced new political opportunities related to HIV and AIDS. On the other hand, while the article demonstrates pastors' agency, it also illustrates that the broad sociocultural context in which these leaders operate means that this agency is not absolute.

To begin, I will clarify my terms. I define successful mobilisation broadly as any church activities that directly relate to HIV and AIDS, such as organised home-based care programmes, HIV prevention efforts, AIDS awareness campaigns, support for orphans and vulnerable children (OVCs), and/or community advocacy. Because a large number of African churches have done nothing to address HIV and AIDS, this broad definition is appropriate. I determine the success of mobilisation in light of the organisation's stated objectives. That is, if the goal of a particular church is to provide home-based care, then I assess the success of mobilisation based on that specific goal. My definition does not presuppose that once mobilisation begins, it will continue. The cases below illustrate both that successful mobilisation can have different effects on the ground and that it can change with time. I utilise the term "church organisational structures" to mean rules and processes that situate power in decision-making. The concept of frames describes schemata for interpreting situations and mobilising action (Snow et al. 1986), while the term "political opportunities" refers to changes in the political and institutional environment such as transitions in state power, economic adjustments, and the rise of new global issues that create moments in which movements can organise or change their focus (Van Stekelenburg and Klandermans 2009, 25; Tarrow 1989).

Leadership by pastors is not the only factor that has led churches to respond to HIV and AIDS in Africa. The increased availability of donor AIDS funding after 2001, the development of collective identity (particularly among Pentecostals), and the formation of effective organisations with the capacity for communication and programme administration and with linkages to the global AIDS movement also contributed to mobilisation (Friedman and Mottiar 2004; Gusman 2009; Patterson 2011). But I maintain that leadership plays a role in mediating these factors. The article focuses on leadership for theoretical, empirical, and policy-related reasons. From a theoretical perspective, leadership has been inadequately analysed in social movements, particularly because of the dominance of the political process perspective in the literature. Scholars' concern about overemphasising agency and downplaying the role of mass mobilisation if they focus on leadership has also led to this lacuna (Morris and Staggenborg 2004). On the other hand, research on organisational cultures and political transitions shows that leadership is crucial, particularly when issues are ill-defined, there are few precedents for how to respond to a particular crisis, and it is unclear who the major players in a response should be (Warren 2001; Sorensen 2007; Trice and Beyer 1991). Viewing AIDS as a type of new and ill-defined crisis situation, this article elucidates how leadership matters in fostering particular responses to the disease.

From an empirical perspective, political and religious leaders play a large role in African society, because of executive-centred political systems and the crucial role of religion on the continent (van de Walle 2001; Ellis and ter Haar 2004). Individuals such as Treatment Action Campaign founder Zackie Achmat, Uganda President Yoweri

Museveni, and former Bostwana President Festus Mogae have been crucial in Africa's response to the disease. At the grassroots level, community activists assert that leadership is essential for successful HIV and AIDS activities.[1] However, there is little analysis of what those leaders actually do to bring about successful mobilisation. Finally, on the policy front, to meet UNAIDS' objective of greater political commitment to the disease, an analysis of successful leadership activities is essential.

This article begins with a focus on theoretical insights into social movements and leadership that are crucial for understanding church HIV and AIDS efforts in Zambia and Ghana. I then describe my methodology. Next I contrast the two country cases in order to highlight the ways that context influences leaders' actions. The work then delves into a three-pronged argument: I maintain that pastors with successful church mobilisation (1) employed their own church structures to urge activities, (2) utilised frames that resonated with their intended audiences, and (3) capitalised on political opportunities to address the disease. In doing so, I illustrate how these strategies exemplify the themes of extraversion, anti-politics, and political mobilisation. Extraversion is the process by which African institutions may "exploit, occasionally skilfully" their poverty and dependence on the West to gain resources (Bayart 1993, 25–26). Anti-politics alludes to the assertion by James Ferguson (1990) that issues in the development realm such as poverty and AIDS become depoliticised as donors, non-governmental organisations (NGOs), and faith-based organisations (FBOs) treat them as technical challenges and ignore the ways these issues link to questions of representation, participation, and power. In contrast, political mobilisation is the process by which such organisations engage in debates over resources and representation, sometimes to the exclusion of others. The conclusion raises future research questions about church HIV and AIDS mobilisation.

II.   Social movements, leadership, and church responses to HIV and AIDS in Africa

Social movements are a form of collective action that seek to affect political, social, economic, and/or cultural change. They incorporate a variety of activities and strategies. As dynamic processes, movements work outside of the state, although they do not necessarily challenge the state through confrontation. Movements exhibit some level of organisation, although this can vary greatly between movements. They also may alternate between periods of activism and dormancy, waxing and waning historically (Snow, Soule, and Kriesi 2004, 6–11). As strategic decision-makers, leaders play a crucial role in these dynamic processes; they mobilise resources, found organisations, offer frames for understanding issues, and respond to incentives and opportunities (McCarthy and Zald 1977). Leaders who successfully mobilise resources may urge greater participation in a movement; in turn, participation may increase movement resources. Leaders not only rely on their charisma or personalities to motivate, but they also utilise their previous experiences, cultural traditions, and social networks (Morris and Staggenborg 2004, 179–180).

These aspects of social movements and leadership are evident in African church mobilisation on HIV and AIDS. Church responses have involved collective action among church leaders, congregants, and/or community members to develop programmes (such as home-based care) or to advocate for particular HIV policy positions (such as limiting condom advertisements). HIV and AIDS activities have included HIV awareness campaigns, congregation-based support groups for people living with HIV, and the distribution of anti-retroviral treatment (ART) at mission hospitals. This variety of actions reflects both labour specialisation and the fact that church participants in the AIDS movement often do not agree about how best to fight the disease. Churches involved with HIV and AIDS also seek to affect change. Gideon Byamugisha, the first African religious leader to declare his HIV positive status, emphasises this point: "[Activism] is a dynamic but coherent process that seeks to achieve sociocultural, economic, educational, spiritual and political change [... to create a world] free from new HIV and AIDS related infections, illnesses and deaths" (Byamugisha 2010, 11). Religious groups may promote this change in a variety of ways, including through cooperation and collaboration with the state, particularly in Africa's neopatrimonial political arena (Ellis and van Kessel 2009).

African pastors have unique qualities that give them the potential to serve as leaders in HIV and AIDS mobilisation. They are very respected and trusted in Africa, a continent where religion is highly salient (Little and Logan 2008), religious institutions are trusted (Gallup News Service 2007), and most other types of non-state organisations are weak. As intermediaries between the spiritual and physical worlds, pastors are perceived to have unique powers such as the gifts of healing, prophecy, speaking in tongues, and/or spiritual intercession. Because spiritual power is as real in Africa as physical power, and because few (if any) other community members can claim such spiritual linkages, pastors have a unique form of legitimacy (Meyer 2004; Ellis and ter Haar 1998, 191–192). Pastors' charisma and popularity mean they often have connections to other civil society groups, state officials, local elites, and donor agencies. Pastors may be the most, if not the only, educated citizens in a community (Green 2003). Because of these traits, people turn to pastors for both spiritual and material help. Afrobarometer (2009, 11) found that on average forty per cent of respondents in eighteen African countries had contacted a religious leader about a problem at least once during the last year. One HIV-positive Pentecostal church member in Lusaka demonstrated this reliance: "When I don't have any money for food, I go to the pastor and he helps me".[2] This dependence may be rooted in the traditional norm that leaders are expected to care for followers materially (Haynes 2009). Thus, "good pastors" are defined not only in terms of their preaching or teaching skills, but also in terms of their ability to address material issues in people's lives. Because HIV and AIDS affect the lives of some churchgoers in Africa, there may be implicit pressure on pastors to meet societal expectations on the issue.

III. Methodology

Data for this work come primarily from over two hundred semi-structured interviews that I conducted in Zambia in 2007, 2009, and 2011, and in Ghana in 2008. I chose interviewees based on their affiliation with church-based organisations that I identified through newspaper articles and interviews with others involved in HIV and AIDS efforts. While I focused my interviews on church leaders, participants in church-organised HIV and AIDS programmes, and church pastors, I also met with secular AIDS activists, government representatives, and bilateral and multilateral donor officials in order to situate church activities in a broader context. Interviewees were asked about church activities on HIV and AIDS, the factors that shaped church mobilisation, church leadership on the disease, and church-donor relations. Because I wanted interviewees to share their honest opinions, I assured them of anonymity in any publications.[3]

In addition to interviews, I also examined documents from two organisations highlighted in this study, the Jubilee Centre in Zambia and the Christian Council of Ghana. And I observed church services led by Zambian pastors Joshua Banda and Lawrence Temfwe. Because Catholic Church activities on HIV and AIDS have been well documented (Rasmussen 2011; Amanze 2007; Joshua 2010; Kelly 2010), this article focuses on mainline Protestant and Pentecostal church responses. I acknowledge that African Independent Churches are not included in this study.

IV.   Contrasting contexts: Zambia and Ghana

Zambia and Ghana provide three major contrasts that help contextualise the leadership of pastors on HIV and AIDS. The first revolves around the epidemic. The countries differ greatly in their HIV prevalence, or the percentage of people aged 15 to 49 who are estimated to be HIV positive. Zambia's HIV rate has remained stubbornly high, while Ghana's rate (which was already low at roughly 3%) declined slightly between 2001 and 2006. In 2009, Zambia's HIV rate was 15.2% and Ghana's was 1.9%. In terms of ART access, approximately 40% of HIV-positive Ghanaians who needed ART could access it in 2009, compared to 68% of Zambians (Ministry of Health, National AIDS Council, and UNAIDS 2011; UNAIDS 2010a). Because of the higher prevalence rate in Zambia and the large number of individuals who have been infected or affected, stigma in Zambia is lower than in Ghana (Mwinituo and Mill 2006).

A second contextual difference is each country's external linkages. Social movement actors may use such linkages to mobilise labour, messages, and financial resources in advocacy (Keck and Sikkink 1998). Africa's reliance on global institutions for health and development projects may weaken the continent's social movements or serve as a resource for them (Ellis and van Kessel 2009, 7). In terms of Zambia and Ghana, external AIDS funding has been more evident in the former than the latter, although both countries rely heavily on donor money. In 2008, 84% of Ghana's AIDS funding and 85% of Zambia's came from external sources (Ministry of Health, National AIDS Council, and UNAIDS 2011; UNAIDS 2010a). Between 2003 and 2009, Zambia received over $1.12 billion from the US President's Emergency Plan for AIDS Relief (PEPFAR) and $324 million from the Global Fund to Fight AIDS, Tuberculosis and Malaria (the Global Fund). Ghana, on the other hand, received roughly $114 million from the Global Fund. Ghana was not a PEPFAR-focus country (Patterson 2010).

Third, Zambia and Ghana contrast in their religious demographics. Both are majority Christian, and both have diverse Christian populations, including Catholics, mainline Protestants (e.g., Presbyterians, Methodists), mission-introduced Pentecostals (e.g., Apostolic Faith, Assemblies of God), African Independents (e.g., Zionists), and neo-Pentecostals (e.g., Winners' Chapel). Both have also experienced the expansion of Pentecostalism, with Pentecostal churches increasingly competing for members, connections to (and funding from) American evangelical churches, and prestige (Kapenda Lumbe 2008; Gifford 2004; Kalu 2008). However, there is a discernible difference in the size of each country's Christian majority. In Zambia, 82% of the population identifies itself as Christian, while in Ghana the figure is only 55% (Barrett, Kurian, and Johnson 2001). Zambia's constitution declares that the country is a "Christian nation"; on the other hand, church leaders in Ghana have sought inter-faith cooperation on a variety of high-level issues, such as the 2008 highly contested presidential election (Ranger 2008; Okyerefo, Fiaveh, and Asante 2011).

These contextual differences have implications for pastors' ability to lead on HIV and AIDS. Stigma in Ghana makes a response more difficult, as does the relative lack of donor resources. Additionally, Ghana's lower HIV rate means that churches have engaged in far fewer types of activities, focusing primarily on AIDS awareness, HIV prevention, and stigma reduction. Ghanaian church leaders have sought to cooperate with Muslim leaders on high-level HIV and AIDS initiatives. In Zambia, donor attention, lower stigma, and the high HIV prevalence have created an environment in which pastors can mobilise members for a variety of AIDS-related activities. Additionally, since religious minorities are a relatively small group in Zambia, they have not figured into some of the most high-level AIDS activities in the country – those conducted by Pentecostal pastors. Because of these contextual differences, church understandings of successful mobilisation were narrower in Ghana than they were in Zambia.

V. Pastors and church mobilisation against HIV and AIDS

This section examines the specific ways that pastors have capitalised on church organisational structures, framed AIDS messages, and reacted (positively or negatively) to opportunity structures in order to mobilise a response to HIV and AIDS. In this analysis, I will highlight how the specific contexts of Ghana and Zambia shaped these pastoral activities. Although mobilisation differed in each country, the cases show that church efforts did have an effect on the ground. In both cases, mobilisation changed with time: in Ghana, this meant a decline in high-level and public activities, while in Zambia, it meant greater professionalisation in AIDS efforts.

A. *Pastors and church organisational structures*

To illustrate how pastors utilised church organisational structures to foster HIV and AIDS mobilisation, I will focus on early Protestant church efforts in Ghana and Zambia. For Ghana, I analyse the Compassion Campaign, an effort that started in 2000 and was led by the ecumenical Christian Council of Ghana (CCG), an organisation with fifteen mainline Protestant denominations as its members. In Zambia, I investigate the HIV/AIDS-related activities which began in the late 1990s at the Northmead Assembly of God in Lusaka. Both the Zambian and Ghanaian efforts emerged at a time when Protestant churches were doing little to address the matter of HIV and AIDS, when the disease was beginning to gain greater global attention, and when there were no clear precedents about how religious institutions should engage the issue. In this period of issue transition, leadership was an important variable for mobilisation.

The Compassion Campaign in Ghana included AIDS education workshops for religious leaders, as well as public media campaigns to raise AIDS awareness and combat stigma. It sought to bring Muslim leaders into some of its training efforts. It was the first high-level church effort in Ghana, and it received substantial support from the US Agency for International Development (USAID). Its goal was twofold. First, the programme sought to increase knowledge among religious leaders about basic facts on HIV transmission and AIDS and to urge them to show greater compassion toward people with the disease. Second, the campaign wanted to diminish attitudes of stigma in the general population through TV commercials, billboards, and public radio discussions of HIV and AIDS (Compassion Campaign 2002). Donors felt relatively confident in providing the CCG with campaign funds because of its long history, well-defined organisation, and highly respected leadership.[4] The campaign's approach was relatively narrow; there were no support, care, or treatment aspects, and the public prevention message was relatively obtuse, since it emphasised that "AIDS is real" but did not provide explicit information on modes of HIV transmission.[5]

Interviewees assert that the campaign had positive effects. One HIV-positive activist argued that when religious leaders publicly appeared with HIV-positive people in TV commercials they challenged the AIDS stigma in society.[6] A government official also said that the campaign led to a decline in stigma, since before the campaign "we had all these pastors condemning people with AIDS".[7] Church facilitators for the workshops reported that there were higher levels of general knowledge on HIV and AIDS among pastors after the campaign.[8] Additionally, an academic study credited the campaign with the decline in negative societal attitudes about people living with HIV and AIDS between 2001 and 2003 (Boulay, Tweedie, and Fiagbey 2008). Thus, the campaign was successful in meeting its narrow objectives.

Pastors capitalised on the CCG structure for HIV and AIDS mobilisation in two ways. First, pastors used the CCG's external linkages to gain information and moral support for their activities. Because the CCG has close ties to mission hospitals, it was able to include health-care professionals, such as doctors, nurses, and social workers, in its discussions on HIV and AIDS. At CCG meetings, these health-care experts passionately described their observations: AIDS patients facing imminent death felt desolate, lonely, and unloved, and these patients yearned for compassion and dignity in their final days.[9] As clinic staff grappled with the epidemic on the ground, most Ghanaian churches refused to discuss the disease, because they believed that people with the disease were "dying of sin".[10] These health-care professionals provided crucial information that helped pastors recognise the AIDS problem and define a role for the church beyond stigma and silence.

Additionally, the CCG has close linkages to international ecumenical bodies, such as the World Council of Churches and the All Africa Conference of Churches. CCG pastors used these connections to gain moral support and technical information on the disease for the Compassion Campaign. The CCG pastors used the fact that the World Council of Churches instituted its "The Church in Africa Has AIDS" campaign in 2001 as a way to justify their increased activities around the disease, particularly in a country with a high AIDS stigma. One former CCG worker speculated that without this external support, the Compassion Campaign would have gone nowhere.[11] Pastors' reliance on these external linkages shows that their agency in the Compassion Campaign was not absolute. On the other hand, pastors utilised these built-in structures to their advantage in mobilising the Compassion Campaign.

A second advantage of the CCG structure that pastors utilised was its ecumenical membership, which enabled pastors to act relatively early to address HIV and AIDS without putting themselves at great risk. It helps to remember the historical and epidemiological context to appreciate this fact. Before 2001, few African government leaders had spoken publicly on HIV and AIDS, and global attention to and donor funding for the disease was minimal. Additionally, few Ghanaians personally knew individuals with the disease and stigma was quite high (Afrobarometer 2004). The ecumenical nature of the campaign made it less likely that a society with high levels of stigma would criticise particular denominations or that individual congregations would condemn a specific pastor's actions on HIV and AIDS.[12] The Ghana Compassion Campaign illustrates how pastors can utilise ecumenical structures in risky environments to mobilise HIV and AIDS activities.

The HIV and AIDS activities of the 2000-member Northmead Assembly of God Church in Lusaka, Zambia highlight a pastor's use of congregational decision-making structures. This mobilisation was possible because, as is typical in many Pentecostal churches (Kalu 2008), decision-making in the congregation revolves around the pastor, Bishop Joshua Banda. The church has a governing board of individuals chosen by the bishop, who also chairs the board. Increasingly approached by HIV-positive congregants for support and counselling in the late 1990s, Bishop Banda began to publicly discuss HIV and AIDS in his sermons. At that point, few churches beyond the Catholics had HIV and

AIDS programmes; among Protestant (and particularly Pentecostal) churches, there was a vacuum in leadership. The bishop urged a group of HIV-positive congregants to form the first church-based support group for people living with HIV in Zambia (the "Circle of Hope"). The bishop's initial actions may have partly been a response to societal expectations that good pastors should show concern for both the spiritual and material conditions of their followers. By 2001, the church had several HIV and AIDS efforts, including abstinence-focused prevention programmes and HIV testing and counselling (*Post*, June 5, 2005). By 2005, the church oversaw income-generating projects for women at risk of HIV infection, and it had a farm where OVCs lived and were educated. In 2005, the church accessed PEPFAR funding to open the Circle of Hope ART clinic (Ndhlovu 2007).[13] Thus, the goals of the Northmead Church mobilisation – educating about HIV prevention and providing social services to people living with or affected by HIV and AIDS – were broader than those of the Compassion Campaign in Ghana. These efforts had a tangible impact on the community: by 2007, roughly 3800 HIV-positive people were receiving home-based care through the church, approximately 100 women were involved in income-generation projects, and over 40 homeless OVCs lived on the farm. By 2011, the clinic provided treatment to roughly 2000 people in five poor Lusaka neighborhoods.[14]

Bishop Banda was able to mobilise his congregation to develop many of these programmes with limited concern that these initiatives would be thwarted by the congregation. While some in the church did criticise these efforts as "too worldly",[15] the bishop's central role on the church's governing board gave him more leeway to act. Since their inception, the bishop has played a crucial role in the direction of these programmes: he sits on the boards of the clinic and the other programmes, and he has personally chosen prominent church and community leaders to serve as clinic board members.[16] As one staff member at the Circle of Hope clinic said, "While the bishop may not be here often, he knows everything that occurs here"[17]. While these programmes' governance structures facilitate action, they may also raise questions about wider participation in decision-making.

To summarise, leaders utilised particular church structures to mobilise action in both the Compassion Campaign of Ghana and the Northmead Assembly of God in Zambia, though these organisational structures differed in each case. In the Compassion Campaign, pastors utilised the Protestant ecumenical organisation with its external linkages to global ecumenical councils and health-care professionals to promote its AIDS education campaign. In contrast, the pastor-centred decision-making process within the Northmead Assembly of God enabled Bishop Banda to mobilise his congregation in its path-breaking and multi-faceted response to the disease in Zambia.

B.   *Pastors and frames for HIV and AIDS mobilisation*

Leaders play a crucial role in framing issues for mobilisation, particularly when issues are new or ill-defined. For example, Friedman and Mottiar (2004) demonstrate that the Treatment Action Campaign's success in HIV and AIDS mobilisation in South Africa resulted from its leaders' ability to frame the disease not as a problem of sexual morality but as a human rights issue. Because individuals vary greatly in the ways they perceive problems, frame alignment is a necessary process to encourage movement participation. I analyse what Snow et al. (1986) term "frame extension" (a process through which leaders approach an issue in a new way so as to mobilise participants) and "frame transformation" (an approach in which leaders link a narrow issue to broad and different understandings to reach out to new participants). The continuous debate about the ways in which churches should address the disease, even though AIDS cases have existed in the two countries since the mid-1980s, leads pastors to frame the disease in diverse ways.

Both the Northmead Assembly of God in Zambia and the Compassion Campaign in Ghana illustrate frame extension. In the Zambia case, Bishop Banda extended the church's frame of evangelism to urge church mobilisation on HIV and AIDS. The bishop acknowledged that when the church opened the ART clinic, some church members criticised the effort as too worldly, too biomedical, and potentially too expensive. In response, the bishop stressed that God wants all people to live full lives; he said that the poor, sick, and hungry will not be receptive to the Gospel message if they do not have their material needs met.[18] In a Sunday service, the bishop explained that the HIV-positive people whom the clinic serves are a potential group of non-evangelised individuals and that the clinic is a way for the church to reach this population.[19] The bishop used an important tenet of Pentecostalism – evangelism – to mobilise his church for HIV and AIDS activities.

Similarly, the Compassion Campaign took a common tenet of Christianity – Jesus Christ's acceptance of and love for the poor, sick, and marginalised – and built its campaign around this theme. The campaign's public slogan – "Who are you to judge?" – was rooted in the well-known New Testament story of the adulterous woman who was going to be stoned by the crowd before Jesus intervened.[20] Some of the aforementioned health-care workers described the negative effects of ostracism, exclusion, and discrimination that resulted from judging people with HIV and AIDS. These stories and the broader Ghanaian context of high stigma shaped pastors' desire to frame a message around compassion and acceptance. The campaign extended the theme of compassion to the new issue of AIDS with the goal of reducing stigma. But on the other hand, the context of high stigma and low HIV prevalence meant that the compassion framework did not challenge Ghanaians to mobilise in order to care for, support, or provide medical treatment for people with the disease (Patterson 2011). The overall message was anti-political: it did not tackle issues of societal inequality or demand greater state action on HIV and AIDS. Instead, it called on individual Ghanaians to alter their personal attitudes toward their HIV-positive fellow citizens.

A few pastors transformed HIV and AIDS to encompass broader issues of poverty, community development, and good governance. In these cases, mobilisation was no longer solely about the disease. This approach was most evident in the Jubilee Centre in Ndola, Zambia and its dynamic leader, Pentecostal pastor Lawrence Temfwe. The organisation helps networks of churches in Lusaka and the Copperbelt work together to combat poverty; HIV and AIDS efforts such as income-generation projects and the provision of assistance to OVCs are included under the umbrella of poverty reduction. These networks of pastors have also worked with their communities to sign memoranda of understanding (MOUs) with political officials about how local and national government officials will address community needs. These MOUs have included demands for schools, roads, ART facilities, and land titles (Chipulukusu/Mapalo Community 2006). The organisation's frame for mobilisation uses a common trait among all community members – their poverty – to bring people together.[21] In doing so, the Jubilee Centre and the pastors it trains transform AIDS from a single issue into a problem that results from high poverty and limited government attention to citizens' needs.

Pastors were crucial in developing frames for mobilisation in the above examples. Pastors on the CCG were pragmatic; they had prior experience negotiating with the state during Ghana's transition from military rule to democracy (Ranger 2008). They knew that mainline Protestant mobilisation would not be possible if they framed HIV and AIDS in a way that threatened the belief systems of Christians and non-Christians or if their frames demanded that people living in Ghana's environment of high stigma engage in direct action to fight the disease. Bishop Banda has been heralded as a visionary in his ability to generate interest in HIV and AIDS among Pentecostals (*Post*, 5 June, 2005; Phiri 2007).[22] And in the words of one Jubilee Centre leader, "Pastor Temfwe is gifted at bringing people together and helping them see issues in new ways".[23]

While pastors provided the framework, it was necessary that their messages would resonate with their audiences in order for mobilisation to occur. Bishop Banda's ability to link HIV and AIDS to evangelism appealed to Pentecostals who feel called to spread the Gospel. Bishop Banda is somewhat unusual among evangelical pastors, because he utilised evangelism to create a niche for his church mobilisation. Many other Pentecostal pastors have been hesitant to approach the AIDS issue, because of its links to sexual behavior. When they have spoken on the disease, their approach has tended to be narrow and to only stress sexual morality (Pfeiffer 2004). While Bishop Banda did not ignore these messages about morality, they were not the main frame for mobilising congregants to support the clinic, the OVC programme, and the income-generation efforts for people at risk of HIV infection. The very fact that the bishop was Pentecostal then gave him further leverage in his mobilisation, in a country where Pentecostal churches are rapidly growing and where Christians dominate society.

For the Jubilee Centre, its transformative message appealed to both HIV-positive and HIV-negative individuals because it did not rely on sero-status as an identity for action. While this transformative frame had the danger of ignoring the specific needs of HIV-positive people, it had the advantage of avoiding HIV stigma and discrimination. According to one church leader working with the Jubilee Centre, this message was particularly appealing to church members because of the disease's continued association with promiscuity.[24]

The frames incorporated by Bishop Banda and Pastor Temfwe contrast, despite the fact that they are both Pentecostal pastors. The distinctive frames may reflect the cultural context in which Pentecostal churches increasingly compete for members and prestige. Bishop Banda's frame did not directly challenge political power structures or state policies, although his church was involved in HIV and AIDS policymaking as I illustrate below. Rather, this frame sought to provide services and the Gospel message to unreached peoples. As such, it echoes the idea that African NGOs and FBOs act as depoliticised development partners. Pastor Temfwe, on the other hand, urged churches to engage in the political process. While the Jubilee Centre provided some material support to churches for community projects, it focused on empowering church members as citizens. The goal, however, was to open channels of cooperation and communication with political officials, not to directly confront them.[25] In doing so, the Jubilee Centre churches engaged in political activism through the power-broking networks that epitomise African politics (van de Walle 2001).

C. Political opportunity structures and pastoral leadership

This section asserts that pastors who successfully respond to HIV and AIDS embrace political opportunities for mobilisation. Because of Africa's dependence on foreign assistance, changes in donor attention to the continent create one such political opportunity (Ellis and van Kessel 2009). In the case of HIV and AIDS, media coverage of the disease, celebrity campaigns to highlight the issue, global activism, and high-level discussions in the United Nations had pushed the disease into public consciousness by

2001. The Global Fund and PEPFAR were tangible funding results. These programmes (and other bilateral donor efforts) meant that resources for HIV and AIDS increased greatly; between 2001 and 2009, this funding rose from $1.6 billion to $15.9 billion (UNAIDS 2011). Greater appreciation for the role of religion in the development enterprise accompanied this funding opportunity (Thomas 2005). As a result, roughly 20% of PEPFAR money has gone to global FBOs such as World Vision and their local partners (Patterson 2006). Some African church institutions (such as the Churches Health Association of Zambia) received millions of dollars from the Global Fund and PEPFAR. As recipients of large sums of money, African churches and FBOs were also incorporated into high-level discussions at UNAIDS and given seats on national AIDS councils (WHO 2007; Patterson 2011).

Leaders have heightened influence with new opportunity structures, because situations are fluid, patterns for responding to a problem are unclear, and the set of actors to address the problem are often not well defined. Leaders may embrace new opportunities to urge church mobilisation on HIV and AIDS, or they may demobilise church activities. In the context of increased global attention to HIV and AIDS in the new millennium, leaders in the Northmead Assembly of God and the CCG mobilised around the opportunity. But the case of the CCG also demonstrates how leaders may choose to demobilise when opportunity structures become discouraging to church activities. While demobilisation does not detract from the CCG's early successes, it does demonstrate that mobilisation may not be continuous.

1. Pastors embrace opportunities: the Northmead Assembly of God in Zambia

Although the Northmead Assembly of God began low-level HIV and AIDS activities in the late 1990s, it did not increase its efforts until 2000, when Bishop Banda collaborated with several other pastors to form the Expanded Church Response (ECR) in Zambia. Believing that church cooperation was essential for HIV and AIDS work, World Vision-Zambia encouraged the ECR's establishment. At this point, there were few church HIV and AIDS efforts beyond Catholic home-based care programmes. The issue arena was fluid and the actors were undefined. While the ECR's founders (four Pentecostal pastors led by Bishop Banda) took the initiative, the establishment of the organisation was somewhat controversial. Mainline Protestant church leaders asserted that Bishop Banda had not worked through the "proper channels" of the established ecumenical councils.[26] By 2007, the ECR worked with local congregations to build capacity for grassroots advocacy and AIDS awareness programmes. In 2009, the ECR became a direct recipient of PEPFAR funding for programmes that provide support and care for people living with and affected by HIV and AIDS (ECR, n.d.).[27]

The ECR's success catapulted Bishop Banda into a leadership role on HIV and AIDS in Zambia. His church gained greater attention in the media, particularly when former US First Lady Laura Bush visited Zambia in 2007, and when Bishop Banda was appointed to the National AIDS Council (Phiri 2007). Thus, the church's initial mobilisation through the ECR led to more access to AIDS resources. In 2005, the Northmead Church became one of two Pentecostal churches in Lusaka that was given PEPFAR funding to begin an ART clinic.[28] This achievement was possible because the bishop understood the changing dynamics of HIV and AIDS efforts in Zambia and, particularly, the goal of PEPFAR to bring more FBOs into the response to HIV and AIDS. The nebulous, fluid context that existed with the initiation of massive donor programmes in the new millennium provided an arena in which the bishop could define a new role for his church.

The theme of extraversion is evident in the formal and informal HIV and AIDS activities of the Northmead Church. On a formal level, the bishop capitalised on the prevailing belief among Western governments, donors, and AIDS experts that Africa could not address HIV and AIDS without massive foreign assistance. This theme was evident in President George W. Bush's 2003 speech that announced PEPFAR, an announcement shaped by conversations with African leaders including Bishop Banda.[29] President Bush termed PEPFAR "a work of mercy beyond all current international efforts to help the people of Africa" (Gerson 2013). But extraversion was also exemplified in the informal networks that African church officials built with Western churches and FBOs. These fluid networks have brought together non-denominational, evangelical, and socially conservative churches in the West and Pentecostal churches in Africa (Hearn 2002; Miller and Yamamori 2007). They emerged with the mobilisation of evangelical Christians in the West, who tended to stress the images of innocent, weak, and marginalised Africans in their portrayal of the disease ("Close Encounters with HIV" 2006). For the Northmead Church, these external connections that flowed from such images led the church to host mission groups from American churches and Christian universities. Aware of the benefits of such networks, church leaders throughout Zambia looked for such connections. For example, one Pentecostal pastor in a poor Lusaka neighbourhood asked me: "Can you help us get connected to American sources for funding? We know that you aren't a donor, but we are looking for connections".[30]

While African actors depend on external connections and resources, donors also need African institutions to implement programmes and meet agency objectives. Donor officials in Zambia quickly admit that if they had to implement home-based care or OVC programmes, they would not have the resources or manpower to do so.[31] In Ghana, donors relied on churches to educate citizens in early HIV and AIDS campaigns because of the churches' legitimacy and wide reach in the country.[32]

Much of PEPFAR and the Global Fund's reliance on non-state actors, including African churches, for HIV and AIDS programme implementation rests on the idea that these organisations are not political. That is, they are assumed to engage in service delivery without challenging power structures, advocating for interests, or lobbying for resources. As Stephen Joshua (2010) found with Catholic HIV and AIDS efforts in South Africa, professionalisation can lead church AIDS programmes to resemble any other NGO effort. In one sense, this apolitical nature is partly evident in the Circle of Hope clinic linked to the Northmead Assembly of God: it is staffed by nurses, clinical officers, counsellors, data-entry specialists, and a programme manager. Staff members administer HIV tests, meet clients, dispense ART medicines, fill out reports, and counsel patients about adherence to medication.[33] By 2011, this church-based mobilisation had become more professionalised: the clinic had moved far from the church's neighbourhood in order to better serve populations in need; fewer church members volunteered at the clinic; and only three of twenty clinic staff members were congregation members.[34] Despite this professionalisation, the congregation was still somewhat involved in the clinic through representation on the clinic's governing board, regular church fund-raising efforts, and continued spiritual and moral support.[35] Professionalisation illustrates how mobilisation may take on different forms with time.

On the other hand, the HIV and AIDS mobilisation at the Northmead Assembly of God also had political aspects. The formation of the ECR excluded other churches and set in motion a process by which the Northmead Assembly of God gained resources and representation in policymaking. Through its heightened position, the church was then able to shape HIV and AIDS policies, and particularly to advocate for abstinence in prevention programmes, through Bishop Banda's position on the National AIDS Council. Because PEPFAR has heightened attention to and funding for abstinence campaigns, conservative churches such as Northmead have gained a greater voice in prevention debates and more access to AIDS funds ("Senate Passes PEPFAR Reauthorization Legislation" 2008; Patterson 2006; Phiri 2007). The fact that donors such as PEPFAR, UNAIDS, and the Global Fund have increased programming for abstinence and fidelity campaigns demonstrates that church mobilisation not only responds to externally-presented opportunity structures, but it can also define those structures. If donor programmes are intended to be successful then their organisers must consider the ideas of major societal actors, such as powerful church leaders like Bishop Banda, who now have the resources to mobilise others and the representation to express their opinions. In this process, churches engage in the political act of policy definition.

2. Pastors embrace then refuse opportunity structures: the Compassion Campaign in Ghana

In 2000, pastors in the CCG recognised donors' concern that the HIV prevalence in West Africa could become as high as it was in southern Africa. In 2001, this concern manifested itself in a $25 million loan from the World Bank to Ghana to establish the Ghana AIDS Commission and to design a multi-sectoral HIV and AIDS strategy. In 2002, the country's largest bilateral donor, USAID, provided $20 million for combating HIV and AIDS, over one third of the funding that the American agency provided to Ghana in that one year (Patterson 2007). Leaders in the CCG responded positively to these opportunities with the Compassion Campaign, a three-year effort. The campaign's narrow focus on AIDS awareness comported with donors' concern for HIV prevention, the prevailing trends of denial and stigma in society, and the need for Muslim–Christian cooperation in order to educate the wider population.

By 2008 (the year in which this research was conducted), the opportunity structures around HIV and AIDS in Ghana had changed. It had become apparent that the country's HIV prevalence was not rapidly increasing, and that the large donor programmes like PEPFAR and the Global Fund were not going to give millions to countries with low HIV rates. In low HIV prevalence countries, donors moved from HIV and AIDS awareness efforts for the general population to programmes that targeted at-risk populations such as commercial sex workers. Donors also focused less on HIV and AIDS and more on malaria and maternal mortality. By 2008 USAID money for the disease had dropped by two thirds from 2002 (USAID 2008).[36] The epidemic also seemed to fall off the national political agenda. The Ghanaian president rarely spoke about the disease in public after 2003, and the Ghana AIDS Commission declined in power from its high-level position in the president's office to its low-level placement in the Ministry of Women and Children.[37]

In this new opportunity structure, church leaders' attention waned and church efforts diminished. Most pastors did not speak about HIV and AIDS, and church leaders who had been involved with the Compassion Campaign moved on to other health and development issues. This was particularly true for the church-based medical professionals who had been so passionate about the disease in 2000.[38] Because Ghana's prevalence did not increase, church leaders, like the general population, did not view HIV and AIDS to be a crucial issue.[39] Pastors responded to this new opportunity structure with demobilisation. To be clear, this decline in interest did not mean that the initial campaign did not meet its objectives. As demonstrated above, the campaign did educate church leaders on the basic facts about HIV and AIDS and help to reduce public stigma. Instead, the decreased interested in HIV and AIDS five years after the campaign ended illustrates that mobilisation is not static.

The Compassion Campaign contrasts with the Northmead Church example because its participants did not rely on a strategy of extraversion to attract new AIDS funding when donor money ended. While the CCG had tried to access some resources, these efforts had yielded meagre results.[40] Perhaps this outcome reflected the low priority that HIV and AIDS was for many CCG leaders by 2008 because of the country's low HIV rates. While the decline of the campaign may appear to be apolitical, it is possible to interpret this demobilisation as a reaction to donors' new focus on marginal populations with whom church leaders may not have wanted to be associated. Here it is important to remember that the initial campaign had not focused on at-risk populations; instead, it had emphasised heterosexual transmission of HIV, the broad HIV risk to all Ghanaians, and the need to show compassion to people with the disease (without questioning how they acquired the virus). By 2008, the broader AIDS agenda had changed. One multilateral donor official explained this new dynamic: "There is a reason the churches [now] say nothing on AIDS. They don't want to be linked to a disease that affects sex workers, people with multiple partners, or men who have sex with men".[41]

To be fair, some churches remained active on HIV and AIDS long after the Compassion Campaign. One mainline Protestant denomination developed income-generating projects for women living with HIV, another Protestant denomination provided HIV prevention messages to church youth, and the CCG continued local AIDS awareness campaigns in rural Ghanaian churches.[42] In some mega-churches, Pentecostal pastors stressed the need for HIV testing and for greater sexual morality among congregants, particularly youth.[43] None of these efforts were high level or very publicly visible, though. And with the exception of a handful of individual congregations, these efforts did not embrace donors' new focus on at-risk populations.[44] Through these local-level activities (and through churches' unwillingness to work with at-risk populations), the churches involved with the Compassion Campaign engaged the politically contentious process of defining societal values and shaping popular perceptions of the disease.

The demobilisation that occurred after the official end of the Compassion Campaign raises three points about church leadership on HIV and AIDS. First, in order to sustain efforts, leadership must be continuously refreshed and reinvigorated; for this to occur, an investment must be made in leadership development. Church officials who had worked on the Compassion Campaign complained that donors would not support HIV and AIDS training in theological schools or seminaries. And because the disease was no longer a leadership priority, it was hard for individual congregations to commit to such educational efforts.[45] Second, part of the decline in CCG pastors' interest in HIV and AIDS may have reflected the fact that church members did not expect pastors to meet their needs related to the disease. Unlike in Zambia, it seemed that few Ghanaian congregants looked to their pastors to provide material, spiritual, or social help on HIV and AIDS.

Third, the Ghana case shows that the ways in which issues are framed matter for both short-term and long-term mobilisation. Discouraging judgemental attitudes helped the Compassion Campaign gain traction in a religiously diverse country with a high AIDS stigma, but it also reflected the subjective interpretation that AIDS is a problem outside the church and that HIV-positive "others" need compassion. Not only did the campaign reflect those attitudes, but it also helped to perpetuate them.[46] As of 2008, many pastors and churchgoers still thought that "good Christians" do not contract HIV, even though Ghanaian churches do have HIV-positive members, many of whom face great stigma.[47] Over time, the perception that the epidemic does not negatively affect the church did not push church leaders to claim the AIDS problem as their own and to develop care, support, advocacy, and treatment programmes. The compassion theme had a short-term benefit, but did not provide an effective frame for long-term mobilisation, particularly when donor funding declined and the country's HIV rate did not increase.[48]

The Ghana case illustrates that mobilisation is dynamic; it cannot be assumed that once a movement begins it will continue at its same level of activity. To be clear, this transformation does not diminish the campaign's earlier successes in educating pastors on basic HIV and AIDS facts, and challenging the public stigma towards the disease. But the transformation does show how changes in political priorities and the epidemiological context, as well as inadequate frames for action, may hamper long-term mobilisation. By 2008, donors' focus on at-risk groups, less interest in and fear of the disease in the population, the decline in HIV prevalence, and challenges in the ways in which HIV and AIDS were understood made it difficult for pastors in the CCG to sustain interest in mobilisation beyond somewhat ad hoc efforts. The case illustrates that the larger context for mobilisation matters, since it influences leaders' agency. This decline in agency meant that churches did not lead the country's response to HIV and AIDS as they had at the start of the new millennium.

VI. Conclusion

This article has analysed the ways in which pastors in Ghana and Zambia utilise church organisational structures, frames, and opportunity structures in HIV and AIDS mobilisation. The work demonstrated that in Ghana, church leaders used ecumenical structures and links to global ecumenical bodies and health-care providers to facilitate their mobilisation. In Zambia, the Pentecostal pastor Bishop Banda could mobilise on HIV and AIDS because he was relatively autonomous in church decision-making. The work illustrated that pastors have framed AIDS mobilisation with biblical messages that resonate with church members. However, as in the case of the Jubilee Centre, framing was sometimes implicitly political and sought to situate HIV and AIDS in the context of government responsibilities in order to promote social justice. The opportunities that emerged for increased AIDS funding and programmes after 2001 had diverging effects on Ghanaian and Zambian churches: in the former, church activities first increased and then declined, while in the latter, they ramped up.

These findings raise three future research questions about the leadership of church mobilisation on HIV and AIDS. The first relates to the dynamism of social movements. This article has demonstrated that church leaders may frame issues to urge participation, use strategies of extraversion to access resources, allow their ministries to become professionalised, and directly engage in political debates. Less positively, these same leaders may struggle with movement dynamics over time, as larger policy, social, and epidemiological contexts affect their agency. Churches in Ghana and Zambia illustrate many of these themes, sometimes alone or in combination. By 2011, churches faced a new global AIDS landscape. The global recession, the popular perception in the West that HIV and AIDS in Africa is no longer a problem, and the inability of treatment programmes to keep up with new HIV infections pushed the disease off the political agenda in industrialised countries. In 2010, funding for PEPFAR stagnated; US commitment to the Global Fund declined by $50 million; and Global Fund grants were on average 12% smaller than in 2009 (McNeil 2010). Future research should investigate how leaders respond during such times of declining global interest.

A second area of inquiry centres on the effects of pastor-driven mobilisation on the involvement of HIV-positive people in church HIV/AIDS-related activities. David Maxwell (2000) points out that power centralisation in Pentecostal churches can hamper participatory decision-making and heighten opportunities for corruption. What does pastor-centred mobilisation mean for the involvement of people living with HIV and AIDS in such church-based programmes? What changes in resources, opportunity structures, organisational structures, or socio-cultural contexts would be necessary in order for HIV-positive people to take over this leadership position from pastors? Because one of the goals of the global AIDS movement is to empower HIV-positive individuals to participate in policy decisions that directly affect their lives, this question deserves greater attention (UNAIDS 2010b).

Finally, more research is needed on the effect of HIV and AIDS mobilisation on churches and pastors themselves. Catrine Christiansen (2010) finds that when Ugandan churches have received large amounts of funding for HIV and AIDS, their pastors have lost legitimacy with their congregations. While congregants know the church has gained resources, they often feel that the members do not directly benefit from these monies. In the future, it may be inaccurate to state that pastors are highly trusted in Africa. How might such a loss in pastoral legitimacy hamper all pastors' future ability to urge their followers to address Africa's multiple socio-economic problems, such as unemployment, gender inequality, and public health challenges? If the church is to be a constructive institution that combats poverty and underdevelopment in Africa, such a question deserves greater attention.

Acknowledgements

An earlier version of this article was presented at the 2010 Summer School on Religion, AIDS, and Social Activism in Africa held at the Working Group on the Social and Political Aspects of AIDS in Uganda, Child Health and Development Centre, Makerere University, Kampala, Uganda, 5–9 July 2010. The summer school was sponsored by the Calvin Center for Christian Scholarship. Research for this paper was funded by the Fulbright African Regional Research Program, the Calvin College Alumni Association, the McGregor Fellowship Program, the Nagel Institute for the Study of World Christianity, the Paul Henry Institute for the Study of Christianity and Politics, and the Calvin College semester in Ghana program. I am grateful to Marian Burchardt, Louise Mubanda Rasmussen, the Uganda 2010 summer school participants, and two anonymous reviewers for their insightful comments.

Notes

1. Interview with church community AIDS mobiliser, by author. Lusaka, 10 March 2011.
2. Interview with HIV-positive individual, by author. Lusaka, 8 March 2011.
3. Two interviewees gave me permission to use their names.
4. Interview with former Compassion Campaign official, by author. Accra, 25 September 2008.
5. Interview with denominational AIDS coordinator, by author. Accra, 10 November 2008; interview with multilateral donor official, by author. Accra, 8 October 2008.
6. Interview with AIDS activist, by author. Accra, 14 October 2008.
7. Interview with Ghana AIDS Commission official, by author. Accra, 10 October 2008.
8. Interview with former Compassion Campaign official, by author. Accra, 25 September 2008; interview with CCG official, by author. Accra, 21 October 2008.
9. Interview with denominational AIDS coordinator, by author. Accra, 10 November 2008.
10. Interview with former CCG leader, by author. Accra, 27 August 2008; interview with denominational AIDS coordinator, by author. Accra, 10 November 2008; interview with CCG official, by author. Accra, 21 October 2008.
11. Interview with former CCG worker, by author. Accra, 2 September 2008.

12. Interview with CCG official, by author. Accra, 21 October 2008; interview with former denominational AIDS coordinator, by author. Kumasi, Ghana, 2 December 2008.
13. Interview with Circle of Hope clinic staff member, by author. Lusaka, 23 February 2011; interview with Circle of Hope clinic board member, by author. Lusaka, 29 March 2011; interview with Bishop Joshua Banda, by author. Lusaka, 17 February 2011. More information on the Northmead Assembly of God is available at http://www.northmeadassembly.org.zm (accessed 25 June 2011).
14. Interview with Bishop Joshua Banda, by author. Lusaka, 14 August 2007; interview with Circle of Hope clinic staff member, by author. Lusaka, 23 February 2011.
15. Interview with Bishop Joshua Banda, by author. Lusaka, 17 February 2011.
16. Interview with Circle of Hope clinic board member, by author. Lusaka, 29 March 2011.
17. Interview with Circle of Hope staff member, by author. Lusaka, 2 March 2011.
18. Interview with Bishop Joshua Banda, by author. Lusaka, 17 February 2011.
19. Author's notes from observing a Northmead Assembly of God Sunday morning service. Lusaka, 5 June 2011.
20. See John 8:1–11 for this story.
21. Interview with Pastor Lawrence Temfwe, by author. Ndola, Zambia, 23 May 2011.
22. Interview with Circle of Hope clinic staff member, by author. Lusaka, 18 March 2011.
23. Interview with Jubilee Centre staff member, by author. Ndola, Zambia, 21 May 2011.
24. Interview with church leader, by author. Ndola, Zambia, 21 May 2011.
25. Interview with Jubilee Centre-trained pastor, by author. Lusaka, 31 May 2011.
26. Telephone interview with former Christian Council of Zambia official, by author. Lusaka, 19 April 2011.
27. Interview with ECR founding pastor, by author. Lusaka, 14 August 2007; interview with ECR staff member, by author. Lusaka, 31 March 2011.
28. Interview with Circle of Hope clinic staff member, by author. Lusaka, 23 February 2011.
29. Interview with Bishop Joshua Banda, by author. Lusaka, 17 February 2011.
30. Interview with Pentecostal pastor, by author. Lusaka, 23 April 2011.
31. Interview with bilateral donor official, by author. Lusaka, 8 June 2011.
32. Interview with former Compassion Campaign official, by author. Accra, 25 September 2008.
33. Author's notes from observing Circle of Hope clinic operations. Lusaka, 2 March 2011, 8 March 2011, and 17 March 2011.
34. Interview with Circle of Hope clinic staff member, by author. Lusaka, 23 February 2011; interview with Circle of Hope clinic staff member, by author. Lusaka, 12 March 2011.
35. Interview with Bishop Joshua Banda, by author. Lusaka, 17 February 2011.
36. Interview with Ghana AIDS Commission official, by author. Accra, 10 October 2008.
37. Interview with multilateral donor official, by author. Accra, 8 October 2008.
38. Interview with former Ghanaian AIDS NGO official, by author. Accra, 30 November 2008; interview with former denominational AIDS coordinator, by author. Accra, 10 November 2008.
39. Interview with former denominational AIDS coordinator, by author. Kumasi, Ghana, 2 December 2008.
40. Interview with CCG official, by author. Accra, 21 October 2008.
41. Interview with multilateral donor, by author. Accra, 8 October 2008.
42. Interview with denominational women's coordinator, by author. Accra, 4 December 2008; interview with denominational AIDS coordinator, by author. Accra, 2 September 2008; interview with CCG official, by author. Accra, 21 October 2008.
43. Interview with Pentecostal pastor, by author. Accra, 11 November 2008; interview with Ghana AIDS Commission official, by author. Accra, 10 October 2008.
44. Interview with former denominational AIDS coordinator, by author. Kumasi, Ghana, 2 December 2008; interview with Ghanaian FBO official, by author. Kumasi, Ghana, 2 December 2008.
45. Interview with former denominational AIDS coordinator, by author. Kumasi, Ghana, 2 December 2008; interview with former CCG leader, by author. Accra, 27 August 2008.
46. Interview with denominational women's coordinator, by author. Accra, 4 December 2008; interview with former Compassion Campaign official, by author. Accra, 25 September 2008; interview with Ghanaian FBO youth worker, by author. Accra, 29 August 2008.

47. Interview with Ghanaian FBO youth worker, by author. Accra, 29 August 2008; interview with denominational women's coordinator, by author. Accra, 4 December 2008.
48. Interview with multilateral donor official, by author. Accra, 8 October 2008; interview with former Compassion Campaign official, by author. Accra, 25 September 2008.

Bibliography

Afrobarometer. 2004. "Public Opinion and HIV/AIDS: Facing up to the Future?" Briefing Paper 12. Accessed June 3, 2006. http://www.afrobarometer.org/index.php?searchword=HIV%2FaIDS& ordering=&searchphrase=all&Itemid=39&option=com_search

Afrobarometer. 2009. "Are Democratic Citizens Emerging in Africa?" Briefing Paper 70. Accessed May 27, 2010. http://www.afrobarometer.org/papers/AfrobriefNo70_21may09.pdf

Amanze, James, ed. 2007. *Christian Ethics and HIV/AIDS in Africa*. Gaborne: Bay Publishing.

Barrett, David, George Kurian, and Todd Johnson. 2001. *World Christian Encyclopedia: A Comparative Survey of Churches and Religions in the Modern World*. New York: Oxford University Press.

Bayart, Jean-François. 1993. *The State in Africa: The Politics of the Belly*. London: Longman.

Boulay, Marc, Ian Tweedie, and Emmanuel Fiagbey. 2008. "The Effectiveness of a National Communication Campaign Using Religious Leaders to Reduce HIV-Related Stigma in Ghana." *African Journal of AIDS Research* 7 (1): 133–141.

Byamugisha, Gideon. 2010. "Understanding Religious Involvement in the Ugandan AIDS Response." Pamphlet prepared for the conference of the International Research Network on AIDS and Religion in Africa, Kampala, Uganda, July 5–9.

Chipulukusu/Mapalo Community. 2006. "Memorandum of Understanding with Officials, Ndola, Zambia." Unpublished document. Ndola, Zambia.

Christiansen, Catrine. 2010. "Development by Churches, Development of Churches: Institutional Trajectories in Rural Uganda." PhD diss. Department of Anthropology, University of Copenhagen.

"Close Encounters with HIV". 2006. *Christianity Today*, February 1. http://www.christianitytoday.com/ct/2006/february/17.30.html

Compassion Campaign. 2002. *Notes from Sunyani Training*. Accra: Christian Council of Ghana.

Ellis, Stephen, and Gerrie ter Haar. 1998. "Religion and Politics in Sub-Saharan Africa." *The Journal of Modern African Studies* 36 (2): 175–201.

Ellis, Stephen, and Gerrie ter Haar. 2004. *Worlds of Power: Religious Thzought and Political Practice in Africa*. New York: Oxford University Press.

Ellis, Stephen, and Ineke van Kessel. 2009. "Introduction: African Social Movements or Social Movements in Africa?" In *Movers and Shakers: Social Movements in Africa*, edited by Stephen Ellis, and Ineke van Kessel, 1–16. Leiden: Brill Publishers.

Expanded Church Response. n.d. *Factsheet*. Lusaka, Zambia: Expanded Church Response.

Ferguson, James. 1990. *The Anti-Politics Machine: "Development," Depoliticization, and Bureaucratic Power in Lesotho*. New York: Cambridge University Press.

Friedman, Steven, and Shauna Mottiar. 2004. "A Moral to the Tale: The Treatment Action Campaign and the Politics of HIV/AIDS." Paper for the Centre for Policy Studies. Durban, South Africa: University of KwaZulu-Natal.

Gallup News Service. 2007. "Africans' Confidence in Institutions—Which Country Stands Out?" *News Release*. Accessed February 18, 2008. http://www.gallup.com/poll/26176/Africans-Confidence-Institutions-Which-Country-Stands-Out.aspx

Gerson, Michael. 2013. "George W. Bush's Words That Saved Millions". *Washington Post*, February 11. http://www.washingtonpost.com/opinions/michael-gerson-george-w-bushs-words-in-state-of-union-saved-millions-of-people/2013/02/11/5e899754-7483-11e2-aa12-e6cf1d31106b_story.html

Gifford, Paul. 2004. *Ghana's New Christianity: Pentecostalism in a Globalizing African Economy*. Bloomington: Indiana University Press.

Goodwin, Jeff, and James Jasper. 2004. *Rethinking Social Movements: Structure, Meaning, and Emotion*. New York: Rowman & Littlefield Publishers.

Green, Edward. 2003. *Rethinking AIDS Prevention: Learning From Successes in Developing Countries*. Greenport, CT: Praeger.

Gusman, Alessandro. 2009. "HIV/AIDS, Pentecostal Churches, and the 'Joseph Generation' in Uganda." *Africa Today* 56 (1): 66–86.

Haynes, Naomi. 2009. "My Wealth, Your Health: Prosperity Theology and the Praxis of Care Among Zambian Pentecostals." Paper presented at the conference of the International Research Network on AIDS and Religion in Africa, Lusaka, Zambia, April 15–17.

Hearn, Julie. 2002. "The 'Invisible' NGO: US Evangelical Missions in Kenya." *Journal of Religion in Africa* 32 (1): 32–60.

Joshua, Stephen Muoki. 2010. "A Critical Historical Analysis of the South African Catholic Church's HIV/AIDS Response Between 2000 and 2005." *African Journal of AIDS Research* 9 (4): 437–447.

Kalu, Ogbu. 2008. *African Pentecostalism: An Introduction*. New York: Oxford University Press.

Kapenda Lumbe, John Muntunda. 2008. "Origins and Growth of Pentecostal and Neo-Pentecostal Church Movements in Zambia Between 1989 and 2000." MA thesis, University of South Africa.

Keck, Margaret, and Kathryn Sikkink. 1998. *Activists Beyond Borders: Advocacy Networks in International Politics*. Ithaca, NY: Cornell University Press.

Kelly, Michael. 2010. *HIV and AIDS: A Social Justice Perspective*. Nairobi: Paulines Publications Africa.

Little, Eric, and Carolyn Logan. 2008. "The Quality of Democracy and Governance in Africa: New Results from Afrobarometer Round 4." Working Paper 108, Accessed June 15, 2009. http://www.afrobarometer.org/papers/AfropaperNo108_21may09_newfinal.pdf

Maxwell, David. 2000. "'Catch the Cockerel before Dawn': Pentecostalism and Politics in Post-Colonial Zimbabwe." *Africa: Journal of the International African Institute* 70 (2): 249–277.

McAdam, Doug, John McCarthy, and Mayer Zald. 1996. *Comparative Perspectives on Social Movements: Political Opportunities, Mobilizing Structures and Cultural Framings*. Cambridge: Cambridge University Press.

McCarthy, John, and Mayer Zald. 1977. "Resource Mobilization and Social Movements: A Partial Theory." *American Journal of Sociology* 82 (6): 1212–1242.

McNeil, Donald. 2010. "As the Need Grows, the Money for AIDS Runs Far Short." *New York Times*, May 9. http://www.nytimes.com/2010/05/10/world/africa/10aidsmoney.html?_r=0

Meyer, Birgit. 2004. "Christianity in Africa: From African Independent to Pentecostal-Charismatic Churches." *Annual Review of Anthropology* 33 (1): 447–474.

Miller, Donald, and Tetsunao Yamamori. 2007. *Global Pentecostalism: The New Face of Christian Social Engagement*. Los Angeles: University of California Press.

Ministry of Health, National AIDS Council, and UNAIDS. 2011. *Zambia Country Progress Report. UNGASS 2010 Reporting*. Accessed May 30, 2011. http://www.unaids.org/en/dataanalysis/monitoringcountryprogress/2010progressreportssubmittedbycountries/zambia_2010_country_progress_report_en.pdf

Morris, Aldon, and Suzanne Staggenborg. 2004. "Leadership in Social Movements." In *The Blackwell Companion to Social Movements*, edited by David Snow, Sarah Soule, and Hanspeter Kriesi, 171–196. London: Blackwell Publishing.

Mwinituo, P., and J. Mill. 2006. "Stigma Associated with Ghanaian Caregivers of AIDS Patients." *Western Journal of Nursing Research* 28 (4): 369–382.

Ndhlovu, Japhet. 2007. "Combating HIV: A Ministerial Strategy for Zambian Churches." PhD diss., University of Stellenbosch, South Africa.

Okyerefo, Michael Perry Kweku, Daniel Yaw Fiaveh, and Kofi Takyi Asante. 2011. "Religion as a Tool in Strengthening the Democratic Process in Ghana." *Journal of African Studies and Development* 3: 124–130.

Patterson, Amy S. 2006. *The Politics of AIDS in Africa*. Boulder, CO: Lynne Rienner Publishers.

Patterson, Amy S. 2007. "Advocacy in the AIDS Fight: The Role of Churches in Zambia." Paper presented at the African Studies Association Conference, New York, NY, October 18–21.

Patterson, Amy S. 2010. "Church Mobilisation and HIV/AIDS Treatment in Ghana and Zambia: A Comparative Analysis." *African Journal of AIDS Research* 9 (4): 407–418.

Patterson, Amy S. 2011. *The Church and AIDS in Africa: The Politics of Ambiguity*. Boulder, CO: First Forum Press.

Pfeiffer, James. 2004. "Condom Social Marketing, Pentecostalism, and Structural Adjustment in Mozambique: A Clash of AIDS Prevention Messages." *Medical Anthropology Quarterly* 18 (1): 77–103.

Phiri, Isaac. 2007. "Abstinence Brings 'Dignity'." *Christianity Today*. June 29. Accessed May 30, 2011. http://www.christianitytoday.com/ct/2007/juneweb-only/126-52.0.html?start=2

Piot, Peter. 2006. "Statement at the UN General Assembly High Meeting on AIDS." New York, May 31. Accessed August 11, 2011. http://www.unaids.org/en/media/unaids/contentassets/dataimport/pub/speechexd/2006/20060531_sp_piot_hlm_en.pdf

Ranger, Terence, ed. 2008. *Evangelical Christianity and Democracy in Africa*. New York: Oxford University Press.

Rasmussen, Louise Mubanda. 2011. "From Dying with Dignity to Living with Rules: AIDS Treatment and 'Holistic Care' in Catholic Organisations in Uganda." PhD diss. Centre of African Studies, University of Copenhagen.

"Senate Passes PEPFAR Reauthorization Legislation." 2008. *Kaiser Daily HIV/AIDS Report*, July 17. http://www.kaiserhealthnews.org/Daily-Reports/2008/July/17/dr00053344.aspx?p=1

Snow, David, E. Burke Rochford, Steven Worden, and Robert Benford. 1986. "Frame Alignment Processes, Micromobilization, and Movement Participation." *American Sociological Review* 51 (4): 464–481.

Snow, David, Sarah Soule, and Hanspeter Kriesi, eds. 2004. *The Blackwell Companion to Social Movements*. London: Blackwell Publishing.

Sorensen, Georg, ed. 2007. *Democracy and Democratization: Processes and Prospects in a Changing World*. Boulder, CO: Westview Press.

Tarrow, Sidney. 1989. *Democracy and Disorder: Protest and Politics in Italy 1965–1975*. Oxford: Clarendon Press.

Thomas, Scott. 2005. *The Global Resurgence of Religion and the Transformation of International Relations*. New York: Palgrave MacMillan.

Trice, Harrison, and Janice Beyer. 1991. "Cultural Leadership in Organizations." *Organization Science* 2 (2): 149–169.

UN (United Nations). 2001. "Declaration of Commitment on HIV/AIDS." Accessed August 8, 2011. http://www.unaids.org/en/media/unaids/contentassets/dataimport/publications/irc-pub03/aids declaration_en.pdf

UNAIDS (Joint United Nations Program on HIV/AIDS). 2010a. "Ghana's Progress Report on the United Nations General Assembly Special Session (UNGASS) Declaration of Commitment on HIV and AIDS." Accessed March 3, 2011. http://data.unaids.org/pub/Report/2010/ghana_2010_country_progress_report_en.pdf

UNAIDS (Joint United Nations Program on HIV/AIDS). 2010b. "Greater Involvement of People Living with or Affected by AIDS." Background Statement. Accessed May 4, 2011. http://www.unaids.org/en/PolicyAndPractice/GIPA/default.asp

UNAIDS (Joint United Nations Program on HIV/AIDS). 2011. "AIDS at 30: Nations at the Crossroads", Accessed May 4, 2011. http://www.unaids.org/en/resources/presscentre/pressreleaseandstatementarchive/2011/june/20110603praids30/#d.en.60161

US Agency for International Development (USAID). 2008. "Ghana: HIV/AIDS Health Profile." Accessed February 11, 2009. http://www.usaid.gov/missions/gh

van de Walle, Nicolas. 2001. *African Economies and the Politics of Permanent Crisis*. New York: Cambridge University Press.

Van Stekelenburg, Jacquelien, and Bert Klandermans. 2009. "Social Movement Theory: Past, Present and Prospects." In *Movers and Shakers: Social Movements in Africa*, edited by Stephen Ellis, and Ineke van Kessel, 17–43. Leiden: Brill Publishers.

Warren, Mark. 2001. *Dry Bones Rattling: Community Building to Revitalize American Democracy*. Princeton, NJ: Princeton University Press.

World Health Organization (WHO). 2007. "Faith-Based Organizations Play a Major Role in HIV/AIDS Care and Treatment in Sub-Saharan Africa." Accessed July 5, 2009. http://www.who.int/mediacentre/news/notes/2007/np05/en

"Zambia: Bishop Banda Clocks 10 Years as Northmead Assemblies Leader." 2005. In *The Post*, June 5. http://allafrica.com/stories/200506060858.html

"To donors, it's a program, but to us it's a ministry": the effects of donor funding on a community-based Catholic HIV/AIDS initiative in Kampala

Louise Mubanda Rasmussen

Department of Society and Globalisation, Roskilde University, Denmark

Résumé

En rapprochant les notions de mouvement social de la mobilisation des ressources et de l'identité collective, cet article analyse le rôle des ressources matérielles externes dans le choix des orientations de l'action collective contre le VIH/sida au sein de la *Christian Caring Kamwokya* (KCCC), une initiative catholique à assise communautaire basée à Kampala. Depuis sa formation à la fin des années 80, en tant que communauté de chrétiens offrant des « soins holistiques » aux personnes vivant avec le VIH/sida, la KCCC s'est transformée, dans le sillage de l'augmentation des financements externes, en une organisation non-gouvernementale (ONG) et professionnelle de développement. Au cours de cette transformation, les idéaux de soins holistiques ont peu à peu été éclipsés par des rationalités néolibérales sur le développement et par des préoccupations biopolitiques. C'est pourquoi l'article soutient qu'une mobilisation fructueuse des donateurs peut avoir des conséquences imprévues sur la nature de l'action collective religieuse contre le VIH/sida.

Abstract

Combining social movement approaches to resource mobilization and collective identity, this article investigates the role of external material resources in shaping the direction of collective action against HIV/AIDS within the Kamwokya Christian Caring Community (KCCC), a Catholic community-based initiative in Kampala. From its origins in the late 1980s as a community of Christians providing "holistic care" to people living with HIV/AIDS, the KCCC has in the wake of increasing external funding been transformed into a professional development non-governmental organization (NGO). In the process, the ideals of holistic care have gradually been overshadowed by neo-liberal development rationalities and bio-political concerns. The article therefore argues that successfully mobilizing donor funding can have unintended consequences for the nature of religious collective action against HIV/AIDS.

I. Introduction

Based on ten months of ethnographic research with Catholic HIV/AIDS projects in Uganda, this article analyzes the case of the Catholic community-based initiative in Kampala, called Kamwokya Christian Caring Community (KCCC). Located in an impoverished area of Kampala, the KCCC began in the late 1980s as a community of Christians providing "holistic care" to people living with HIV/AIDS. But in the wake of increasing external funding over the last three decades, the organization has been transformed into a professional development non-governmental organization (NGO). The article shows that professionalizing as a development NGO has contributed to changing the KCCC's approach towards HIV/AIDS treatment and care, and has also challenged its sense of collective identity as a community of Christians enacting the Gospel. On this basis, the article argues that successfully mobilizing donor funding can have unintended consequences for the nature of religious collective action against HIV/AIDS.

It is a well-established theme in discussions of civil society in Africa that channeling development funding towards "civil society organizations" may turn these organizations into implementers of donor policy and mere service providers, rather than being the autonomous promoters of social and political change assumed by the very same donors (e.g., Aubrey 1997; Hulme and Edwards 1997; Hearn 2001; Igoe and Kelsall 2005). Scholars have also begun to explore the effects that donor funding has on religious organizations (e.g., Christiansen 2010; Joshua 2010; Gifford 2009). This article brings a novel approach to these discussions by combining social movement theory with the concept of "transnational governmentality" (Ferguson 2006) to explore how becoming a professional player in this transnational field can redirect how religious actors in Africa conceptualize collective action.

Using social movement perspectives on resource mobilization, the article investigates the role of external material resources in shaping the direction of collective action against HIV/AIDS in the KCCC. Examining external material resources raises questions about the effects these exchange relationships have on the goals and activities of social movements (Edwards and McCarthy 2009, 118). I combine this perspective with a constructivist approach to the role of collective identity in social movements (Melucci 1996), which helps me to analyze how the effects of exchange relationships with donors are experienced from the perspective of the people who have volunteered and worked for the KCCC for decades. Examining how the resultant transformation of the KCCC reconfigures these participants' collective identity illustrates some of the unintended consequences that mobilizing donor funding can have for religious organizations.

In the context of the growing interest among international development agencies in faith-based organizations (FBOs), it has become highly relevant to explore the effects of external material resources on religious collective action. From the beginning of the new millennium, many development agencies began to direct funding to and collaborate more closely with various FBOs, which increasingly came to be seen as promising partners in the search for sustainable development solutions (Haynes 2007, 3; Marshall and Van Saanen 2007). In the field of HIV/AIDS, this trend has been profound. The U.S. President's Emergency Plan for AIDS Relief (PEPFAR) and the Global Fund to Fight HIV/AIDS, Tuberculosis and Malaria – along with smaller funding initiatives – have directed substantial shares of their funding towards FBOs in Africa (Patterson 2011, 28–30).[1]

Accessing such funding opportunities entails that religious organizations become part of a web of transnational governmentality, which during the last decades has been characterized by neo-liberal development rationalities (Ferguson 2006). With this term, I refer to techniques of government that focus on how to govern through the creation of "responsible" individuals and communities (Ferguson 2010, 172). Additionally, thanks to the way in which HIV/AIDS activists have successfully framed the limited access to antiretroviral (ARV) treatment in developing countries as a humanitarian emergency, international HIV/AIDS programs have in recent years been dominated by a humanitarian, bio-political logic premised on the need to save as many lives as possible with ARVs (Nguyen 2009; Rasmussen and Richey 2012). The access to ARV treatment has given local organizations new opportunities to provide treatment and care for people living with HIV/AIDS. But the treatment comes along with particular rationalities of government within which the effects of external material resources on the KCCC also take shape.

It has become almost conventional wisdom that the involvement of a wide variety of civil society organizations was central to the successful decline of HIV prevalence in Uganda (see Allen and Heald 2004; Richey and Haakonsson 2004; Parkhurst 2001).[2] Religious organizations, including the Catholic Church, played important roles in this "multi-sectoral" HIV/AIDS response from the outset (Seidel 1990). The Ugandan HIV/AIDS "success" illustrates how the combination of donor funding for a growing number of "local" NGOs and the semi-authoritarian politics of a regime such as Yoweri Museveni's (Tripp 2010) may contribute to depoliticizing the fight against HIV/AIDS and render AIDS NGOs into service providers that do not question the status quo (O'Manique 2004; Hearn 2001; Ferguson 1994). The transformation of the KCCC in the wake of increased external funding exemplifies this larger trend. However, this pattern may have particular consequences for religious organizations, especially with regard to the collective identities underpinning collective action.

I begin the article with a methodology section that accounts for the implications of using the KCCC as a case study, and which briefly describes the fieldwork on which this article is based. The next section includes a theoretical discussion on how to combine social movement perspectives on resource mobilization and collective identity with an approach to transnational governmentality. This is followed by a background section, which introduces the politics of HIV/AIDS in Uganda and the role of the Catholic Church in the Ugandan HIV/AIDS response. The analysis of the KCCC then illustrates how successfully mobilizing donor funding has contributed to a professionalization of the organization and to a redirection of its approach to HIV/AIDS treatment and care. Its holistic approach has gradually been overshadowed by neo-liberal development rationalities and bio-political concerns which, together with the professionalization, has challenged the employees' sense of collective identity as a community of Christians enacting the Gospel.

II.   Methodology

This article builds upon ten months of fieldwork in 2008, 2009 and 2010. I conducted ethnographic research with three Catholic HIV/AIDS projects, one being situated in Kampala and two in Arua diocese in Northwest Uganda. Permission to conduct the research was granted by the Uganda National Council for Science and Technology in March 2008.

In Kampala, I studied the KCCC – the main focus of this article. In the context of Catholic HIV/AIDS initiatives in Uganda, the KCCC represents a particular Kampala phenomenon – that of semi-independent Catholic AIDS-NGOs. Outside the capital, most Catholic HIV/AIDS projects operate within existing health institutions or are coordinated by the diocese. Many of these Kampala-based NGOs, like the KCCC, are characterized by the fact that they started as initiatives among the laity and slowly transformed into professional NGOs.[3] Thus, the KCCC is not exemplary of Catholic action against HIV/AIDS in Uganda as a whole. I have chosen to analyze the KCCC in this article because of the way its transformation exemplifies the unintended consequences for such initial "grassroots" initiatives that mobilize donor funding. As such, the case raises larger questions about the potential for translating Catholic lay-mobilization into sustained HIV/AIDS activism.

During my time with the KCCC, I observed program activities, staff meetings, and morning prayers; I interviewed program coordinators, counselors, community workers, and clients, and conducted two focus group discussions with various staff members. And I observed counseling sessions and accompanied community workers on home visits over a three-month period. Additionally, an assistant conducted interviews with elderly members of the local Catholic Church in Kamwokya. In this article, all interviewees are identified by pseudonyms, while some well-known figures, such as the founder of the organization, are identified by their real names.

III. Theoretical perspectives on resource mobilization, collective identity and transnational governmentality

The resource mobilization approach to social movements contends that the mobilization of various resources (material and non-material) is central to the growth, decline and change of social movements (van Stekelenburg and Klandermans 2009, 24). Edwards and McCarthy (2009) argue that it is crucial to distinguish between different resource types and the different ways in which resources are accessed. The way resources are accessed implies different exchange relationships, which can have different consequences for social movement activities and goals because of the way these relationships facilitate and constrain particular kinds of collective action (Edwards and McCarthy 2009, 135).

Internal moral, cultural, and organizational resources such as pastoral leadership, biblical framing, and church organizational structures have been identified as central to Christian mobilization against HIV/AIDS in Africa (Patterson 2011). However, external material resources often play a key role if religious organizations are to expand small-scale mobilization of congregations into wider activist efforts. In the context of the greater availability of donor funds for FBOs engaged in HIV/AIDS-related activities in the new millennium, it is important to explore the effects of external material resources on religious collective action against HIV/AIDS.

Inspired by the work of James Ferguson (2006; Ferguson and Gupta 2002), I argue that exchange relationships with international development donors are characterized by the workings of a particular kind of "transnational governmentality". With the term "transnational", Ferguson (2006, 40) points to how many "local" NGOs in Africa are part of transnational networks, together with international NGOs, foreign donor governments and UN agencies. These networks, he points out, have taken over a large part of basic service provision from African states. With the term "governmentality", Ferguson builds upon Michel Foucault's (2002a, 2002b) analysis of how a plurality of agents are involved in governing how people govern themselves. In his later works, Foucault developed an approach to the study of power, which builds on the notion that the exercise of power is "less a confrontation between two adversaries or their mutual engagement than a question of 'government'" (Foucault 2002b, 341). With the term "government", Foucault conceptualizes the exercise of power as a matter of both recognizing and seeking to shape the freedom of those governed. Here, "government" refers to the very broad meaning that the term had in sixteenth-century Europe, when it referred not only to formal political structures or the management of states but also to how the conduct of individuals or groups could be directed – to ways of acting upon others' possible actions. The idea is thus that "[t]he exercise of power is a 'conduct of conducts' and a management of possibilities" (Foucault 2002b, 341). The notion of governmentality makes it possible to examine how a plurality of agents, including those with no involvement in the formal political system, participates in governing both themselves and others (Englund 2006, 37). Additionally, the term governmentality denotes an analytical attention to the different ways in which the problem of how to govern is rationalized – that is, to different rationalities of government (Foucault 2009; Dean 2004).

The spread of transnational governmentality networks comprising local and international NGOs, foreign donor governments and UN agencies from the 1990s onwards has taken place in a context where "civil society" came to be seen as the new panacea for Africa's development (Igoe and Kelsall 2005, 1). From a Foucaultian perspective, the interest in using civil society organizations to achieve "sustainable development" is evidence of neo-liberal rationalities of government in the way this method is thought to make local actors responsible for and capable of achieving development, rather than foreign donors (cf. Foucault 2009). These rationalities are not necessarily equal to neo-liberalism as economic ideology, but should be understood as techniques of government that focus on how to govern through the creation of "responsible" communities and citizens (Ferguson 2010, 172). As the discourse on sustainable development proclaims, individuals and communities in Africa should no longer be passive recipients of charity or handouts, but must become self-activating and responsible for their own development (Fisher 1997; Kelsall and Mercer 2003; Swidler and Watkins 2009). The question this article explores is what facilitations and constraints may be placed on religious organizations when they become integrated into transnational governmentality networks dominated by neo-liberal development rationalities.

The article will not only explore how becoming a professional player in this transnational field can affect how religious groups conceptualize collective action, but it also pays particular attention to how these processes affect collective identities. I assume that a shared sense of "we-ness" that distinguishes the group from others is particularly central to religious mobilization against HIV/AIDS (Melucci 1996, 73–74; Gusman 2009). Therefore, examining the effects of development professionalization on collective identities is highly relevant. Studies of women's groups in developing countries illustrate how the formalization and professionalization that follow from becoming reliant on donor funding may alter not only the group's approach to social change but also the sense of collective identity that initially led to the mobilization of collective action (Lebon 1996; Aubrey 1997; Markowitz and Tice 2002). Melucci (1996, 70) defines collective identity in the following way:

> Collective identity is an interactive and shared definition produced by a number of individuals concerning the *orientations* of their action and the *field* of opportunities and constraints in which such action is to take place (original emphasis).

Thus, collective identity not only has implications for the direction of collective action but also for the group members' interpretations of their possibilities and responsibilities for action. Discussions of community mobilization in Africa, in connection with donor-funded projects, often revolve around how to ensure that people do not participate only for opportunistic or selfish reasons, as it is feared that participation will cease as soon as the donor funding stops (see Akintola 2011; Harrison 2002; People in Aid 2007; Swidler and Watkins 2009). The question of whether religious organizations can sustain a collective identity informed by religious motivations in the face of development professionalization is highly relevant to such discussions (see also Vander Meulen et al. this issue), especially when in the recent decade faith-based volunteerism has been turned into a strategic asset in transnational non-governmental governmentality (Burchardt 2013, 48).

IV. Background: the politics of HIV/AIDS in Uganda and the Catholic Church

A. The politics of HIV/AIDS in Uganda

In Uganda, the first AIDS cases were identified in 1982 in the Rakai district in the southwest. Formal HIV/AIDS responses began in 1986, when the National Resistance Movement (NRM) took power and Museveni was installed as President, after almost two decades of political chaos and armed conflicts.

The fight against HIV/AIDS was early on a central part of Museveni's agenda to rebuild social cohesion through his "broad-based" movement government (de Waal 2003). Museveni spoke about AIDS as a threat to everyone and encouraged Ugandans to come together and fight the disease (Richey 2005). In 1992, the Uganda AIDS Commission, placed directly under the President, was established to coordinate a "multi-sectoral approach" to HIV/AIDS (Uganda Aids Commission 1993). When Uganda achieved a significant decline in HIV prevalence in the early 2000s and was hailed as an HIV/AIDS success story (Parkhurst 2005), many observers retrospectively interpreted this success as stemming from the diversity of approaches to HIV prevention that were promoted by the government, along with the participation of a wide variety of local and international NGOs, religious groups, and other social and cultural actors (Parkhurst 2001; Allen and Heald 2004; Richey and Haakonsson 2004).

But whereas the NRM government seemingly encouraged the mobilization of various groups towards the fight against HIV/AIDS, it did not (until recently) encourage any engagement in party politics. The NRM government initially banned party politics, officially to address the ethnic and religious "sectarianism" that had haunted the country in the 1970s and 1980s (Carbone 2008). This strategy included diminishing the close linkages between the mainline churches and opposition parties (Kassimir 1995, 131).[4] Though a multi-party system was reintroduced in 2006, Aili Mari Tripp (2010, 2–5) characterizes Museveni's regime as *semi-authoritarian*. On the one hand, formal democratic institutions are in place, but on the other, democratic institutions are often subverted for undemocratic ends, civil rights are violated, and the regime increasingly uses corruption, patronage, and violence to remain in power.

In this context, it seems that HIV/AIDS has functioned as a depoliticized arena where Museveni found it safe to encourage mobilization. According to Putzel (2004, 27) and Parkhurst (2001, 78), Museveni actively sought not to antagonize religious leaders in the HIV/AIDS fight. He made sure to accommodate their views by "quietly" promoting condoms and by inviting these leaders to be part of national coordination efforts. This can be interpreted as an attempt by Museveni to empty HIV/AIDS of much of its contentious potential. At the same time, Hearn (2001, 51) has generally observed that the Ugandan government allows civil society organizations to get involved in policy processes as long as "they confine themselves to the space and issues allowed by government" and do not get involved in "politics". As such, there have been ample opportunities for religious groups to organize collective action against HIV/AIDS, as long as mobilization could not be construed as overtly contesting state authority or be connected to party politics.

During the 1990s, a massive influx of donor funds for HIV/AIDS interventions began to come into the country (Parkhurst 2005, 586). Though large flows of international funds into a growing number of "local" NGOs can be seen as a threat to state authority (cf. Leusenkamp 2010), Museveni seemed to have played this "aid dependency" to his own political advantage. By maintaining state authority around the coordination of HIV/AIDS, while largely relying on international NGOs, foreign donors and local churches for implementation and financing, Museveni has been able to take credit for the successful decline in HIV prevalence, which has helped him build legitimacy and mute international criticism (Rau 2006; Parkhurst 2005). Moreover, the strengthening of NGOs vis-à-vis state institutions, in terms of social service delivery, was in line with the larger macro-economic policy the Ugandan government had committed to in its structural adjustment plans (O'Manique 2004, 137–139). This particular network of transnational governmentality has thus provided opportunities for local religious AIDS initiatives to expand by mobilizing resources from foreign donors. But because of the circumscribed maneuvering room for civil society organizations, this expansion may more easily take the direction of a form of service provision, which does not challenge the political status quo (see Hearn 2001), or more precisely the neo-liberal economic and social agenda in which the Ugandan AIDS response has been tightly circumscribed (O'Manique 2004, 137).

The trajectory of The AIDS Support Organization (TASO), the most well-known Ugandan AIDS NGO, exemplifies this trend. TASO was formed in 1987 by a small group of people living with or personally affected by HIV/AIDS. From its early role in advocating "Positive Living" and opposing the government's initial AIDS campaigns based on fear (Seidel 1990, 66–67), TASO has today become a professional service delivery NGO offering HIV/AIDS treatment and care in eleven service centers across the country.[5]

In recent years, funding from PEPFAR for HIV/AIDS treatment, care and prevention programs in Uganda has been the subject of much debate. The emphasis which PEPFAR initially placed on abstinence and faithfulness in its funding of HIV prevention programs led some critics to argue that it had contributed to steering the Ugandan HIV/AIDS policy away from its successful multifaceted prevention approach (e.g., Epstein 2007; Human Rights Watch 2005). The debate also concerns to what extent Museveni himself changed his position in response to these changes in United States (US) policy. Some observers emphasize how President Museveni and his wife Janet "backtracked" to a conservative anti-condom stance in response to PEPFAR (e.g., Evertz 2010).[6] Others claim that Museveni had continuously downplayed the role of condoms (Allen 2006, 21). What this very polarized debate tends to have obscured is that PEPFAR was an initiative meant to rapidly expand the access to ARV treatment in Africa. From 2005 to 2008, 70–79% of the funds were devoted to treatment and care interventions.[7] The implications that such large-scale funding for ARVs have for local organizations' approach to HIV/AIDS treatment and care are crucial to consider. Only focusing on PEPFAR's controversial HIV-prevention politics may lead us to overlook important dilemmas of the rapid ARV treatment expansion.

B. *The role of the Catholic Church in the Ugandan HIV/AIDS response*

The Catholic Church holds a central social, political, and cultural position in Uganda (Gifford 1998; Kassimir 1999). In terms of membership, the Catholic Church is the largest denomination – closely followed by the Church of Uganda (Anglican).[8] Though the duopoly of these two mainline churches has been shaken by a dramatic growth of various Pentecostal and charismatic churches since 1986 (Kassimir 1999, 249), the Catholic Church continues to constitute a sociopolitical factor in the country, and is an important player in HIV/AIDS politics. This position is connected to the church's early and broad involvement with HIV/AIDS (Patterson 2011, 54–59), its large membership base, its prominent role as a health-provider, and the transnational ties of the organization itself, which give the church a greater financial strength than the Anglican Church, and which have led to a significant presence of foreign missionaries (see Gifford 2009), who have been central figures in a number of HIV/AIDS initiatives.

Early on, the Uganda Catholic Medical Bureau (UCMB) and the Catholic bishops participated in HIV/AIDS campaigns that urged Christians both to "respect God's laws" regarding sex (Seidel 1990, 68) in order to prevent the spread of HIV, and to reach out in compassion to those suffering from the disease (Catholic Bishops of Uganda 1989; Seidel 1990). As a health care provider, the church was involved in setting an agenda for using home-based care to deal with the growing number of chronic AIDS patients (Nsambya

Home Care 2007).[9] In the 1990s, increasing flows of international funding allowed a number of Catholic hospitals across the country to begin comprehensive treatment and care programs. This funding also allowed a number of community-based initiatives in Kampala, including the KCCC, to expand their activities. Since 2004, many Catholic NGOs and health facilities have engaged in the provision of ARV treatment, largely with the help of PEPFAR funding (Orach 2005). In 2009, Catholic providers of ARVs included four NGO-like organizations, all of their twenty-seven hospitals, and a number of larger health centers.[10]

PEPFAR funding for ARV programs has to some extent been contingent upon implementing organizations' promotion of abstinence and faithfulness into their HIV-prevention programs, which has given the Catholic Church and other faith-based organizations an advantage in the competition for funds. But, since this article examines the effects of mobilizing external material resources for the KCCC's approach to HIV/AIDS treatment and care, it focuses on a number of other dynamics, aside from whether abstinence, faithfulness or condoms are promoted as HIV prevention methods.

V. The case of the Kamwokya Christian Caring Community

I now turn to the analysis of how the mobilization of external material resources has contributed to redirecting the KCCC's approach towards HIV/AIDS treatment and care and has challenged the employees' sense of being a community of Christians enacting the Gospel. With this analysis, I argue that successfully mobilizing donor funding can have unintended consequences for the nature of religious collective action against HIV/AIDS. The discussion first describes how the KCCC initially developed into an HIV/AIDS initiative through the activities of small Christian communities (SCCs) in an impoverished area of Kampala, and then discusses the effects that mobilizing donor funding has had on the KCCC.

A. Beginnings: establishing a "Caring Christian Community"

In this sub-section, I present the ways in which informants from the KCCC narrated the beginning of the organization as being connected to a unique Christian community-based approach that evolved into a model for holistic HIV/AIDS care. These narratives should not be read as objective histories, but as particular collective-building narratives that have come to produce an ideal of holistic care, which managers, counselors and community workers in the KCCC today orient themselves towards in debates about how to provide treatment and care to people living with HIV/AIDS.

The KCCC is situated in a "slum" area called Kamwokya, which is one of oldest slum areas in Kampala. Kamwokya began to grow in the 1970s and 1980s during the time of civil unrest and displacement. It is also one of the more attractive slum areas in Kampala, because of its central location just to the northeast of the city center and its vibrant informal economy, which has attracted an ethnic mix of people from all over the country, searching for economic opportunities (Wallman 1996).

The story of how the KCCC began is extremely central to how the organization presents itself externally and internally. In my first visits to the organization and in initial interviews with program coordinators, the story of how the KCCC began was repeated over and over. The details of the story varied from informant to informant, but emphasis was always placed on its origins in Kamwokya's SCCs and the pivotal role of Sr Dr Miriam Duggan, a Franciscan Missionary Sister from Ireland, who was previously the medical superintendent of Nsambya Hospital. The emphasis on the foundation of the KCCC in SCCs illustrates how a particular collective identity revolving around being a community of Christians enacting the Gospel has been built and is constantly evoked.

Establishing SCCs is a strategy which was begun in the 1970s by Catholic Church leaders across Africa, who were inspired by the base communities in Latin America. In the SCCs, Catholics were to organize themselves into small, neighborhood cells, where they engaged in Bible reading, prayers and "self-help" projects. The rationale was that lay-Catholics would be encouraged to take more responsibility for their own Christian formation and socialization, leading to a form of "spiritual empowerment", which it was hoped would mobilize them into wider social and political action (Kassimir 1998, 69–70). In Uganda, the SCCs have not been established as voluntary organizations, but as the lowest branch of the church's administrative system to which all Catholics living in a village belong. Therefore, many Catholics perceive the SCCs as basically an administrative unit (Kassimir 1998, 70–71; Christiansen 2010).

Prior to 1987, the SCCs in Kamwokya functioned mostly as administrative units. But in 1987, the newly arrived priest Fr Tony Darragh, who had attended a course on "community ministries", introduced the idea of SCCs as forums for everyday Christian action to the parishioners. The response was slow at first, but soon the number of church members that were active in their respective *kabondo* (the Luganda term for SCCs) started growing (Williams and Tamale 1991, 20).

In 1988, the *bubondo* (plural of *kabondo*) in Kamwokya became connected to the mobile team from Nsambya Hospital's HIV/AIDS program, slowly redirecting their efforts to care for neighbors in need with regard to HIV/AIDS care (Williams and Tamale 1991, 20–22). In 1990, three Franciscan Missionary sisters, including Sr Duggan, moved to Kamwokya. According to KCCC informants, these sisters provided medical resources that were central to transforming the practices of the *bubondo* into an encompassing HIV/AIDS intervention. With the help of Sr Duggan, a small clinic was opened by the church, and here clinic staff could refer patients to Nsambya Hospital. Additionally, there was a group of volunteers who would meet at the church every day after morning mass, divide themselves into small groups, and visit "the sick".[11]

When volunteers visited the sick, they provided practical assistance and spiritual support. Informants mentioned practical help like washing clothes, bathing the sick person, cleaning the house, and fetching water. There was also a monthly collection at the church to buy basic food items for the poor, which were distributed by *kabondo* members (Williams and Tamale 1991, 11). In terms of spiritual support, the volunteers would lead prayers, read Bible passages, or sing a hymn.[12] A number of informants stressed how, for the sick, the mere presence of these caregivers had a spiritual significance. This included the three pastoral workers/counselors – Damian, Anthony and Charles – who spoke of a "sacrament of presence"[13] and about "journeying" with the people living with HIV/AIDS.[14] Journeying implied being with them and supporting them in whatever they went through, including helping them to die with dignity.

Informants described these initial treatment and care practices as stemming from the resolve of the *bubondo* to "put the Gospel into reality".[15] As Damian argued, they were trying to find a way of *practically* enacting the Christian obligation to love your neighbor in their day-to-day lives in Kamwokya:

> It was just the values we had in Christianity that motivated us to reach out to our people … there was that love, that drive, that love of Christ, you know, love one another as I have loved you …. We would read a scripture, after reading it, then apply it in our day-to-day life. God is to help people, let's go and help. It was practical, what we share is what we do.[16]

The biblical passage which informants most often referred to in such discussions was Matthew 25:35–36,[17] which emphasizes the centrality of material help and mere presence in caring for the suffering and lonely as a reflection of one's love of Christ. Thus, as the above points also illustrate, for KCCC informants the notion of being a community of Christians enacting the Gospel is closely connected to a "holistic" approach to HIV/AIDS treatment and care that combines material, spiritual, and medical assistance.

According to "the beginning narrative", this approach developed into an encompassing practice of "holistic care", as the volunteers were journeying with people living with HIV/AIDS and realized the extent of the often wide-ranging social problems that they faced. Community work coordinator, Christine, explained:

> This was chronic illness which didn't have even a treatment that so many of them couldn't work … many of them they do petty trade, and if they don't work, they don't have anything to eat, the children will not go to school, they will not pay house rent, and the moment you don't pay house rent, they send you out of the house …. So many of them used to be in a no hope situation and very sick … and also we found it very difficult that you cannot even give treatment, because when somebody has not eaten, even the treatment will not, will weaken …. So all the programs you see here … those have been lessons learnt … on the long road we are moving on with these HIV/AIDS patients.[18]

This quote exemplifies the ideal of holistic care, which is central to how the KCCC identifies itself as a community-based initiative that stands out from others. According to this ideal, social, medical and spiritual support must be combined in order to provide AIDS patients with a comprehensive form of healing.

The KCCC is certainly not alone in using the term "holistic care" in Uganda;[19] in fact the term is so widespread that it may be considered just an empty catchphrase. However, it is important to note that "holistic care" resonates with Catholic notions of health care as an imitation of Christ's mission – as a practice aiming to restore wholeness, which points towards the final healing of a broken creation (Cochran 1999, 28–29). More importantly, as illustrated above, to KCCC informants the notion of developing a "unique" holistic care approach on the basis of Catholic lay-mobilization is central to how they claim and understand how the organization was founded.

During my research in 2008 and 2009, the notion of being a Christian community committed to holistic care was still actively evoked in the organization. For example, each day started with morning prayers for all employees and volunteers, which included praise songs, prayers and official announcements. In the focus group discussions, old and new employees presented holistic care as the essence of their Christian community-based approach. Pastoral worker/counselor, Anthony, who started as a volunteer during the KCCC's beginning years, explained:

> When we are reaching out to the sick … we look at this person we are caring for in a holistic way … there is a lot of needs, there is social need, there is spiritual need, there are psychological needs and there are physical needs, so the approach we use on this person is to be holistic … so as Christians, we have been looking … the whole person will be collectively helped, yeah, that is our approach.[20]

Rose, a counselor who started working for the KCCC in 2004, and who is also a Catholic, explained in a similar way:

> As a Christian you need to treat him wholly, holistic care, that's what one should approach, you treat the psycho-part, the body … the social, the mental part, and the economic comes afterwards, at least when the mind is set, he will even appreciate the medicine.[21]

Despite the prominence of these ideals of holistic care in such normative discourses, the effects of mobilizing donor funds that I discuss in the following section include, however, a redirection of the KCCC's holistic approach to treatment and care, and a challenge to the notion of being a community of Christians enacting the Gospel.

B. Effects of mobilizing donor funding

During the 1990s and 2000s, the KCCC expanded its services in Kamwokya with a wide portfolio of programs that were aimed at providing holistic care for people living with HIV/AIDS. Many of these programs started as impromptu initiatives, but with the help of donor funding they gradually turned into more formal programs. These programs include, among others, a Child Welfare Department (which at the time of research provided school fees for 1300 orphans and vulnerable children), a primary school, foster homes, a vocational training centre, a micro-credit program, a youth HIV-prevention and sports center, accommodation for homeless clients, a post-HIV test club, a community mental-health program, a clinic open to both HIV-positive clients and the general public, and various food support programs.

Along with this expansion of services, the number of people the KCCC serves has also dramatically increased from a few hundred households situated in Kamwokya in the early 1990s to approximately 5000 people living with HIV/AIDS from all over Kampala district at the time of research. Many of the programs mentioned above were also gradually opened up to the general public and not only people living with HIV/AIDS.

This expansion illustrates just how successful the KCCC has been in mobilizing donor funding from a wide range of smaller, primarily faith-based, European and American organizations, as well as, in recent years, the US Agency for International Development (USAID) and PEPFAR. In the process of expanding, the KCCC was transformed from a Catholic lay-initiative into an NGO that calls itself "a Caring Christian Community". The organization was registered as an NGO with the Ministry of Internal Affairs in 1994, and this is when it officially took on the name of the "Kamwokya Christian Caring Community".

In the following subsections, I first analyze how professionalizing as a development NGO has raised questions among the employees about their collective identity. Then I analyze how the neo-liberal development rationalities and bio-political concerns that currently dominate this field of transnational governmentality have contributed to redirecting the KCCC's approach to HIV/AIDS treatment and care.

1. Professionalization and its challenge to collective identities

During the 1990s, as the KCCC transformed from a Catholic lay-initiative into an NGO, it shifted from being based on volunteer work to employing paid staff. From 1993, the volunteers started to receive a salary, and gradually the work of the KCCC was divided into different professional areas of expertise. Those working for the KCCC are no longer "volunteers", but "counselors", "nurses", "social workers", and "program coordinators". Most of the initial volunteers were Catholics. At the time of research, most of the 140 full-time employees were Catholic, but there are also a number of Anglicans and a few Muslim and Pentecostal employees.[22]

In 2008 to 2009, the KCCC appeared to be quite a professional organization, which, however, was struggling with implementing further formalized organizational procedures in collaboration with some of its key donors. In 2008, the management began developing a new strategic plan for 2009–2013 (KCCC 2008). As part of this strategic plan, each department had to develop both quantitative targets and qualitative standards for its work.

However, the counselors objected to setting quantitative targets for how many clients they should counsel in a day. Despite this fact, one counselor contended that they had to abide with this requirement, because "the donors want numbers".[23] The community workers, who go on home visits to ARV clients, objected to the growing demand that the management placed on them to fill out forms and write reports to document their work. Most of the community workers have limited English skills, so completing this paperwork challenged them. These demands also reinforced their experience of being repeatedly questioned for not doing their work well enough. When some of the data the clinic collects to monitor the ARV program showed increasing mortality rates and an increasing number of clients "lost to follow-up", the executive director blamed the community workers for not doing their work well enough. The director also claimed that the donors had begun to question what the use of the community workers were when they could not "ensure life continuation".[24]

What is central to these professionalization exercises in the KCCC is how they reflect what it means for a local organization to be in exchange relationships with international donors. The organization becomes increasingly geared towards demonstrating account-ability to its donors, as it becomes preoccupied with showing that the donated money has been efficiently used for meeting the programmatic objectives that have been spelled out in collaboration with their donors (see also Harrison 2002, 591; Mosse 2005, 211).

Additionally, as a professional development NGO, the KCCC is now almost entirely dependent on donor funds in order to continue its various programs and for the management and staff members to maintain their own jobs.[25] Donor funding is fickle, as it is usually provided for time-specific projects and donors may withdraw funding as their priorities change. On a brief follow-up visit in 2010, one of the managers asked me to help search for other donors, as they had been forced to significantly scale down the services offered by the Child Welfare Department after one of their major donors withdrew funding in the wake of the global financial crisis. In other words, being in exchange relationships with donors appears to cause local organizations to become geared towards continuously cementing their relationships with existing donors while also searching for new ones.

These exchange relationships tend to make upward accountability (to donors) more important than downwards accountability (to communities) (Fisher 1997, 454), and for the KCCC it seems that the connection to the community roots have been lost in the process. Long-time *kabondo* member Clarence claimed that the KCCC had forgotten about the *bubondo* in Kamwokya: "They've left us out completely and it's now politics, and we have left them, because they even have their own *kabondo*".[26] The marginalization of the *bubondo* is indicative of how the professionalization has affected the KCCC as an organization, raising questions for the original volunteers about whether it still functions as a caring community of Christians. This change is reflected in how the counselors who were originally trained as pastoral workers discussed the neglect of pastoral care. They found that pastoral care had been neglected to such an extent that, at the beginning of 2009, they began to discuss with the management about how to revive it.

Damian and Anthony invited me to attend a home visit with a woman who has been a client with the KCCC since 1994. During this visit, Anthony and Damian demonstrated how a home visit used to take place. Anthony asked us all to raise our hands to pray for the Holy Spirit to protect the client, while he laid his hand on the client's head and led a praise song. Afterwards, both he and Damian said a prayer for the client. During the visit, Anthony and Damian shared their frustrations with me. They argued that pastoral care has been neglected because home visiting had been left entirely to the community workers, who "don't have the capacity for praying and counseling".[27] More broadly, they talked about the neglect of pastoral care as an unintended consequence of the professionalization of the KCCC. They said:

> Damian: Every day we must thank God to get in touch with [the] Holy Spirit. We have to make them appreciate God to appreciate this treatment. These newcomers don't know our program, they are only interested in the salary. Before we were just volunteers. We started getting salaries slowly by slowly from something like 1993 to 1994. We were all doing home visiting from Francis[28] to Sr Miriam.

> Anthony: After becoming professionals we forgot about home visiting. We need to revitalize it, because when you visit like this it gives them new hope.[29]

Damian and Anthony thus connected the neglect of pastoral care with the changing motivations of the KCCC workers. According to them, whereas the initial volunteers were motivated by the Christian obligation to "love thy neighbor", the employees today are just interested in the salary. Though the newcomers all participate in the morning prayers and a number of them identify with the "unique" Christian approach of the KCCC, from Damian and Anthony's perspective, professionalization has raised questions about the sense of "we-ness" that distinguishes this "community of Christians" from others (Melucci 1996). Damian summarized how, from his perspective, being in exchange relationships with donors poses a challenge to functioning like a ministry that enacts God's will: "In the language of donors it is a program, but actually it's a ministry, we are his [God's] neck, his hands, his arms. We have to go back to our roots".[30] Apart from these effects of professionalization, it is also important to consider which rationalities of government dominate the field of transnational governmentality that the KCCC has become part of in the process of becoming a professional development NGO, and how these rationalities have contributed to redirecting the organization's approach to HIV/AIDS treatment and care.

2. From providing holistic care to helping clients "follow the rules"

In 2004, the KCCC received funding from PEPFAR to provide ARV treatment to its clients. The access to ARVs has provided the KCCC with distinct new opportunities for providing treatment and care to people living with HIV/AIDS. The organization has moved from helping people to "die with dignity" and "journeying" with chronically ill persons to now providing potentially life-prolonging and life-transforming medicines to a much larger number of people. At the time of research, the KCCC provided ARV treatment to approximately 1500 people living with HIV/AIDS. These new opportunities form an important context to how the KCCC's approach to HIV/AIDS care and treatment has changed over the years. But what I argue in this section is that in choosing to access this funding, the KCCC has become part of a transnational governmentality network focused on the bio-political project of "saving" as many lives as possible with ARV treatment (Nguyen 2009), which has had implications for how the organization can and does practice HIV/AIDS treatment and care.

In connection with the introduction of ARV treatment into the KCCC, five new counselors and thirty-three community workers were recruited and trained to deal with the new counseling and follow-up recruitments of the treatment. Today, counselors and community workers focus on educating, counseling, and disciplining the clients to follow "the rules" of ARV treatment and Positive Living: taking medicine every day at the same time, coming on time for clinical appointments, eating a balanced diet, avoiding smoking, drinking, unprotected sex, and overworking, disclosing HIV status, and maintaining a positive attitude (see also Allen et al. 2011 on counseling in TASO).

In the context of poverty and social inequalities, many clients in fact struggle to follow these rules (for example, struggling to get enough to eat or affording transport to the clinic to come in time for their appointments). Though the access to ARVs represents a great improvement for the many whose lives it has helped prolong, benefiting from the medicine's life-prolonging potential hinges on one's ability to follow "the rules" well (Rasmussen 2011, chapter 9; Meinert, Mogensen, and Twebaze 2009; Kalofonos 2010). In this context, some KCCC informants argued that a form of holistic care, which complements ARV treatment with social and spiritual support, was even more essential than before.[31] By being part of the transnational project of saving lives with ARVs, the KCCC has had to balance holistic care with these bio-political ambitions, as well as with the neo-liberal rationalities characterizing international development assistance. As a consequence of these negotiations, both the material and pastoral aspects of how the KCCC conceptualizes holistic care have been challenged.

During the home visit with Damian and Anthony, Damian explained that one of the client's daughters is on their school sponsorship program. He said:

> When fees are paid for, she feels ok. If not, it will stress her. If there are basic needs not addressed you can keep counseling without it helping. Sometimes you need to have other practical interventions like rent, food but it's not sustainable, which donor will fund that?[32]

This statement points to how the KCCC, in recent years, has had to negotiate holistic care with donor definitions of what constitutes a sustainable intervention. The notion of sustainability is one of the central tenets of neo-liberal development rationalities. The doctrine of sustainability posits that communities and individuals must be empowered and made responsible so that they can continue with the activities when the donor and its funding departs. This doctrine has implications for the kind of activities that donors are willing to fund. Generally, giving material assistance and employing staff are deemed unsustainable, while conducting training and mobilizing volunteers are deemed sustainable (Swidler and Watkins 2009, 1184–1185).

What precisely makes projects sustainable is open to some negotiation between donors and receiving organizations. Particularly in a context which can be claimed to be a humanitarian emergency, organizations may be able to legitimize some forms of material assistance. For example, prior to the introduction of ARV treatment, in many projects in Uganda, food support was provided to people living with HIV/AIDS, both to mitigate the socio-economic effects of living with the disease and to improve their health. The food support continued in many programs during the first years of the ARV treatment scale-up, defined as an essential therapeutic supplement to the treatment. But in the context of the rapidly growing number of ARV clients who had to be on the treatment for life, many donors changed their policy (see World Food Programme 2006, 2009).

In the KCCC, two large food support programs, initiated in 2001 and funded respectively by USAID and WFP, were discontinued in 2006, because they were no longer considered sustainable. Many clients were perplexed by this change. They were continuously asking the counselors and community workers (and me) things like "is there hope for us to get porridge and oil as we used to get?"[33] Many of the community workers and counselors also regretted the development. But some counselors, and especially the management and the program coordinators, agreed with the donors' premise that food support in the long run is an unsustainable intervention, which only leads to passive, dependent clients. The home visiting coordinator explained:

> There is also that dependency syndrome, waiting to be given. We tell them: "It's high time, you start supporting yourself, you have been given the medicine for free, so at least you can also work for yourself". You see we found that food support was not sustainable.[34]

Some of the KCCC's other social support programs have undergone a similar change during the process of their expansion. For example, the micro-credit program, which initially provided grants and interest-free loans to people living with HIV/AIDS in order to help them start undertaking "income-generating activities" has been restructured in the name of sustainability. According to some informants, the program had created the attitude that this was "church money", which the clients did not need to pay back, and therefore the program was suffering both from poor repayment rates and increasing demand. The program's donors gave the KCCC a final grant and asked KCCC to come up with a new program that could continue without any more funding.[35] In response, the program was transformed into an independent Savings and Credit Co-operative (SACCO), which functions as a revolving fund, and which is directed towards everyone living in Kampala district, not just people with HIV/AIDS. With SACCO, a person first has to open a savings account and after two months he or she can apply for a loan. But to get a loan, that person has to provide security and have one or two guarantors. Most of the clients found these new loan requirements either unattainable or frightening. According to the SACCO director, 25% of their members are people living with HIV/AIDS,[36] but in my experience – and recognized by the KCCC as well – the loans have become largely inaccessible to their poorest clients (Ntale and Cunningham 2008, 45).

The school-fees support program has not undergone such a restructuring process. But as the Child Welfare Department expanded and began generally helping orphans and vulnerable children rather than focusing on children whose parents have HIV/AIDS, the number of people trying to access this support has grown substantially. Every day five to ten people come to the office asking for help, many from outside Kamwokya.[37] Because the waiting list to access school-fees support is very long, there were, in my experience, few instances where school fees came to function as a much-needed form of support to impoverished people living with HIV/AIDS.

As a consequence of these developments, there is a significant shift in how the material aspects of HIV/AIDS treatment and care are conceptualized in the KCCC. In the early years, the volunteers aimed to "feed the hungry, give drinks to the thirsty, visit the sick" – that is, to demonstrate God's love through material assistance and their mere presence. Today, the appropriate role of counselors and community workers is defined as a matter of counseling clients on how to use their own means (or their social networks) to address any socio-economic barriers they face in following the rules, so that they may ensure successful ARV treatment.

Within this rationality of government, there is some space for pastoral care, since counseling clients on how to overcome social and economic barriers to treatment success is defined as "psychosocial" support. In the realm of psycho-social support, counselors and community workers provide prayers and consolation, which stress that "God will make a way for you".[38] But when the pastoral workers/counselors regretted that pastoral care had been neglected because home visiting had been left in the hands of the community workers, this reflects how the practice of home visiting has been redefined in the KCCC in the context of ARV treatment (Rasmussen 2011, chapter 8). The point is not whether the community workers have the capacity for praying and counseling, but rather that the community workers' primary responsibility is to carry out ARV treatment follow up. Their core responsibility is to monitor whether clients follow the rules, especially with regards to drug adherence. Therefore, most home visits concentrate on pill counting, checking adherence cards, and reminding the clients of their next appointment at the clinic. As reflected in the way the executive director questioned the community workers for not working hard enough to "ensure life continuation", they are in fact held accountable for how effectively they help to "save lives" with ARVs. The disciplining tasks with which the community workers are charged in order to ensure ARV treatment success leave little room for the pastoral, care-oriented home visits that were central to the KCCC's beginnings.

Studies of TASO also suggest that staff members are faced with the challenge of maintaining their "personal touch" in the process of expanding the organization's ARV program (Abaasa et al. 2008). In the KCCC it is especially the material and pastoral aspects of the holistic approach to HIV/AIDS care that are challenged, in the context of the dominant form of government currently being centered on enabling and disciplining each client to govern him or herself responsibly (according to "the rules") in order to ensure ARV treatment success.

Despite the dilemmas of providing ARVs, there were no informants in the KCCC who directly regretted their introduction. On the contrary, some informants talked about the flows of funding that have made the provision of ARVs possible as a prayer being answered.[39] While some of the initial volunteers more generally recognize the unintended consequences of mobilizing donor funding, there were no explicit calls for severing ties with donors, which in a way reflects how much the professionalization process has affected the organization.

VI. Conclusion

From the beginning of the new millennium, religious organizations in Africa were offered many new opportunities for international funding for HIV/AIDS initiatives. The analysis of the Catholic community-based initiative in Kampala called the Kamwokya Christian Caring Community has illustrated that mobilizing donor funding can have unintended consequences for the nature of religious collective action against HIV/AIDS.

The analysis has demonstrated how external material resources have shaped the direction of collective action in the KCCC. First, it has illustrated that being in exchange relationships with donors has professionalized the KCCC as a development NGO that is focused on demonstrating accountability to its donors and continuously searching for new opportunities for funding. In the process, long-term employees have experienced that their sense of being a community of Christians enacting the Gospel has been severely challenged. At the same time, the exchange relationships with donors are characterized by the workings of a particular kind of transnational governmentality, which is dominated by neo-liberal development rationalities and a bio-political ambition to "save lives" with ARV treatment. Consequently, the ideals of holistic care so central to how the KCCC's employees define their approach as uniquely Christian-community-based have been sidelined by a form of government that focuses on enabling and disciplining each client to govern him or herself responsibly in order to ensure ARV treatment success.

Since similar contradictory experiences with accessing donor funding have been reported from other Catholic HIV/AIDS initiatives in Eastern and Southern Africa (see Fikansa 2009; Czerny 2007; Joshua 2010), the KCCC's experience raises larger questions about the potential of translating Catholic lay-mobilization into sustained HIV/AIDS activism.

Acknowledgements

An earlier version of this paper was presented at the 2010 Summer School on Religion, AIDS, and Social Activism in Africa held at the Working Group on the Social and Political Aspects of AIDS in Uganda, Child Health and Development Centre, Makerere University, Kampala, Uganda, 5–9 July 2010. I am grateful to Amy Patterson, Marian Burchardt and the summer school participants for the comments and suggestions they made towards the improvement of the paper. The fieldwork in Uganda was made possible with financial support from the Danish Council for Development Research, the Nordic Africa Institute and University of Copenhagen's fund for Theology Students and Candidates. But most importantly, this paper could not have been written without all the programme coordinators, counsellors, community workers and clients in Uganda who agreed to offer their time and experiences to participate in my research. I am equally indebted to my assistants Norah Kirabo, Nelly Arikuru and Jimmy Candia for the invaluable help they provided during the fieldwork.

Notes

1. For example, out of PEPFAR's funding obligations in its focus countries in 2005, on average 10% went to FBOs. This figure covers a great variation between countries, with 30% going to FBOs in Kenya and 0.2% in Botswana. In Uganda, FBOs received 12–13% of the funding. FBOs in the focus countries on average received more funding for treatment than for care and prevention (Oomman, Bernstein, and Rosenzweig 2008, 9).
2. In the early 1990s, the HIV prevalence in Uganda was around 10–20%, but by 2002 the rate had declined to around 5% (UNAIDS 2002; Parkhurst 2005).
3. This includes Meeting Point, Reach Out Mbuya, and Youth Alive (which started as an initiative within the KCCC and became an independent NGO in 1995). An exception to this trend is Nsambya Home Care, which started as a department in Nsambya Hospital.
4. Since the time of independence, the Uganda People's Congress (UPC) had been connected to the Anglican Church and the Democratic Party (DP) to the Catholic Church.
5. See www.tasouganda.org
6. From Museveni's initial reluctance to actively promote condoms, his views were gradually moderated (Allen 2006, 21), and social marketing of condoms was initiated in 1991 (Green et al. 2006, 341).
7. This included around 45% for ARV treatment and around 30% for "care", which includes palliative care for HIV and TB patients, HIV counseling and testing and care for orphans and vulnerable children; see http://www.pepfar.gov/about/c19,388.htm
8. The 2002 national census recorded 42% Catholic, 36% Anglican, 4% Pentecostal and 15% Muslim; see http://www.ubos.org/
9. Interview with Catholic health official, by author. Kampala, 25 March 2008.
10. Interview with Catholic health official, by author. Kampala, 18 February 2009.
11. Interview with Damian (pastoral worker/counselor), by author. Kampala, 28 April 2008.
12. Interview with Christine (community work coordinator), by author. Kampala, 21 April 2008.
13. Interview with Damian, by author. Kampala, 28 April 2008; interview with Anthony (pastoral worker/counselor), by author. Kampala, 2 February 2009.
14. Charles (pastoral worker/counselor), during focus group discussion, facilitated by author. Kampala, 16 June 2008.
15. Fundraising coordinator, in conversation with author. Kampala, 1 April 2008; interview with Christine, by author. Kampala, 21 April 2008.
16. Interview with Damian, by author. Kampala, 28 April 2008.
17. "For I was hungry and you gave me food, I was thirsty and you gave me drink, a stranger and you welcomed me, naked and you clothed me, ill and you cared for me, in prison and you visited me" (Matthew 25:35–36, The African Bible, Nairobi: Paulines).
18. Interview with Christine, by author. Kampala, 21 April 2008.
19. Other organizations in Uganda that use the notion of "holistic care" include TASO, Hospice Africa Uganda and Mildmay. Traditional and Modern Health Practitioners Together against AIDS (THETA) has a "Holistic Care Clinic" in Kamwokya.
20. Focus group discussion, facilitated by author. Kampala, 16 June 2008.
21. Focus group discussion, facilitated by author. Kampala, 16 June 2008.

22. Generally the presence of staff, as well as international volunteers, with different religious backgrounds did not appear to cause major conflicts, as long as they respected the general Christian ethos of the organization.
23. Author's notes from participant observation in counseling office, 27 January 2009.
24. Author's notes from observation of morning praise and announcements, 27 January 2009.
25. For example, during one morning praise session, the fundraising coordinator urged the staff to be creative in terms of using resources cost-effectively (such as saving on paper, electricity and water), because their donors were challenged financially in the wake of the global financial crisis. He said: "The more we save on such things, the more people can keep their job. If you want to lose your job, then make sure the organization loses money aimlessly" (Author's notes from observation of morning praise and announcement, 23 January 2007).
26. Interview with Clarence (long-time *kabondo* member), by research assistant. Kampala, 22 December 2009.
27. Damian in conversation with author during participant observation of home visit, 2 February 2009.
28. Francis is today the executive director of the KCCC.
29. Author's notes from participant observation of home visit, 2 February 2009.
30. Author's notes from participant observation of home visit, 2 February 2009.
31. Focus group discussions, 12 June 2008 and 16 June 2008.
32. Author's notes from participant observation of home visit, 2 February 2009.
33. Author's notes from participant observation of home visit, 12 December 2008.
34. Home visiting coordinator, in conversation with author. Kampala, 19 December 2008.
35. Interview with Anthony, by author. Kampala, 2 February 2009.
36. Interview with SACCO director, by author. Kampala, 2 May 2008.
37. Interview with Child Welfare coordinator, by author. Kampala, 22 April 2008.
38. Author's notes from participant observation of home visit, 9 January 2009.
39. Interview with community worker Doris, by author. Kampala, 5 February 2009; interview with Anthony, by author. Kampala, 2 February 2009.

Bibliography

Abaasa, Andrew M., Jim Todd, Kenneth Ekoru, Joan N. Kalyango, Jonathan Levin, Emmanual Odeke, and Charles A. S. Karamagi. 2008. "Good Adherence to HAART and Improved Survival in a Community HIV/AIDS Treatment and Care Programme: The Experience of the AIDS Support Organization (TASO), Kampala, Uganda." *BMC Health Services Research* 8 (1): 241.

Akintola, Olagoke. 2011. "What Motivates People to Volunteer? The Case of Volunteer AIDS Caregivers in Faith-Based Organizations in KwaZulu-Natal, South Africa." *Health Policy Planning* 26 (1): 53–62.

Allen, Tim. 2006. "Aids and Evidence: Interogating Some Ugandan Myths." *Journal of Biosocial Science* 38 (1): 7–28.

Allen, Tim, and Suzette Heald. 2004. "HIV/AIDS Policy in Africa: What Has Worked in Uganda and What Has Failed in Botswana?" *Journal of International Development* 16 (8): 1141–1154.

Allen, Caroline, Martin Mbonye, Janet Seeley, Josephine Birungi, Brent Wolff, Alex Coutinho, and Shabbar Jaffar. 2011. "ABC for People with HIV: Responses to Sexual Behaviour Recommendations Among People Receiving Antiretroviral Therapy in Jinja, Uganda." *Culture, Health & Sexuality* 13 (5): 529–543.

Aubrey, Lisa. 1997. *The Politics of Development Cooperation: NGOs, Gender and Partnership in Kenya.* London: Routledge.

Burchardt, Marian. 2013. "Faith-Based Humanitarianism: Organizational Change and Everyday Meanings in South Africa." *Sociology of Religion* 74 (1): 30–55.

Carbone, Giovanni. 2008. *No-Party Democracy? Ugandan Politics in Comparative Perspective.* Boulder/London: Lynne Rienner Publishers.

Catholic Bishops of Uganda. 1989. *The AIDS Epidemic – Message of the Catholic Bishops of Uganda. 8th September 1989*. Kampala: Uganda Episcopal Conference.

Christiansen, Catrine. 2010. "Development by Churches, Development of Churches – Institutional Trajectories in Rural Uganda." PhD thesis, Department of Anthropology, University of Copenhagen.

Cochran, Clarke E. 1999. "Institutional Identity; Sacramental Potential: Catholic Healthcare at Century's End." *Christian Bioethics* 5 (1): 26–43.

Czerny, Michael F. 2007. "ARVs When Possible." In *AIDS in Africa – Theological Reflections*, edited by Bénézet Bujo, and Michael Czerny, 95–103. Nairobi: Pauline Publications Africa.

de Waal, Alex. 2003. "How Will HIV/AIDS Transform African Governance?" *African Affairs* 102 (406): 1–23.

Dean, Mitchel. 2004. *Governmentality – Power and Rule in Modern Society*. London: Sage.

Edwards, Bob, and John D. McCarthy. 2009. "Resources and Social Movement Mobilization." In *The Blackwell Companion to Social Movements*, edited by David A. Snow, Sarah A. Soule, and Hanspeter Kriesi, 116–152. Malden, MA: Blackwell Publishing.

Englund, Harri. 2006. *Prisonors of Freedom: Human Rights and the African Poor*. Berkeley, CA: University of California Press.

Epstein, Helen. 2007. *The Invisible Cure: Africa, the West and the Fight Against AIDS*. New York: Farrar, Straus and Giroux.

Evertz, Scott H. 2010. "How Ideology Trumped Science: Why PEPFAR Has Failed to Meet Its Potential." http://www.americanprogress.org/wp-content/uploads/issues/2010/01/pdf/pepfar.pdf

Ferguson, James. 1994 [1990]. *The Anti-politics Machine: "Development", Depoliticization, and Bureaucratic Power in Lesotho*. Minneapolis: University of Minnesota Press.

Ferguson, James. 2006. *Global Shadows – Africa in the Neoliberal World Order*. Durham and London: Duke University Press.

Ferguson, James. 2010. "The Uses of Neoliberalism." *Antipode* 41: 166–184.

Ferguson, James, and Akhil Gupta. 2002. "Spatializing States: Toward an Ethnography of Neoliberal Governmentality." *American Ethnologist* 29 (4): 981–1002.

Fikansa, Chandra. 2009. "Reflections on the Contradictions of ARVs From a Practitioner Perspective." Presentation at the Conference Prolonging Life, Challenging Religion, Lusaka, Zambia, 15–17 April.

Fisher, William F. 1997. "Doing good? The Politics and Antipolitics of NGO Practices." *Annual Review of Anthropology* 26 (1): 439–464.

Foucault, Michel. 2002a [1978]. "Governmentality." In *Michel Foucault – Power. Essential Works of Foucault 1954–1984 Volume 3*, edited by James D. Faubion, 201–222. London: Penguin Books.

Foucault, Michel. 2002b [1982]. "The Subject and Power." In *Michel Foucault – Power. Essential Works of Foucault 1954–1984 Volume 3*, edited by James D. Faubion, 326–348. London: Penguin Books.

Foucault, Michel. 2009 [1978–79]. *The Birth of Biopolitics – Lectures at Collège de France 1978–1979*, edited by Michel Senellart, and translated by Graham Burchell. Houndsmills, Basingstoke, Hampshire: Palgrave Macmillan.

Gifford, Paul. 1998. *African Christianity. Its Public Role*. London: Hurst & Company.

Gifford, Paul. 2009. *Christianity, Politics and Public Life in Kenya*. London: Hurst & Company.

Green, Edward, Daniel T. Halperin, Vinand Nantulya, and Janice A. Hogle. 2006. "Uganda's HIV Prevention Success: The Role of Sexual Behavior Change and the National Response." *AIDS and Behavior* 10 (4): 335–346.

Gusman, Alessandro. 2009. "HIV/AIDS, Pentecostal Churches, and the 'Joseph Generation' in Uganda." *Africa Today* 56 (1): 67–86.

Harrison, Elisabeth. 2002. "The Problem with the Locals: Partnership and Participation in Ethiopia." *Development and Change* 33 (4): 587–610.

Haynes, Jeffrey. 2007. *Religion and Development: Conflict or Cooperation?* Houndmills, Basingstoke, Hampshire: Palgrave Macmillan.

Hearn, Julie. 2001. "The 'Uses and Abuses' of Civil Society in Africa." *Review of African Political Economy* 28 (87): 43–53.

Hulme, David, and Michael Edwards, eds. 1997. *NGOs, States and Donors: Too Close for Comfort?* Houndmills, Basingstoke, Hampshire: Macmillan Ltd. in association with Save the Children.

Human Rights Watch. 2005. "The Less They Know the Better – Abstinence-Only HIV/AIDS Programs in Uganda." *Human Rights Watch* 17 (4): 1–79.

Igoe, Jim, and Tim Kelsall. 2005. *Between a Rock and a Hard Place – African NGOs, Donors and the State*. Durham, North Carolina: Carolina Academic Press.

Joshua, Stephen Mouki. 2010. "A Critical Historical Analysis of the South African Catholic Church's HIV/AIDS Response Between 2000 and 2005." *African Journal of AIDS Research* 9 (4): 437–447.

Kalofonos, Ippolytos A. 2010. "'All I Eat is ARVs': The Paradox of AIDS Treatment Interventions in Central Mozambique." *Medical Anthropology Quarterly* 24 (3): 363–380.

Kamwokya Christian Caring Community. 2008. *Moving Beyond Service Provision to Facilitating Civil Society Development – Strategic Plan 2009–2013*. Kampala: KCCC.

Kassimir, Ronald. 1995. "Catholics and Political Identity in Toro." In *Religion & Politics in East Africa – the Period Since Indepedence*, edited by Holger Bernt Hansen, and Michael Twaddle, 120–140. London: James Curry.

Kassimir, Ronald. 1998. "The Social Power of Religious Organisation and Civil Society: The Catholic Church in Uganda." In *Civil Society and Democracy in Africa – Critical Perspectives*, edited by Nelson Kasfir, 54–83. London: Frank Cass & Co. Ltd.

Kassimir, Ronald. 1999. "The Politics of Popular Catholicism in Uganda." In *East African Expressions of Christianity*, edited by Thomas Spear, and Isaria N. Kimambo, 248–274. Oxford: James Curry.

Kelsall, Tim, and Claire Mercer. 2003. "Empowering People? World Vision & 'Transformatory Development' in Tanzania." *Review of African Political Economy* 30 (96): 293–304.

Lebon, Nathalie. 1996. "Professionalization of Women's Health Groups in Sao Paulo: The Troublesome Road Towards Organizational Diversity." *Organization* 3 (4): 588–609.

Leusenkamp, Alexander M. 2010. "Religion, Authority and Their Interplay in the Shaping of Antiretroviral treatment in Western Uganda." *African Journal of AIDS Research* 9 (4): 419–427.

Markowitz, Lisa, and Karen W. Tice. 2002. "Paradoxes of Professionalization: Parallel Dilemmas in Women's Organizations in the Americas." *Gender & Society* 16 (6): 941–958.

Marshall, Katherine, and Marisa Van Saanen. 2007. *Development and Faith – Where Mind, Heart and Soul Work Together*. Washington, DC: The World Bank.

Meinert, Lotte, Hanne O. Mogensen, and Jenipher Twebaze. 2009. "Tests for Life Chances: CD4 Miracles and Obstacles in Uganda." *Anthropology & Medicine* 16 (2): 195–209.

Melucci, Alberto. 1996. *Challenging Codes: Collective Action in the Information Age*. Cambridge: Cambridge University Press.

Mosse, David. 2005. *Cultivating Development – An Ethnography of Aid Policy and Practice*. London: Pluto Press.

Nguyen, Vinh-Kim. 2009. "Government-by-Exception: Enrolment and Experimentality in Mass HIV Treatment Programmes in Africa." *Social Theory & Health* 7 (3): 196–217.

Nsambya Home Care. 2007. *Nsambya Home Care 1987–2007*. Kampala: St. Raphael of St. Francis Nsambya Hospital.

Ntale, Charles Lwanga, and Angela Cunningham. 2008. *Independent Evaluation Report. Kamokwya Christian Caring Community, Uganda, January 2004–December 2007*. UK: Development Research & Training, Uganda and Kairos Consultancy.

O'Manique, Colleen. 2004. *Neoliberalism and AIDS Crisis in Sub-Saharan Africa – Globalization's Pandemic*. Houndmills, Basingstoke, Hampshire: Palgrave Macmillan.

Oomman, Nandini, Michael Bernstein, and Steven Rosenzweig. 2008. *The Numbers Behind the Stories: PEPFAR Funding for Fiscal Years 2004 to 2006*. Washington, DC: Center for Global Development. http://www.cgdev.org/files/15799_file_theNumbersBehindTheStories.PDF

Orach, Sam Orochi. 2005. "ART in Uganda Catholic Health Facilities: Opportunities and Challenges." *Health Policy and Development* 3: 21–27.

Parkhurst, Justin O. 2001. "The Crisis of Aids and the Politics of Response: The Case of Uganda." *International Relations* 15 (6): 69–87.

Parkhurst, Justin O. 2005. "The Response to HIV/AIDS and the Construction of National Legitimacy: Lessons from Uganda." *Development and Change* 36 (3): 571–590.

Patterson, Amy S. 2011. *The Church and AIDS in Africa – the Politics of Ambiguity*. Boulder, CO: Lynne Rienner Publishers.

People in Aid. 2007. "Motivating Staff and Volunteers Working in NGOs in the South." http://www.peopleinaid.org/pool/files/pubs/motivating-staff-and-volunteers-working-in-ngos-in-the-south.pdf

Putzel, James. 2004. "The Politics of Action on AIDS: A Case Study of Uganda." *Public Administration and Development* 24 (1): 19–30.

Rasmussen, Louise Mubanda. 2011. "From Dying with Dignity to Living with Rules: AIDS Treatment and 'Holistic Care' in Catholic Organisations in Uganda." PhD thesis, Centre of African Studies, University of Copenhagen.

Rasmussen, Louise Mubanda, and Lisa Ann Richey. 2012. "The Lazarus Effect of AIDS Treatment: Lessons Learned and Lives Saved." *Journal of Progressive Human Services* 23 (3): 187–207.

Rau, Bill. 2006. "The Politics of Civil Society in Confronting HIV/AIDS." *International Affairs* 82 (2): 285–295.

Richey, Lisa Ann. 2005. "Uganda – HIV/AIDS and Reproductive Health." In *Where Human Rights Begin*, edited by Wendy Chavkin, and Ellen Chesler, 95–126. Piscataway: Rutgers University Press.

Richey, Lisa Ann, and Stine Jessen Haakonsson. 2004. *Access to ARV Treatment: Aid, Trade and Governance in Uganda*, DIIS Working Paper 2004:19. Copenhagen: Danish Institute for International Studies.

Seidel, Gill. 1990. "'Thank God I Said No To AIDS': On the Changing Discourse of AIDS in Uganda." *Discourse and Society* 1 (1): 61–84.

Swidler, Ann, and Susan Cotts Watkins. 2009. "'Teach a Man to Fish': The Sustainability Doctrine and Its Social Consequences." *World Development* 37 (7): 1182–1196.

Tripp, Aili Mari. 2010. *Museveni's Uganda – Paradoxes of Power in a Hybrid Regime*. Boulder, Colorado: Lynne Rienner Publishers.

Uganda Aids Commission. 1993. "The Multi-Sectoral Approach to Control HIV/AIDS in Uganda." www.aidsuganda.org

UNAIDS. 2002. *Report on the Global HIV/AIDS Epidemic*. Geneva: Joint United Nations Programme on HIV/AIDS.

van Stekelenburg, Jacquelien, and Bert Klandermans. 2009. "Social Movement Theory: Past, Present and Prospects." In *Movers and Shakers – Social Movements in Africa*, edited by Stephen Ellis, and Ineke van Kessel, 17–43. Leiden: Brill.

Wallman, Sandra. 1996. *Kampala Women Getting by – Wellbeing in the Time of AIDS*. London: James Curry.

Williams, Glen, and Nasaali Tamale. 1991. "The Caring Community – Coping with AIDS in Urban Uganda." In *Strategies of Hope no. 6*. London and Nairobi: Action Aid, Catholic Overseas Development Agency UK and African Medical and Research Foundation.

World Food Programme. 2006. "HIV/AIDS & Care and Treatment – Food in the Response to AIDS." http://www.wfp.org/food_aid/doc/39149_Care_Treatment.pdf (no longer available online).

World Food Programme. 2009. "Country Strategy for WFP in Uganda (2009–2014)." http://www.wfp.org/sites/default/files/Draft%20-%20Uganda%20Country%20Strategy%202009-2014.pdf

HIV/AIDS activism, framing and identity formation in Mozambique's *Equipas de Vida*

Rebecca J. Vander Meulen[a], Amy S. Patterson[b] and Marian Burchardt[c]

[a]Mission Department, Anglican Diocese of Niassa, Mozambique, Africa; [b]Department of Politics, University of the South, Sewanee, TN, USA; [c]Max Planck Institute for the Study of Religious and Ethnic Diversity, Göttingen, Germany

Résumé

Cet article examine sous un angle ethnographique la mobilisation basée sur la religion autour du VIH et du sida au Mozambique. Il explique les stratégies de mobilisation et leurs résultats dans le cas des équipes communautaires de riposte au VIH de l'Église anglicane du diocése de Niassa, dans le nord du Mozambique. En faisant intervenir des points de vue constructivistes issus de la théorie des mouvements sociaux, en particulier ceux qui se concentrent sur la formulation des processus et des identités collectives, cet article illustre la maniére dont ces points de vue peuvent être utilisés dans l'étude des contextes africains et montre la complexité des motivations sous-jacentes au volontariat. Bien que les dirigeants religieux insistent sur les cadres bibliques et le libre-arbitre des communautés pour motiver la participation, cet article soutient que ces cadres entrent en concurrence avec la dépendance et des attitudes divergentes au sein de la culture en général à l'égard du volontariat. Le premier cadre théologique que les dirigeants religieux utilisent pour mobiliser les équipes de riposte au VIH se concentre sur la compassion et facilite la participation de volontaires issus d'autres courants religieux.

Abstract

This article ethnographically explores faith-based mobilization around HIV and AIDS in Mozambique. It explains mobilization strategies and their outcomes in the case of the community-based HIV response teams of the Anglican Church in the Diocese of Niassa in Northern Mozambique. Engaging constructivist perspectives from social movement theory, especially those focusing on framing processes and collective identities, this article illustrates how such perspectives can be used in the study of African settings and shows the complexity of motivations behind volunteerism. While church leaders stress biblical frames and community agency to motivate involvement, this article argues that these frames compete against dependency and diverging attitudes within culture at large towards volunteerism. The primary theological frame that church leaders use to mobilize the HIV-response teams focuses on compassion and facilitates the participation of volunteers from other faith perspectives.

I. Introduction

Thousands of activists voluntarily participate in community-based HIV-response teams within the Anglican Diocese of Niassa in Mozambique. These teams, known as "*Equipas de Vida*" or "Life Teams", manage and develop their own community-based HIV-response activities in the northern half of Mozambique, where national HIV prevalence was 12% of the adult population in 2009. In reference to social movement approaches to framing (Snow et al. 1986) and collective identities (Melucci 1996), this article uses the *Equipas* as a case study to analyze mobilization strategies and their outcomes. While church leaders stress biblical frames and community agency to motivate involvement, these frames compete against dependency and attitudes within the culture at large towards volunteerism. Though volunteerism may be motivated by a transformed identity, volunteerism can also emerge from material poverty that drives a need for the pursuit of present or future material compensation. The examination is situated within the context of Mozambique's historical underdevelopment of civil society, its high proportion of donor funding earmarked for HIV-related activities, and ongoing debates in the literature about the nature of volunteerism in AIDS work.

Underlying the approach of diocesan leaders is the philosophy that voluntary activism is a legitimate mechanism for community action. Diocesan leaders have first aligned the theological frame that social action is a manifestation of one's faith and Christian identity with the underlying community-held frame that spirituality is not disconnected from daily life. Leaders have also recognized that local communities have inherent capacity that is essential in addressing local problems. Diocesan leaders have facilitated this frame resonance through the strategic use of frame-aligning language and didactic tools. As a result, more than four thousand volunteers currently participate in more than two hundred *Equipas de Vida* in northern Mozambique.

Frame alignment has facilitated significant community-level social action by transforming participants' sense of service into a new sense of individual and collective identity. This newly articulated identity both derives from and perpetuates a sense of satisfaction and solidarity within the team and the community. Though frame alignment is critical in initiating action, the maintenance of action is propelled by its resulting identity formation. Through volunteering, activists have begun to define part of their identity as being *Equipa de Vida* activists, and this identity continues to urge their action. Such identity creation and satisfaction are not universally adequate enough to sustain continued volunteerism; some activists leave in the absence of financial compensation.

This article contributes a case study to four bodies of literature. First, it examines how religious leaders utilize theological principles to frame social policy and social mobilization. Theological principles as mobilization frames have a long history; for example, Levine (1992) details how liberation theology propelled action among poor Latin Americans through groups such as the Landless Workers' Movement in Brazil. Similar studies exist on the role of religious leaders in the United States (US) civil rights movement (see Marsh 2005). This study adds an African case to this body of literature. Secondly, some policy-oriented literature argues that a community must be assessed not through the lens of its needs, but from the perspective of its existing strengths in skills and social capital. Scholars such as Freire (1970) and Werner (1982) have analyzed the ways that local insight and capacity could better shape effective development. This study investigates the effects of mobilization framed around ideas of local capacity in the specific context of Mozambique. Thirdly, this article contributes to the literature on volunteers in African development, and particularly the controversy over paying volunteers for their efforts (see Swidler and Watkins 2009). This article asserts that volunteerism is influenced by multiple factors: framing, identity transformation, and material benefits. Through an acknowledgement of the complexity of these motivations, the article provides greater nuance to the debate over volunteerism in Africa. Finally, the article adds to the body of literature on the role of the church in responding to HIV, presenting the case of a mainline church, which places more of an emphasis on earthly physical struggles than do many Pentecostal and African Independent Churches discussed in existing literature.

II. Methodology

This article is based on ethnographic research conducted independently (without sponsorship) by the author Rebecca Vander Meulen within the Diocese of Niassa between 2003 and 2011, as well as on an analysis of existing Anglican Church reports, proposals, and policy documents. It is supported by interviews with approximately 65 informants, all of whom had, at some point, been volunteer activists within the Diocese of Niassa. Recorded interviews from these activists were conducted by six different people, including Vander Meulen, diocesan staff, and diocesan volunteers. No noticeable patterns emerged in terms of the responses given to any single interviewer. Before beginning interviews, interviewers explained that the questions were being asked in order to better understand why people are and are not involved in the *Equipas de Vida*. The activists were chosen through convenience sampling (with the intention of speaking both with activists currently involved in HIV-response work and with those who had previously done work with the *Equipas* but later quit). Though interviewers were authorized to ask additional, follow-up questions, all interviewers used the same basic interview questions (which are presented in Appendix 1). Respondents were not obligated to participate and received no compensation for their participation in the interviews. Participants were also informed about the academic use of their responses. No Institutional Review Board (IRB) approval was required for this study. Interviewees provided oral consent to be interviewed and for interviews to be recorded. For further protection of interviewees, their anonymity is preserved in this publication. Though this research specifically focuses on the activist mobilization work of the Diocese of Niassa, it bears similarities to the work of thousands of faith-based programs on HIV and AIDS found in communities across Africa.

III. Contextual background

Historical events have challenged the current manifestation of social efficacy in Mozambique. Centuries of autocratic Portuguese colonialism (replete with slavery, the establishment of inefficient government bureaucracies, control over civil society, and the confinement of secondary education and medical care to a minute minority of the population), a protracted war for independence (and the widespread destruction of the country's assets by many Portuguese people upon their forced departure), and a brutal civil war from 1977 to 1992 have taken their toll on Mozambique's social fabric (Waterhouse 1996). During the civil war, many Mozambicans were forced to watch or participate in the brutal deaths of their elderly parents or young children, and "robbery, or confiscation, became a way of life not only for the Renamo band but for everyone in Mozambique" (Newitt 1995, 576). After the civil war ended, a full two thirds of the country's population lived in absolute poverty (Waterhouse 1996). One result of this history is the latent distrust that many Mozambicans have toward their fellow citizens. Though a 2008 survey found that 91% of Mozambicans trust their relatives "a lot" or "somewhat", only 53% trusted other people they knew to the same extent, and only 32% had "a lot" or "some" trust towards other Mozambicans (Afrobarometer 2009).

Though Mozambique was the world's eighth fastest-growing economy between 2001 and 2010, and is forecasted by the International Monetary Fund to continue as the fourth fastest-growing economy between 2011 and 2015 (*The Economist* 2011), it still suffers from significant social problems: only 55% of adults can read, only 21% of the rural population has access to any improved water source, and only 38% of the urban population has improved sanitation (World Bank 2011). Mozambique is in the world's top 10 countries in both the number and percentage of people living with HIV, as well as in the number of people dying from an HIV-related cause (Central Intelligence Agency 2009). At the national level, 12% of adults aged 15 to 49 (13% of women and 9% of men) were living with HIV in 2009 (Instituto Nacional de Saúde 2009).

Centuries of struggle and oppression have created conditions in which Mozambicans have had little control over their environment, and in light of so many seemingly intractable social difficulties, many Mozambicans have redefined death and pain as being "normal". David Lewis summarizes David Sogge's assessment of civil society in Mozambique by pointing out three impeding factors: (1) historical colonial tightly-controlled constructs around associations so that "Mozambican ways of associating together hardly ever resemble institutions of civil society known to Westerners"; (2) structural adjustment and related forces that led Mozambicans to perceive that power is exercised primarily from outside the country; and (3) "informal social and political action [that] is widely preferred over formal types" (Lewis 2001, 7). Against this context, common responses to death or illness are that "each person has his time" or that "God has willed it". Against such a backdrop, few initiatives against HIV are truly community-driven – and those which are, are quite counter-cultural. A 2008 survey found that 61% of Mozambicans agreed that "people are like children; the government should take care of them like a parent", while only 21% thought that the Mozambican people should serve as "bosses" who control the government (Afrobarometer 2009). The recognition that government and donors have typically provided assistance in times of crisis contributes to this identity of dependence on resources from outside the community.

Mozambique's historic tragedies and resulting lack of trust, poverty, and perceived helplessness among many citizens have created a climate that challenges the Diocese of Niassa's efforts to encourage poor community members to take action against the sickness, food insecurity, and family disruption caused by HIV. Without having the opportunity to see the progress that is being made globally on social indicators, many rural Mozambicans perceive their own social difficulties as universal and normative. Mobilizing action therefore requires preliminary fundamental deconstruction of certain assumptions, and construction of the belief that locally driven improvement is, indeed, possible.

IV. The case of the *Equipas de Vida* of the Diocese of Niassa

The Diocese of Niassa comprises the 350 Mozambican Anglican congregations (mostly rural) north of the Zambezi River. The Diocese of Niassa created a formal HIV and AIDS program in 2004. Though people living with HIV and AIDS had been included in the care traditionally given to sick people by the church's women's groups, this 2004 decision encouraged congregations to create their own HIV- and AIDS-response teams, now known as "*Equipas de Vida*" or "Life Teams". Each *Equipa de Vida* is responsible for its own internal management and for developing its own community-based HIV-response activities. By 2007, 102 congregations had formed formal HIV- and AIDS-response teams (giving 95% of parishes at least one team); by 2009 this number had surged to two hundred, with over four thousand volunteers. Priests had also begun working to integrate a response to HIV into congregational life. Because *Equipas de Vida*, frequently located in very remote parts of the country, were commonly the first groups to formally respond to HIV in a given community, their first responsibility was to mobilize community leaders around HIV – ideally gaining active support from local decision-shapers.

Equipas de Vida are free to organize themselves without any formal intervention from the diocesan leaders, but many *Equipas de Vida* request training on HIV from a staff member or from an experienced activist based in a different community. *Equipas de Vida* work with their communities to identify key challenges and develop response action plans, together with key community members such as teachers, health professionals, religious leaders, traditional authorities, and people living with HIV. Because community action in the *Equipa de Vida* model is internally driven (rather than externally prescribed), HIV-response work is inherently a manifestation of some desire to take initiative.

Practical responses to HIV vary from community to community and season to season, but are as diverse as the *Equipas* themselves. For example, the Yohanna Abdalla *Equipa* grows vegetables to distribute to orphaned and vulnerable children. A playgroup in Metonha enables orphaned children and those whose parents are living with HIV to play together. A youth drama team from Mocuba travels from church to church, performing dramas about HIV prevention after church services. These projects are typical of the types of congregational-based responses described by various researchers (Paterson 2001; Green 2003; Williams 2004). More formal activism includes speaking out in churches against stigma and discrimination, calling authorities to account on issues that affect vulnerable people (for example, confronting teachers who mistreat orphaned children), and fighting for better access to HIV testing and treatment. In Morrupula, for example, *Equipa de Vida* activists effectively lobbied for hundreds of orphaned and vulnerable children to obtain birth certificates (which are now required for children to study beyond the fifth grade).

Since the *Vida* program began, direct donations from Anglican dioceses and Christian development agencies in other parts of the world, funds from the diocese's provincial Anglican governing body in South Africa, and grants through the Mozambican government have funded costs of staff, training, transport, and basic field materials. These donations have been relatively small, ranging from annual contributions of $500 up to $45,000. In 2004, the diocese provided for one paid staff member to assist in the development of a mobilization strategy; by 2009 the diocesan "technical team" had grown to twelve paid staff members. Though the Diocese of Niassa pays these full-time staff members (who are ultimately accountable to diocesan management), it does not directly pay *Equipa de Vida* volunteers (who are ultimately accountable only to their own communities). Instead, it acknowledges their contributions through further skill training, and it seeks funding for the supplies that these *Equipas de Vida* need to conduct their work. It encourages volunteers not to work to such an extent that their work jeopardizes their agricultural labor, and it encourages teams to undertake only the most essential HIV-related tasks during critical farming seasons.

V. Framing activism

David Snow and his colleagues (Snow et al. 1986) assert that frames, or shared ways of understanding a problem, are needed to motivate action. Social movement leaders play a crucial role in that framing, using a variety of strategies from communication techniques to symbols. Diocesan leaders relied on both biblical frames of compassion and notions of local capacity to motivate action within the *Equipas*. As a result of mobilization, activists developed new forms of identity. In addition to new forms of identity being a motivating and contributing factor for action (see Melucci 1996), new resulting identities emerge through the act of mobilization.

A. *Theological and spiritual frames*

Diocesan leaders utilize the frame that social action is a necessary manifestation of one's faith. The diocesan vision is "to become a communion of communities in Christ Jesus through ministry, mission, and worship" (Diocese do Niassa 2003). Viewing the gospel as "good news", the mission work of the Diocese of Niassa does not focus on proselytizing, but rather on practically spreading the good news of liberation and healing (be that physical or spiritual). Congregations regularly pray "for all who are in affliction, sadness, need, sickness, or whatever other adversity" (Igreja 1988, 43). In addition to prayer, priests weekly exhort their congregations to "love your neighbor as you love yourself" (Igreja 1988, 38). A resolution by the Diocese of Niassa's 2007 Synod (its highest decision-making body) states that "[e]very Christian congregation should take action to bring the conditions of heaven to earth" and that "every believer has something to offer in this work of development" (Diocese do Niassa 2007, 16). Both through formal policy and weekly religious services, officials with the Diocese of Niassa assert that Christian spirituality does not preclude action on HIV and AIDS, but rather demands it.

The population at large in Mozambique also tends to see the world through a spiritual frame. This spiritual world includes deceased ancestors, who are often viewed as the force behind unexpected occurrences or bad dreams, and who may be able to be appeased through graveside ceremonies that include the cleaning of the deceased person's plot and a small meal. This spiritual world also includes sorcerers, who are living people who are approached to conjure up spells against fellow community members who have committed a grievance. For many Mozambicans, daily life is in some way shaped by the fear of the spiritual consequences imposed by elders or deceased ancestors against those who offend. Though these beliefs are not specifically Christian, they are often shared by those who worship in Anglican churches.

Diocesan leaders have used these two values – a general respect for the Bible and its messages of compassion and dignity, and widespread respect for a lifestyle-shaping spirituality – to frame AIDS activism. Though the specific beliefs of diocesan leaders, church members, and the community at large have differed, the common understanding of spirituality as pervasive has facilitated frame alignment. Inherent community respect for things spiritual, coupled with the witnessed or practiced tendency to allow spiritual principles to shape lifestyle choices, creates an environment receptive to biblical teachings on social action.

Leaders in the diocese have also utilized the process of frame transformation, or the development of new values to replace old beliefs in order to facilitate and expand collective action (Snow et al. 1986). Diocesan staff members have taken biblical texts that have traditionally been interpreted with an emphasis on personal piety and interpreted them with an emphasis on love and acceptance. Bible studies illustrating the importance of helping one's neighbor have become standard curricula in diocesan HIV training courses. Though the Bible is often used within the context of HIV to mandate a specific set of rules related to personal sexual behavior, leaders in the Anglican Church of Southern Africa instead apply biblical passages to mobilize compassion toward those living with HIV, even if they have broken biblical guidelines on personal sexual behavior (as traditionally interpreted by the church).

An important strategy in solidifying this biblical frame for HIV work was to train church leadership. In 2005, all clergy participated in a week of mandatory HIV training. This training gave priests knowledge on the biological aspects of HIV's prevention and transmission. It also helped priests accept that conversations around HIV, which are so often characterized by talk of sex, are conversations in which clergy can legitimately engage, despite their formal position in the church. Also in 2005, Anglican youth leaders within the diocese studied HIV-related theology and biology during a weeklong course. Many of these youth then began giving a weekly short talk on HIV during church worship services. To reinforce biblical teachings that support the church's loving response towards HIV, diocesan leaders have prepared and distributed sermon outlines on biblical themes relevant to HIV and AIDS. These sermon notes address, for example, issues of community response and unity. Many of the sermon themes have become commonly mentioned passages among *Equipa de Vida* members.

Equipa de Vida T-shirts serve as persistent signs that reinforce these framing messages; they have also inherently become a symbol of acceptance towards people living with HIV. The bright blue shirts, which proclaim that "in Christ there is no difference between positive and negative" (adapting biblical terminology that "in Christ there is no difference between Greek and Jew, slave and free"), have turned church activists into walking billboards.[1] *Equipa* activist Participant A explains their impact:

> The truth in Christ is that there's no difference [between the HIV positive and HIV negative], in Christ we are all equal. So it was because of this that there was a great impact because of that T-shirt. For example, in Mocuba, I can say this way, after those T-shirts came out, many people looked for the Anglican church just to come to know what that verse meant. After we were in the street, in the road, passing by, people wanted to know, "Where are you from?".[2]

Through these framing strategies, the diocese has mobilized thousands of *Equipa de Vida* activists to serve their neighbors. One activist explains: "My faith is to treat ... all the children, all people as if they were me; I saw a verse there that says to love another person as I would myself".[3] Another describes his motivation:

> For me, I feel that it is a calling of Christ. It's the Christian faith. I feel that faith is what keeps me from abandoning the work, it's based in faith. To believe. Believe in Jesus .... I begin to note what Jesus did, starting from the miracles that Jesus did, doing charitable works, without having to earn any money, I don't know, it's to do a charitable work without asking for any hand-out. What Jesus did was from his faith. I also have to do something. To do something to change some lives. It's not a [financial] exchange.[4]

Despite these attempts by the diocese to develop and reinforce a biblical frame for HIV activism, some priests have remained resistant to addressing HIV in the church. One particularly vocal priest (now retired) found that his personal understanding of HIV and AIDS did not align with frames proposed by diocesan leaders. His resistance seemed to be driven not by a specific concern about sex, but rather by a general concern that the church should not involve itself with material problems. In his opinion, the church's focus should be on spiritual salvation. Despite differing levels of involvement around HIV within clergy of the Diocese of Niassa, after the aforementioned priest retired, no active priests opposed the church's involvement with HIV. Some priests appreciate and advocate for the HIV work in and of itself, and some priests appreciate the church growth that has happened after people are introduced to the Anglican congregation by the practical support that they have received from the *Equipas*. A small group of Anglicans, heavily influenced by religious experiences that they and their families have had in neighboring Malawi (where they developed roots during their time as refugees during the Mozambican war), have formed a self named "evangelism nucleus", which has been more oriented than most

Anglicans towards salvation of the soul. Yet some people from within this group are also active members of their local *Equipas de Vida*, and do not see HIV work and evangelism work as mutually exclusive.

B. *Framing activism in terms of local capacity*

Diocesan leaders also approach social action through the frame that local communities have inherent capacities. This is, in part, based on the theological principle that Christians collectively make up the "body of Christ", and just as each human body part serves a particular function, individual people also each contribute something unique.[5] This emphasis on local capacity echoes a deep history of communal mutual support; as Patel and Wilson explain:

> A tradition of self-help, individual and collective responsibility for the wellbeing of families and kinship groups, predates the colonial era. Communities organized themselves to meet their needs along the lines of self-help programs giving rise later to voluntary groups and a rich tradition of indigenous self-help initiatives. (Patel and Wilson 2004, 24S)

Leaders of the Diocese of Niassa work to amplify the evidence of already manifested social capacity to help community members further recognize their own capacity, perhaps unexpressed up to now.

This frame of capable Mozambicans is in stark contrast to the view among some Mozambicans and foreigners who infer that because the country has rampant poverty, Mozambicans must be impotent in their own development. In fact, it may be pragmatically beneficial for a community to dwell on its own lamentable state, since intentionally emphasizing the existing weaknesses of a community can provoke the provision of deeper external resources, which have been the driving force behind much power and prestige in Africa (Bayart 2000).

Some community activists have come to recognize that they, within their community, already have skills that can not only serve as a useful addition to outside support, but can also be preferable to external inputs in terms of effecting community change. One activist explained:

> Anyone [from the outside] who tries to work without recognizing local resources will not satisfy the needs or priorities of the communities, because the outsider will defend only his own interests. The projects will not have any impact or success in the community.[6]

Though the communities that are part of the Diocese of Niassa are some of the materially poorest in the world, diocesan leaders have encouraged looking beyond material wealth as the only effective means towards community responses to HIV. One activist, frustrated with being considered poor and needy, notes that the assumption that all helpful resources are physical ignores the valuable contribution that people themselves make; he says: "Tell someone who thinks that Mozambicans have nothing to contribute on our own development that we can contribute ourselves, in the form of volunteers".[7] Activist D recognizes the role of external support while still maintaining confidence in the role of his compatriots: "I reject the idea that Mozambicans have nothing to contribute. I believe that Mozambicans have skills, gifts, abilities. Maybe we need help planning and implementing".[8]

While acknowledging that people in under-resourced areas do need financial support and technical training to achieve certain goals, diocesan leaders believe that many community skills have traditionally been overlooked both by Mozambicans and foreigners. "It is a complete lie", says diocesan leader Participant F, "to say that Mozambicans can't help themselves".[9]

To encourage and empower locally driven responses, the Diocese of Niassa urges *Equipas de Vida* to work with community authorities to identify pressing HIV-related problems, along with their possible solutions. Local decision-making allows contextual flexibility. Diocesan *Vida* staff members then help the congregational team strategically plan interventions, and occasionally, when conditions permit, help secure small amounts of funding to assist community efforts. Because each individual *Equipa de Vida* drives its own projects, these projects may seem different in different communities, despite meeting similar objectives.

Diocesan leaders help Mozambicans value their own capacities by facilitating a series of community-wide asset appreciation sessions that use mapping and story-telling activities. The Diocese of Niassa encourages communities to begin with small and achievable goals, in order to facilitate the growth of community confidence. Where geographically feasible, diocesan staff members encourage exchange visits between newly formed *Equipas de Vida* and teams that have already achieved significant results. The Diocese of Niassa does not bring in skills or goods from outside a community until it has identified that these skills do not exist within the community. In light of the cultural value of accepting things as they are, the *Equipas de Vida* – working to change the way things are – are revolutionary.

The language used by diocesan staff members to refer to themselves and to community volunteer activists consistently reinforces the importance of community ownership of local development. Leaders have conceived of activists as agents who develop their own goals, and, as stated by the Diocese of Niassa (2010, 1), "[t]he fieldworkers do not use the *Equipas de Vida* to achieve the objectives of the fieldworkers and the Technical Team, but rather the fieldworkers walk alongside the *Equipas* as they achieve their own objectives".

Leaders of the Diocese of Niassa also challenge hierarchies in society through their language. For example, the job title given to field workers is *adepto*, a Portuguese term referring to a "supporter" or "fan" (such as someone at a sporting event). Using this analogy, the *Equipas de Vida* are the ones who win or lose the game; the *adeptos* serve to support their teams. The words *equipa* and *adepto* become ways in which language serves to reaffirm identity. This language backs up the principle that the Diocese of Niassa sees its few support staff as supporting the work of the activists, not as the activists helping the support staff to achieve broader diocesan goals.

The name *Equipa de Vida* also shapes the work by reinforcing the hope that *Equipas de Vida* intend to convey. Though initially dubbed "AIDS teams", the teams themselves rejected this name because they did not seek to promote AIDS and death, but rather abundant life. They wanted to help people prevent HIV infection and to urge HIV-positive people to live well. As Diocese of Niassa Bishop Mark Van Koevering explains:

> I was holding a clergy conference while the young people were meeting to talk about the rise of HIV in Mozambique. Some clearly made jokes about the young *Equipa de SIDA*, or "Team of Death". To their credit and my delight, the young people came up with a truly Christian rebuttal: "We are not people of death but of life, because God is the God of the living, not the dead". They promptly renamed themselves the *Equipa de Vida*, or "Team of Life". (Meyer 2009, 21)

Though other organizations had previously used the phrase "Choose life, not AIDS", the Diocese of Niassa changed that message into "Choose life in this world with AIDS". This language was changed in recognition that the former message implied that AIDS was the end of life, and that AIDS was a choice someone had made. The change aimed to create a spirit of hopefulness by emphasizing that abundant life is possible even for someone living with AIDS.

The use of the local capacity framework has had several outcomes. First, *Equipa de Vida* members self-report the importance of the *Equipa de Vida* for their own identity. Though most *Equipa de Vida* members are themselves poor, they have developed an identity of agency through their work – thereby helping not only their neighbors but also themselves. One said: "I continue to work in this team because it changes my life".[10] Those who are *Equipa de Vida* members out of a manifestation of their own identity have tended to persevere:

> I am continuing to work in the *Equipa de Vida* because – it's not that I don't have a lot of things to do. I have a lot of things. But if I leave it … I think that my gift does not let me abandon it.[11]

Participant H notes that the *Equipa de Vida* was a way to put into reality part of what he already saw as his identity: "I joined because it was my dream, since I was a child, to help orphan children".[12]

In the process of volunteering, the activists' service often creates a new identity for those mobilized. Active *Equipa de Vida* members have made their work part of who they are. Participant C expresses his inability to stop working:

> I've done a lot of things, and I feel so fulfilled, even though I haven't achieved the full objective …. I continue to work in the *Equipa de Vida* because I still feel secure, and I still feel that now we can do – now it's the phase of trying to counsel our colleagues who are not getting a [HIV] test to understand their health, so … this is the battle that keeps me still in the *Equipa de Vida*. Because I still haven't attained my goals.[13]

Many *Equipa de Vida* members gain a new identity both as they come to see themselves as competent and important actors in their communities and as they are viewed with greater respect by those around them. Once people have become active in their local *Equipa de Vida*, their experiences reinforce their identity. One member said: "One thing that leaves me proud is that I helped orphan children. I kept going back to help, to visit. And this is the thing that leaves me very happy".[14]

An *Equipa de Vida* member who sees another person's life change because of his action feels empowered, and continued action creates additional opportunities to recognize this power. Participant B explains:

> What I did that I'm very proud about in the *Equipa de Vida* is that I took a woman living positively to begin with antiretroviral treatment. In the beginning she was taking medicines and they were making her feel bad. I always took her to the hospital, and from there she is now better. And when she wants to go to the hospital, I always take her.[15]

Equipa activist Participant I notes that upon joining "I felt a little more proud".[16] Many of these activists exemplify what Penner (2002, 463; italics in original) describes: "the most potent direct causes of *Sustained Volunteerism* are people's perceptions of themselves and the roles they occupy (i.e. their *Volunteer Role Identity)*".

This new identity is evident in outward ways. Members of *Equipas de Vida* proudly wear *Equipas* T-shirts, caps, or printed nametags. The most common request by *Equipa de Vida* members to the diocesan staff is for more branded *Equipa de Vida* garments. Though never referred to as such by diocesan leaders, many *Equipas de Vida* have started terming these clothes as their "uniforms", indicating their personal desire to be defined by their role as members of *Equipas de Vida* and to be publicly associated with this role. Several *Equipa de Vida* members even wore these shirts in the cathedral for their service of ordination for priesthood. A handful of communities so highly prize their uniforms that they wear them only while engaged in formal, scheduled *Equipa de Vida* activities, and afterwards store the uniforms in one central location in order to keep the T-shirts in better condition. *Equipas* who carefully limit the use of *Equipa*-labeled clothing explain that this practice respects the dignity of the office of the *Equipa de Vida* member because it prevents family members, who may not publicly live up to the standards of compassion and authority that *Equipa* members believe befit their group, from wearing the shirts (see also Muula, Hofman, and Cumberland [2004] on clothing and identity).

The name *Equipa de Vida* has come to bear weight.[17] In public gatherings, it is common for *Equipa* members to introduce themselves with their *Equipa de Vida* title, describing themselves as a "member of the *Equipa de Vida*" in place of another appropriate title, such as "student at Kankhomba Secondary School". *Equipa de Vida* members regularly request typed documents from the diocesan technical staff which explain that they are *Equipa de Vida* members, as these credentials bear weight with government officials and other leaders. The inclusion of *Equipas de Vida* in community decisions shows their credibility with official local leaders.[18] *Equipas de Vida* members were formally invited to send representatives to community consultations in rural communities when Mozambique's president Armando Guebuza officially visited. Identity and external respect become mutually re-inforcing. Public recognition both stems from and contributes to the development of a clear and pride-inducing identity.

The resulting sense of self-efficacy in some *Equipas* has led them to independently take on community projects that are not directly related to HIV. *Equipas* near Wikihi, for example, together constructed a small primary school, advocated for books to be donated from a neighboring school, and began teaching first grade. This project was particularly rewarding for team members, because they realized their power to teach, despite the fact that many of them had limited educational experiences and literacy skills. The new identity that emerged for many *Equipa* activists urges their continued activism.

VI. Donors, volunteerism, and the *Equipas de Vida*

The work of the *Equipas* is set within a larger context of sizeable donor influence in HIV and AIDS work in Mozambique. In 2008, roughly 82% of Mozambique's AIDS funding came from external sources (Mozambique National AIDS Spending Assessment 2008, 9). Donors have contributed to a prevailing view that volunteerism includes financial payments. This section outlines this context and analyzes the ways in which the Diocese of Niassa tries to counter these patterns of dependence on external financing. This section also addresses additional motives that volunteers have for their activism, thereby demonstrating the complexity of religious AIDS activism in a poverty-stricken context.

A. Donor-driven volunteerism

The active involvement of high-level, high-funded organizations in the HIV field, and their stated intention to work with faith-based groups, feeds into the popular perception in Mozambique that HIV is a field with limitless resources. This donor involvement can significantly shape the identity of local organizations.

First, funding creates a relationship of inequality between donors and recipients. Donors tend to significantly shape the activities of funding recipients through specific budgetary guidelines (Alden 2001). Those who control resources can cause organizations that rely on such resources to alter their pre-existing strategies and priorities, and also affect the time frame for implementation. Depending on external resources "has tended to create organizations which lack downwards accountability, are dependent on donors and are not addressing the wider roles for civil society envisaged in the approach" and causes civil society to become "largely dependent on foreign funds for support [and thus] hamstrung by donor agendas to the extent that the 'implementation of locally initiated programs must often wait for external assistance'" (Alden 2001, 106).

Second, given this linkage between funding and leadership, churches or non-governmental organizations (NGOs) are often seen as implementing sub-contractors, not as independent agents with an authentic voice. As such, there is a tendency among outside policymakers to perceive African civil society as a set of "grassroots NGOs", most of which are funded by the international community or by transnational NGOs such as World Vision. As participants in wider institutions of transnational governmentality, civil society groups can become merely conduits of aid money (Lewis 2001).

These donor–civil society relations can lead local organizations to begin working for the partner, not for themselves. As a result, the quality of the work can decrease, as individual participants' self-interest generally compels more forceful action than does a contract. Edwards and Hulme (1996, 19 in reproduced version) warn: "From a radical perspective [the encouragement of NGOs and grass-roots organizations by official agencies] may lead to cooptation: the abandonment of a mission for social transformation to become the implementer of the policy agendas of northern governments".

These broader trends in donor–civil society relationships have found a specific application in the issue of volunteerism in many other African countries. Volunteers and organizations that draw on volunteers abound, especially in the field of HIV (Omoto and Snyder 1990; Mashimo et al. 2001; Schneider 2008; Simon et al. 2009). However, in most situations, volunteers work to support an organization (Damon 2007), not to achieve a community-driven objective. By using the terms "employees" and "volunteers" interchangeably, Dibie and Dibie (2008) imply that volunteers serve as free labor for NGOs. In some contexts, volunteers substitute for paid employees, doing work on behalf of an organization – work for which the organization would otherwise need to pay someone. Swidler and Watkins (2009, 1188) criticize volunteerism as teaching activists "that as villagers they were not worth being paid".

The understanding of the term "volunteer" is shaped by the practices of those who use the term. In Mozambique, a common assumption is that "voluntary" means that the work will be subsidized at a low level. Even if an organization does not pay its volunteers, it may offer generous benefits. As one official from an NGO receiving U.S. President's Emergency Plan for AIDS Relief (PEPFAR) money explained in correspondence with the Diocese of Niassa:

> The MOH [Ministry of Health] issued a directive to all NGOs [non-governmental organizations] that IP [implementing partner] volunteers may not receive cash stipends. They receive bicycles, back packs and rain ponchos as well as all the necessary materials for the home visits and data collection .... Although no other reward is officially permitted by MOH, [the NGO] provides food vouchers, every-so-often to both volunteers and supervisors, as a means of appreciation.[19]

The continued use of the term "volunteer" in the midst of such "means of appreciation" perpetuates a perception that volunteerism is not free of external incentives.

Some Mozambicans attribute the perception that volunteers must be paid to the practices of organizations with foreign funding which began working in Mozambique soon after the civil war, and which, in a need to achieve urgent results, paid people to carry out basic community development activities that, in a context with less urgency, would have been carried out by subsidy-free volunteers.[20] Government policy has also perpetuated the assumption. When the Mozambican government developed a home-based care system, for example, it used the term "volunteer" to refer to home-based care providers for chronically ill patients. These people were also expected to work with a fixed number of patients with fixed schedules – and were therefore effectively treated as informal employees. Accordingly, the government's home-based care guidelines strongly recommended that anyone doing such home-based care be paid.

B. *Diocesan strategies for promoting volunteerism*

The Diocese of Niassa goes against the dominant practices of "volunteerism" encountered by community members in Mozambique. The most obvious way it does this is by not providing payment or material incentives to its volunteers. In addition to the efforts of the diocesan staff to promote volunteerism through frames of biblical justice and local capacity, diocesan staff members use specific mobilization strategies. Diocesan leaders use five broad strategies to promote HIV-related volunteerism in a context of dependence on external financing and of expectations that volunteers should receive financial compensation.

First, diocesan leaders seek to frame action in the context of other traditionally held volunteer roles. They help make linkages with other non-paid societal tasks such as church catechists (lay leaders) or choir members, traditional chiefs, and family members who care for sick relatives. The link between HIV activity and other church activity was clear to one activist, who said:

> The *Equipa de Vida* is equal to other groups because it also does a charitable work. It cannot be paid ... or have any sort of earnings because it has to be in the same way the Mother's Union does things, and it has no earnings. It's not paid.[21]

Second, diocesan leaders promote HIV-related volunteerism by empowering *Equipas* with decision-making rights. In the same way that grassroots organizations can lose their voice and autonomy when fulfilling the objectives of NGOs, *Equipas de Vida* may lose their voice if they work for, instead of with the support of, diocesan staff. In an effort to maintain autonomous *Equipas*, diocesan staff members train *Equipas* on technical skills such as HIV testing and agricultural techniques – but leave planning and implementation up to the local *Equipa*. This autonomy in operations means that, at times, *Equipas de Vida* develop goals that the diocesan leadership does not support. One lakeside community, for example, identified that a major problem for people living with HIV was that a specific hippopotamus too often trampled on their small agricultural fields. The *Equipa* appealed to diocesan leaders for help in obtaining a gun with which to kill the hippopotamus. The diocesan leaders were not in favor of the hippo-killing strategy and did not help with a gun, but they also did not attempt to ban the efforts.

Third, diocesan leaders seek to counter a sense of inequality and hierarchy that can arise in donor–civil society relations by emphasizing financial transparency in their own work, and by keeping expenses as minimal as possible. Diocesan leaders do not want community members to perceive that they are engaged in HIV- and AIDS- related efforts primarily for financial benefit. When traveling, staff members carry budgets to show local communities. Staff members do not receive per diems for their travel, they typically travel by public transportation or bicycles, and they sleep and eat in the homes of *Equipa de Vida* members. The food at training sessions is not provided by outside professionals, but rather is prepared by local church members and is of similar quality to the food that would be eaten at home. The salaries of field workers are generally equivalent to the salaries that government school teachers earn. Diocesan leaders work with donors who share their philosophy about financial management.

Fourth, the diocese does not conform to the usual NGO practices in that it does not go into the community to recruit volunteers. In terms of recruitment, volunteer candidates present themselves to *Equipas*, and *Equipas* present training requests to technical staff. Teams that began in 2005 continue, and since 2006 there has been a backlog of new communities that are interested in starting an *Equipa de Vida*. Though the Diocese of Niassa recognizes that using volunteers to substitute for employees who would otherwise be paid – especially when such work gets in the way of the volunteer earning a living – may be exploitative or abusive, the Diocese of Niassa operates with the understanding that members of the community are working for themselves. Realistically, no volunteers substitute for employees in this community-defined action. One interviewed activist feared that paying volunteers would weaken the unity of the *Equipas*: "It would be bad for the team, because not everyone would come with that faith of helping. They would come simply with that desire of wanting to gain something, or that they would gain something. This would be bad".[22]

Fifth, diocesan leaders aim to dispel misconceptions about *Equipa de Vida* volunteerism before that volunteerism begins. Deep economic poverty challenges volunteer activism, and poverty touches the lives of the majority of *Equipa de Vida* activists, most of whom are subsistence farmers. Their own economic situations would merit their being recipients of aid, were it available. During orientation meetings, diocesan staff members stress the point that *Equipa* work is voluntary and without payment. Yet the predominant language of NGO work on HIV and AIDS can make these explanations difficult to grasp.

Though interviews revealed that some people occasionally left the *Equipa* due to interpersonal conflicts between team members, or for logistical reasons such as relocation or illness, the most common reason for volunteers leaving their *Equipa* was lack of funding. One *Equipa de Vida* member explained about volunteers who had quit: "If they left, it's because they thought, as soon as they entered the *Equipa de Vida*, they would have a benefit".[23] While continuing to volunteer without payment "because I like it", activist Participant L comments that "payment would be a good thing for the team. A lot more people would be eager to work, if they were paid something". [24] Similarly, activist Participant M notes that, with payment, existing *Equipa* members "would be strong and ready to work".[25]

Just as the word "volunteer" has become associated with financial benefit in the broader Mozambican context, the term "project" has also become synonymous with funding. Diocesan leaders originally encouraged *Equipas* to develop projects, not recognizing the full implications of this word. *Equipas* held off work while waiting for the presumed money. Participant N noted: "The *Equipa de Vida* is different [from ecclesiastical groups like Mother's Union, Anglican youth] because it's a project". When pressed on this difference, her assumptions that "project" implies money became clear:

> They messed up in the beginning, to say that the *Equipa de Vida* is a project. If they had said that the *Equipa de Vida* is a church group and that it's an actual part of the church, that it makes up part of the church, that would be a different situation".[26]

Because of such misunderstandings, the diocesan staff members no longer use the term "project". Contextual frames around funding continually challenge the frames used by diocesan leaders to motivate volunteer activists.

C. *Alternative motives for* Equipa de Vida *involvement*

Though the volunteerism of many *Equipa de Vida* activists is motivated by biblical principles, activated through specific strategies of diocesan staff and reinforced through the development of a new identity, other factors also compel action. This section outlines some of those alternative motives, each of which is worthy of further study.

For some activists, *Equipa de Vida* work results from boredom or out of a sense of routine. Participant O explains: "They [volunteers] don't have anything to do – what to do?"[27] Participant P also says he is involved in an *Equipa de Vida* "because I have nothing else to do".[28] Another *Equipa de Vida* member framed his participation not in terms of biblical frames or a new identity, but simply in the belief that *Vida* activities had become a way of life: "I have not quit, because I really like working. It is the activity of my life. I like to do our work".[29] For one activist, participating in the *Equipa de Vida* is simply the way he spends his time: "Wow, I, as a youth, if I left the group, I wouldn't feel better, I have nothing else to do, other than working in the *Equipa de Vida*."[30]

The search for knowledge also compels action. In a context where few formal training opportunities exist, and where the Internet is still very inaccessible, knowledge is seen as a source of power, and activists crave training opportunities – both for the teaching itself and for its associated prestige. This follows Swidler and Watkins' (2009, 1190) observation about Malawian youth: "Lessons about anatomy and leadership skills fulfilled deep aspirations for identity and status, preserving symbolically the sense of self that the pragmatic demands of their everyday lives continually threatened to overwhelm". One activist explained:

> I entered into the *Equipa de Vida* to gain experiences. To hear what the *Vida* program is addressing. When I entered, I learned how to avoid HIV, and how to deal with orphan children, how to do a test, and how, how to live, how to respect people. Respect yourself and the other. Respect the other as I respect myself.[31]

This activist acknowledges learning about biology, social work, and theology.

Some activists are attracted to *Equipa de Vida* involvement through the peripheral benefits of training. Community members expect training sessions to include free food that is of a higher quality than is typically eaten at home (including elements such as meat or soda). Though the Diocese of Niassa does not serve such food, many training sessions sponsored by government or NGOs do indeed include bounteous food offerings. In some communities, particularly those in which other training sessions have already set precedents, some trainees, disappointed by the food offered through the Diocese of Niassa, do not return for the second day of training.[32] Another potential training-related benefit is a certificate. Because having particular skills may provide HIV-related employment opportunities, certificates become an important way of distinguishing oneself; even in the absence of employment opportunities, they bring the pride associated with external recognition. In the first years of the *Equipas de Vida*, certificates of attendance were commonly given upon the completion of training – but the diocese stopped giving certificates for short courses when it realized that some trainees had no intention of applying HIV skills, but were participating only to receive a certificate. This decision not to award certificates was taken by the diocesan leaders in order to better utilize the limited financial resources allocated to training.

Another factor that attracts some activists to volunteerism is the hope of employment. As Swidler and Watkins (2009, 1189) note, "[m]any perceive that the best available route to a steady job is to volunteer, often for several years and for several organizations" (see also Swart, Seedat, and Sader 2004). Though hiring volunteers is not the norm, one somewhat confusing factor for *Equipa de Vida* activists is that some current diocesan staff members have been hired after having proven their capacity and dedication as volunteer *Equipa de Vida* activists. Though not a widespread occurrence (fewer than 20 staff out of more than 4000 volunteers over the course of six years have been chosen this way), this practice may spur on continued volunteer activism.

Some activists also maintain a hope of funding or material resources. Though the diocese explicitly explains that the work of the *Equipas de Vida* is voluntary, the varying use of the word "volunteer" causes many volunteers initially not to believe that volunteerism means no payment, or though they understand this definition, to hold out hope that this will change. One former activist, Participant O, tells his own story:

> I worked voluntarily. But when I saw that there was no money, I stopped right away .... If, one day, they went back to paying the *Equipas de Vida*, the members of the *Equipa de Vida*, I would also return to work. Because ... money's necessary.[33]

This presumption of funding and the unwillingness to work without funding are sentiments also expressed by community health volunteers working with other institutions in Mozambique. One volunteer in Mecanhelas explained:

> When the project was started, they clearly told us that we were not going to be paid. But when [some] one tells you something, you don't always believe that the situation will be like that forever. Things change. Now we know that they actually meant what they said. We're not being paid just like they said at the beginning. (Quoted in Muula, Hofman, and Cumberland 2004, 25)

Such hope for future payment, despite the lack of present payment, may continue to be a driving factor for years, and is not exclusively a Mozambican phenomenon. Swidler describes such hopes of benefits as critical in the mindsets of many who are volunteering in Africa in AIDS-related activities:

> Despite the appearance of pure volunteerism, some hope of access to resources – money for transportation, possible access to a bicycle, food or an outing for a youth group, an actual soccer ball – is a critical complement to volunteering for those from societies so poor that any extra resource is enormously valuable. (Swidler 2006, 276; see also Smith 2003)

Though such motivations are not the frames Diocese of Niassa leaders use to mobilize activists, they are frames by which some *Equipa* activists are motivated.

VII. Discussion

The existence of the Diocese of Niassa's *Equipas de Vida* raises various questions worthy of further analysis. The first relates to the use of theological principles in social mobilization. Though churches were some of the first institutions to provide care to people living with HIV and AIDS in Africa, churches have also been criticized for contributing to AIDS-related stigma (by emphasizing the role of immoral behavior in HIV transmission) and for avoiding direct teachings about HIV transmission. Even critics within the church recognize that, as a whole, churches have struggled to develop a "theology of AIDS" to mobilize action (Chitando 2007). Instead of uniting around cohesive driving principles, Christian voices have each stressed different frames in mobilization. The *Equipas* frame activities in light of biblical messages of having compassion for one's neighbor, equality before God, and Christian calling. In sharp contrast, many Pentecostal churches, which typically have a theological emphasis on spiritual rebirth, punishment for sin, and holy living, have emphasized sexual morality in their discussions around AIDS. Such churches root their views in literal and culturally transcendent readings of biblical texts against promiscuity, prostitution, and homosexuality (Gusman 2009). Acknowledging that humans are created in God's image, many within the Catholic Church use the concept of the complexity of the human condition as the driving frame behind responding to HIV.

Each of these frames shapes differing responses to HIV and AIDS, with profoundly different social consequences. Though the specific work that *Equipas* do varies from community to community, the *Equipas'* emphasis on compassion tends to lead to a focus on activities that improve the dignity of people who are living with HIV (activities such as providing home-based support for people who are sick, or reducing stigmatizing practices by teaching against misconceptions that drive stigma). In contrast, Pentecostal churches have tended to prioritize prevention efforts, conducting activities such as sexual abstinence campaigns for youth. And the Catholic Church's emphasis on the complex human condition has frequently led to the development of holistic programs that stress care, support, prevention, income generation, advocacy, and AIDS treatment (see Rasmussen, this issue; Patterson 2011). The *Equipas'* compassion frame leads to less controversial AIDS activities than a sexual morality frame would; home-based care, for example, does not necessitate public discussions of sexuality or marital infidelity. Working towards the dignity of people living with HIV (from a compassion frame) is more realistically achievable than working to bring about the holistic well-being of people affected by AIDS – a goal that some *Equipas* maintain, but which they do not yet have the capacity to achieve.

These different theological emphases raise questions about the process of frame transformation necessary to facilitate inter-denominational cooperation against AIDS. Though *Equipas de Vida* are formally church bodies, any community member may participate. *Equipa de Vida* activist Participant G recounts his story: "I heard [about the *Equipas de Vida*] for the first time at my church, the Assemblies of God. They came there and I was convinced by the words they shared there at church".[34]

Especially in smaller communities, where the *Equipas de Vida* have a very visible community profile, members of various faith traditions play an active role. Though *Equipas* were originally envisioned by diocesan leaders as groups of like-minded congregants, the increasing involvement of non-Anglicans led to the formal diocesan decision to welcome non-Anglicans to participate within the teams as long as they "respect the guidelines and expectations of the church" (Diocese do Niassa 2006). The frame of compassion facilitates this cross-denominational mobilization. In this process of frame extension, some existing beliefs (such as the idea that AIDS is God's punishment) are replaced by alternative beliefs (such as the idea that God wants Christians to care for all people). Compassion provides a way to bridge different Christian theologies. More research is needed to assess if the emphasis on compassion is sufficient to sustain non-Anglican (particularly Pentecostal) participation in *Equipas*.

The theological principles undergirding *Equipa* mobilization may be further challenged by the involvement of non-Anglicans who are Muslims. As of 2013, church members generally criticized the idea of excluding Muslims; as one respondent explained: "The *Equipa de Vida* is who contributes to everyone's good. It can't practice discrimination. We should have people from the whole human race together in the same group. Our *Equipa de Vida* was always like that, and still is".[35]

Some *Equipas* report that Muslim members participate in *Equipa* Bible studies, out of respect for the Bible as a book of wisdom; on rare occasions, where there is enough theological literacy, a Muslim leader presents passages from the Koran that echo the theme studied in the Bible. Frame extension that moves beyond biblical concepts facilitates the mobilization of non-Christians. It is the need to provide a public good (care for community members) that motivates action. Thus far, these mixed religious *Equipas* have worked well, but it is uncertain how the inclusion of Muslims will affect the long-term Christian identity of the *Equipas*, or how long the majority-Christian *Equipas* will continue to welcome Muslim involvement hospitably. In the short term, it appears that competing identities among participants – religious and community – have been reconciled so that Muslims may participate. This outcome illustrates the fluidity of identity, and the fact that identity can be contextually situated (Melucci 1996). It remains to be seen whether the Anglican theology of compassion will successfully assert itself in the long run over and against more limiting forms of religiously-based identity politics.

A second theme that emerges from an analysis of the *Equipas* relates to the capacity of these local organizations to meet community needs. As illustrated above, diocesan staff tried to highlight the existing capacity of grassroots organizations for care work. Such efforts help to motivate action and increase participant agency. Yet they also seemed to highlight neoliberal views of civil society that may overemphasize individual agency while downplaying structural roadblocks to exercising that agency (Ferguson and Gupta 2002). Organizational capacity requires motivated members, but it also depends on material resources and institutions that define participants' roles. The *Equipas* illustrate the capacity challenges found in many African organizations: they rely on volunteers who may or may not fulfill their responsibilities, they look to outsiders for training and logistical support, and they lack financial resources (Michael 2004).

Though *Equipas* are currently composed of volunteers whose capacity has been limited by lack of experience and little formal training, mobilization is a dynamic process, and social movements change. Some *Equipas* have begun to grow as they have gained greater autonomy in decision-making, more resources through income-generating activities, and greater respect in their communities. The literature on community-based organizations demonstrates that one factor which may facilitate identity transformation is professionalization. Some of the most successful AIDS organizations in Africa, such as The AIDS Support Organisation (TASO) in Uganda, have grown to become more professional over time. As they develop specific rules for participation, leadership hierarchies, and concrete means for dispute settlement, they also pay staff members to manage projects, interact with donors, and keep records; these staff members have particular skill requirements but may not have the same religious background as the organization itself (see Rasmussen, this issue.) In some cases, professionalization causes groups to move away from their original religious identity in order to meet communal needs (Lebon 1996). Because the oldest *Equipas de Vida* were only eight years old in 2013, this type of professionalization has yet to occur. But as the *Equipas* are given more decision-making power, experiences elsewhere on the continent suggest that they may be more likely to challenge diocesan policies and resource allocation. Increased experiences within the *Equipas* may lead to greater autonomy from diocesan leadership and greater professionalization.

Processes of professionalization also improve organizational capacities to attract outside funding. Because expectations of external funding inevitably mean that priorities of foreign donors become part of local groups' imaginations of "projects", some scholars claim that "community needs" are always social and cognitive projections that are inseparable from politics (Burchardt 2013a). Currently minimal disagreements over definitions of "community needs" may be due to the *Equipas'* profound rootedness in local social relations and their still very limited contact with large-scale donors, a situation which stands in contrast to Marian Burchardt's (2013a) findings in South Africa.

A third theme is the issue of compensation for African development volunteers. The emergence across Africa of home-based care programs with their thousands of volunteers has brought this issue to the forefront of development. Critics point to the "myth of the selfless volunteer", in which donors assume that Africans have a "volunteer spirit" and that they derive emotional and spiritual satisfaction from volunteer work (Maes 2010). This article has demonstrated some of the non-material reasons for volunteer participation, such as Christian identity and social recognition. This understanding of religious identity and recognition as *social rewards* for participation contrasts with Burchardt's (2013a) findings that in urban South Africa, the future-oriented desires of upward social mobility are crucial motivators for participation in Christian activism.

This article, however, does not discount the broader reasons for which unpaid volunteers have quit. The research presented here provides another angle on volunteerism, by situating it in the context of church ministries where *Equipas* are viewed as "equal to other groups". Diocesan leaders have sought to prevent divisions within congregations between church groups that do and do not receive compensation by not paying activists in the *Equipa* groups. Diocesan leaders have also encouraged *Equipa de Vida* members to limit the time they dedicate to their *Vida* work, so that this work does not interfere with their own personal economic activities. Though dedicated *Equipa* members and dedicated choir or Mother's Union members put forth a similar weekly time commitment, members of the choir or Mother's Union have no local precedent that work like theirs should be paid, while *Equipa de Vida* members do have a local precedent for financial remuneration of HIV-related activities, particularly home-based care.

The findings about why *Equipa* members participate in unpaid care activities echo other studies. Naidu, Yvonne, and Dageid (2012) find that religious beliefs motivate care work in KwaZulu-Natal, South Africa, and Akintola (2010) illustrates how intrinsic rewards such as job satisfaction, self-growth, and skill development motivate South African volunteers. Yet, even these benefits may be insufficient if caregivers lack the material resources to feed themselves and their families. While calling for the increased involvement in the delivery of HIV services by people who are not formally trained doctors and nurses, the World Health Organization (WHO) has recommended:

> Countries should recognize that essential health services cannot be provided by people working on a voluntary basis if they are to be sustainable. While volunteers can make a valuable contribution on a short term or part time basis, trained health workers who are providing essential health services, including community health workers, should receive adequate wages and/or other appropriate and commensurate incentives. (WHO 2008, 4)

As this article has demonstrated, poverty, lack of remuneration, and misconceptions about volunteerism can undermine sustainability. The *Equipas'* sustainability may be further influenced by Mozambique's economic growth, which may provide more formal employment opportunities in the future. How will economic development shape the feasibility and acceptability of voluntary work? Donors and policymakers must take into consideration these questions as they design development initiatives for the continent.

Finally, this article adds to knowledge about African churches and AIDS. Much scholarly work on African churches has focused on their (sometimes controversial) involvement in HIV prevention efforts or on actions that stigmatize people living with HIV and AIDS (Patterson 2011). Existing scholarship has given greater emphasis to Pentecostal Christianity. Far fewer studies have examined religious participation in care work, particularly among mainline denominations (Burchardt 2013b). The article has demonstrated the complexity of motivations for participation in care activities. By using the social movement literature as its lens, this case study has helped to bridge the gap between social science research and faith-based practitioners.

VIII.   Conclusion

Mobilization of volunteers for HIV-related work in northern Mozambique was analyzed to reveal the complex motivations for grassroots activities on AIDS, which range from spiritual reasons to the hope of material rewards. The investigation found that church leaders utilize biblical teachings and theologically inspired ideas of local capacity as frames to urge activism. Through their activities, volunteers developed a new identity, something that continued to motivate their participation. The efforts of the Diocese of Niassa, however, are situated within a context in which donor money for HIV has led to power imbalances in donor-civil society relationships, in which payment is expected for volunteerism, and in which there are assumptions that HIV work always has access to large amounts of funding. Diocesan leaders seek to counter assumptions around financial gain through HIV-related activities, though they do not always do so successfully in a context where poverty is pervasive and individuals seek any potential opportunities for employment and resources.

This article raises questions for future research. What factors lead to successful frame transformation? Is this process dependent upon particular contexts or leadership structures? The *Equipa* context is one of high poverty, high HIV rates, and strong support from diocesan leadership. There has been great demand for a service, as well as a willingness of the church to supply that service. Not all contexts may be so conducive to mobilization. Second, while frames are necessary for mobilization, are they sufficient to keep activists engaged? In the case of the *Equipas*, the frame of compassion has been the primary frame to motivate action, but poverty could derail such participation over time. How important are material and social factors, such as opportunities for training or communal respect, in motivating long-term participation? Answers to these questions can inform both theoretical and policy debates on religious AIDS mobilization in Africa. Such findings would build knowledge about appropriate mobilization strategies in Africa and the role of religion in shaping those strategies. Greater knowledge on religious activism will also assist practitioners who work with African faith-based organizations.

Notes

1. See Galatians 3:28.
2. Interview with Participant A (*Equipa de Vida* activist), by Vander Meulen. Lichinga, Mozambique, 27 March 2007.
3. Interview with Participant B (*Equipa de Vida* activist), by Vander Meulen. Lichinga, Mozambique, 12 April 2010.
4. Interview with Participant C (*Equipa de Vida* activist), by research assistant (diocesan staff member). Cuamba, Mozambique, 5 May 2010.
5. See 1 Corinthians 12:12, 21–23.
6. Interview with Participant D (*Equipa de Vida* activist), by Vander Meulen. Lichinga, Mozambique, 2 July 2011.
7. Interview with Participant E (*Equipa de Vida* activist), by Vander Meulen. Lichinga, Mozambique, 2 July 2011.
8. Interview with Participant D (*Equipa de Vida* activist), by Vander Meulen. Lichinga, Mozambique, 2 July 2011.
9. Interview with Participant F (diocesan staff member), by Vander Meulen. Lichinga, Mozambique, 2 July 2011.
10. Interview with Participant G (*Equipa de Vida* activist), by research assistant (*adepto*). Nzinje, Mozambique, 26 April 2010.
11. Interview with Participant C (*Equipa de Vida* activist), by research assistant (diocesan staff member). Cuamba, Mozambique, 5 May 2010.

12. Interview with Participant H (*Equipa de Vida* activist), by research assistant (*adepto*). Sanjala, Mozambique, 24 April 2010.
13. Interview with Participant C (*Equipa de Vida* activist), by research assistant (diocesan staff member). Cuamba, Mozambique, 5 May 2010.
14. Interview with Participant G (*Equipa de Vida* activist), by research assistant (*adepto*). Nzinje, Mozambique, 26 April 2010.
15. Interview with Participant B (*Equipa de Vida* activist), by Vander Meulen. Lichinga, Mozambique, 12 April 2010.
16. Interview with Participant I (*Equipa de Vida* activist), by research assistant (*adepto*). Lichinga, Mozambique, 22 April 2010.
17. Interview with Participant J (*Equipa de Vida* fieldworker), by Vander Meulen. Cobue, Mozambique, 3 December 2009.
18. Interview with Participant J (*Equipa de Vida* fieldworker), by Vander Meulen. Cobue, Mozambique, 3 December 2009.
19. Program Director of a US NGO, email to Diocese of Niassa *Equipa de Vida* coordinator, 15 March 2010.
20. Interview with Participant D (*Equipa de Vida* activist), by Vander Meulen. Lichinga, Mozambique, 2 July 2011.
21. Interview with Participant C (*Equipa de Vida* activist), by research assistant (diocesan staff member). Cuamba, Mozambique, 5 May 2010.
22. Interview with Participant K (*Equipa de Vida* activist), by research assistant (*adepto*). Sanjala, Mozambique, 24 April 2010.
23. Interview with Participant K (*Equipa de Vida* activist), by research assistant (*adepto*). Sanjala, Mozambique, 24 April 2010.
24. Interview with Participant L (*Equipa de Vida* activist), by research assistant (*adepto*). Lichinga, Mozambique, 20 April 2010.
25. Interview with Participant M (*Equipa de Vida* activist), by research assistant (*adepto*). Lichinga, Mozambique, 21 April 2010.
26. Interview with Participant N (*Equipa de Vida* activist), by research assistant (diocesan staff member). Milange, Mozambique, 5 May 2010.
27. Interview with Participant O (*Equipa de Vida* activist), by research assistant (volunteer activist). Lichinga, Mozambique, 20 April 2010.
28. Interview with Participant P (*Equipa de Vida* activist), by research assistant (*adepto*). Sanjala, Mozambique, 24 April 2010.
29. Interview with Participant B (*Equipa de Vida* activist), by Vander Meulen. Lichinga, Mozambique, 12 April 2010.
30. Interview with Participant I (*Equipa de Vida* activist), by research assistant (*adepto*). Lichinga, Mozambique, 22 April 2010.
31. Interview with Participant O (*Equipa de Vida* activist), by research assistant (volunteer activist). Lichinga, Mozambique, 20 April 2010.
32. Interview with Participant B (*Equipa de Vida* activist), by Vander Meulen. Lichinga, Mozambique, 12 April 2010.
33. Interview with Participant O (*Equipa de Vida* activist), by research assistant (volunteer activist). Lichinga, Mozambique, 20 April 2010.
34. Interview with Participant G (*Equipa de Vida* activist), by research assistant (*adepto*). Nzinje, Mozambique, 26 April 2010.
35. Interview with Participant Q (*Equipa de Vida* activist), by Vander Meulen. Mefluluchi, Mozambique, 20 May 2011.

Bibliography

Afrobarometer. 2009. "Popular Attitudes toward Democracy in Mozambique: A Summary of Afrobarometer Indicators, 2002–2008." Accessed July 3, 2011. next.pls.msu.edu/index.php?option=com_docman&task=doc_download&gid=215

Akintola, Olagoke. 2010. "Perceptions of Rewards among Volunteer Caregivers of People Living with AIDS Working in Faith-Based Organizations in South Africa: A Qualitative Study." *Journal of the International AIDS Society* 13 (1): 22.

Alden, Chris. 2001. *Mozambique and the Construction of the New African State: From Negotiations to Nation Building*. New York, NY: Palgrave.

Bayart, Jean-François. 2000. "Africa in the World: A History of Extraversion." *African Affairs* 99 (395): 217–267.

Burchardt, Marian. 2013a. "Faith-Based Humanitarianism: Organizational Change and Everyday Meanings in South Africa." *Sociology of Religion* 74 (1): 30–55.

Burchardt, Marian. 2013b. "'Transparent Sexualities': Sexual Openness, HIV Disclosure and the Governmentality of Sexuality in South Africa." *Culture, Health & Sexuality* 14: 1–14.

Central Intelligence Agency. 2009. *The World Factbook 2009*, Accessed July 6, 2011. https://www.cia.gov/library/publications/the-world-factbook/geos/mz.html

Chitando, Ezra. 2007. *Acting in Hope: African Churches and HIV/AIDS*. Geneva: World Council of Churches.

Damon, Michelle Lynette. 2007. "Management of Volunteers at the Cape Town Association for the Physically Disabled." MSW Thesis, University of Stellenbosch, South Africa.

Dibie, Josephine, and Robert A. Dibie. 2008. "Motivation and Volunteerism in NGOs in Ghana and Nigeria." In *Non-Governmental Organizations (NGOs) and Sustainable Development in Sub-Saharan Africa*, edited by R. A. Dibie, 121–138. Lanham, MD: Lexington Books.

Diocese do Niassa [Diocese of Niassa]. 2003. "Visão da Diocese do Niassa." Unpublished document.

Diocese do Niassa [Diocese of Niassa]. 2006. "Guia das Equipas da Vida, Diocese do Niassa Comunhão Anglicana em Moçambique Programa de Vida! (HIV e SIDA)." Unpublished document.

Diocese do Niassa [Diocese of Niassa]. 2007. "Agenda do Sínodo Diocesano. Resolução 2: O Papel da Igreja sobre o Desenvolvimento." Unpublished document.

Diocese do Niassa [Diocese of Niassa]. 2010. "Quem Somos." Unpublished document.

The Economist. 2001. "Daily Chart: Africa's Impressive Growth." Accessed July 12, 2011. http://www.economist.com/blogs/dailychart/2011/01/daily_chart

Edwards, Michael, and David Hulme. 1996. "Too Close for Comfort? The Impact of Official Aid on Nongovernmental Organizations." *World Development* 24 (6): 961–973, Reproduction available: http://www.tc.columbia.edu/cice/Archives/1.1/11edwards_hulme.pdf (accessed September 4, 2011).

Ferguson, James, and Akhil Gupta. 2002. "Spatializing States: Toward an Ethnography of Neoliberal Governmentality." *American Ethnologist* 29 (4): 981–1002.

Freire, Paulo. 1970. *Pedagogy of the Oppressed*. New York, NY: Seabury Press.

Green, Edward C. 2003. "Faith-Based Organizations: Contributions to HIV Prevention." Paper prepared for the Synergy Project, Washington, DC. Accessed September 5, 2011. www.theglobalfund.org/Documents/library/Library_SESAEPS3_Report_en/

Gusman, Alessandro. 2009. "HIV/AIDS, Pentecostal Churches, and the 'Joseph Generation' in Uganda." *Africa Today* 56 (1): 66–86.

Igreja da Província de África Austral [Church of the Province of Southern Africa]. 1988. *A Santa Eucaristia Oração da Manha e Oração da Tarde*. London: Collins Liturgical Publications.

Instituto Nacional de Saúde and Instituto Nacional de Estatística [National Health Institute and National Statistics Institute]. 2009. *O Inquérito Nacional de Prevalência, Riscos Comportamentais e Informação sobre HIV e SIDA em Moçambique (INSIDA)* [National Survey on Prevalence, Behavioral Risks and Information about HIV and AIDS in Mozambique (INSIDA)]. Maputo: Instituto Nacional de Saúde.

Lebon, Nathalie. 1996. "Professionalization of Women's Health Groups in Sao Paulo: The Troublesome Road towards Organizational Diversity." *Organization* 3 (4): 588–609.

Levine, Daniel. 1992. *Popular Voices in Latin American Catholicism*. Princeton, NJ: Princeton University Press.

Lewis, David. 2001. *Civil Society in Non-Western Contexts: Reflections on the 'Usefulness' of a Concept*, Civil Society Working Paper series, 13. London: Centre for Civil Society, London School of Economics and Political Science.

Maes, Kenneth. 2010. "Examining Health-Care Volunteerism in a Food- and Financially-Insecure World." *Bulletin of World Health Organization* 88 (11): 867–869.

Marsh, Charles. 2005. *The Beloved Community: How Faith Shapes Social Justice, from the Civil Rights Movement to Today*. New York, NY: Basic Books.

Mashimo, Ayako, Hiroko Miura, Shoji Sakano, Akira Hamada, Bang-on Thepthien, and Takusei Umenai. 2001. "The Role of AIDS Volunteers in Developing Community-based Care for People with AIDS in Thailand." *Asia-Pacific Journal of Public Health* 13 (1): 3–8.

Melucci, Alberto. 1996. *Challenging Codes: Collective Action in the Information Age*. Cambridge: Cambridge University Press.

Meyer, Carola. 2009. *Siyakha: Stories of Hope, Vision, Commitment and Courage*. South Africa: Anglican Aids and Healthcare Trust.

Michael, Sarah. 2004. *Undermining Development: The Absence of Power among Local NGOs in Africa*. Bloomington: Indiana University Press.

Mozambique National AIDS Spending Assessment (NASA) for the Period: 2004–2006: Level and Flow of Resources and Expenditures to the National HIV and AIDS Response. 2008. Accessed September 4, 2011. http://www.unaids.org/en/media/unaids/contentassets/dataimport/pub/report/2007/nasa_mozambique_0506_20070408_en.pdf

Muula, A. S., J. Hofman, and Margaret Cumberland. 2004. "What Motivates Community Health Volunteers in Mecanhelas District, Mozambique? Report from a Qualitative Study." *Ghana Medical Journal* 38: 24–27.

Naidu, Thirusha, Yvonne Sliep, and Wenche Dageid. 2012. "The Social Construction of Identity in HIV/AIDS Home-Based Care Volunteers in Rural KwaZulu-Natal, South Africa." *SAHARA-J: Journal of Social Aspects of HIV/AIDS* 9: 113–126.

Newitt, Malyn. 1995. *A History of Mozambique*. Bloomington: Indiana University Press.

Omoto, Allen M., and Mark Snyder. 1990. "Basic Research in Action: Volunteerism and Society's Response to AIDS." *Personality and Social Psychology Bulletin* 16 (1): 152–165.

Patel, Leila, and Theresa Wilson. 2004. "Civic Service in Sub-Saharan Africa." *Nonprofit and Voluntary Sector Quarterly* 33 (4 suppl): 22S–38S.

Paterson, Gillian. 2001. *AIDS and the African Churches: Exploring the Challenges*. London: Christian Aid.

Patterson, Amy. 2011. *The Church and AIDS in Africa: The Politics of Ambiguity*. Boulder, CO: First Forum Press.

Penner, Louis A. 2002. "Dispositional and Organizational Influences on Sustained Volunteerism: An Interactionist Perspective." *Journal of Social Issues* 58 (3): 447–467.

Schneider, Helen, Hlengiwe Hlophe, and Dingie van Rensburg. 2008. "Community Health Workers and the Response to HIV/AIDS in South Africa: Tensions and Prospects." *Health Policy and Planning* 23 (3): 179–187.

Simon, Sandrine, Kathryn Chu, Marthe Frieden, Baltazar Candrinho, Nathan Ford, Helen Schneider, and Marc Biot. 2009. "An Integrated Approach of Community Health Worker Support for HIV/AIDS and TB Care in Angónia District, Mozambique." *BMC International Health and Human Rights*, 9: record 13. Accessed June 20, 2011. http://www.biomedcentral.com/1472-698X/9/13

Smith, Daniel Jordan. 2003. "Patronage, Per Diems and the 'Workshop Mentality': The Practice of Family Planning Programs in Southeastern Nigeria." *World Development* 31 (4): 703–715.

Snow, David A., E. Burke Rochford Jr., Steven K. Worden, and Robert D. Benford. 1986. "Frame Alignment Processes, Micromobilization, and Movement Participation." *American Sociological Review* 51 (4): 464–481.

Swart, LuAnne, Mohamed Seedat, and Farzana Sader. 2004. "Community Volunteerism in Safety Promotion and Implications for Sustained Participation." *African Safety Promotion* 2: 1–15.

Swidler, Ann. 2006. "Syncretism and Subversion in AIDS Governance: How Locals Cope with Global Demands." *International Affairs* 82 (2): 269–284.

Swidler, Ann, and Susan Cotts Watkins. 2009. "Teach a Man to Fish': The Sustainability Doctrine and its Social Consequences." *World Development* 37 (7): 1182–1196.

The World Bank. 2011. "The World Bank: Data: Mozambique." Accessed July 12, 2011. http://data.worldbank.org/country/mozambique

Waterhouse, Rachel. 1996. *Mozambique: Rising from the Ashes*. Oxford: Oxfam.

Werner, David. 1982. *Where There Is No Doctor: A Village Health Care Handbook*. Palo Alto, CA: Hesperian Foundation.

World Health Organization. 2008. *Task Shifting: Rational Redistribution of Tasks among Health Workforce Teams: Global Recommendations and Guidelines*. Geneva: WHO Document Production Services.

Williams, G. 2004. *Guia do Facilitador ao Vídeo O que posso fazer? Ministério e Mensagens de Gideon Byamugisha sobre o HIV/SIDA* [Facilitator's Guide to the Video What can I do? The HIV/AIDS Ministry and Messages of Gideon Byamugisha]. Oxford: Estratégias para a Esperança [Strategies for Hope].

Appendix 1. Interview questions

1. What is your name?
2. Where do you live?
3. How old are you?
4. How did you first hear about the *Equipa de Vida*?
5. Why did you join the *Equipa de Vida*?
6. In what year did you join the *Equipa de Vida*?
7. When you joined the *Equipa de Vida*, what were your expectations related to the *Equipa?*
8. Are you still a part of the *Equipa de Vida*?
    a. (If the response to question 8 is "yes"): Why have you continued to be in the *Equipa de Vida*?
    b. (If the response to question 8 is "no"): Why are you no longer part of the *Equipa de Vida*?
    c. (If the response to question 8 is "yes"): Why do you think others who joined the *Equipa de Vida* have since left the *Equipa*?
9. What do you think about the idea of paying members of the *Equipa de Vida*?
10. Should other church groups be paid? Why or why not?
11. How does your faith influence your work within the *Equipa de Vida*?

The abstinence campaign and the construction of the Balokole identity in the Ugandan Pentecostal movement

Alessandro Gusman

Dipartimento di Culture, Politica e Società, University of Turin, Italy

Résumé

Sur la base de données de travaux de terrain recueillies depuis 2005 en Ouganda, ce document examine les connexions entre la participation des jeunes pentecôtistes à des programmes de prévention du VIH, en accordant une attention particulière à l'« *abstinence campaign* », et le processus de construction d'une identité au sein du mouvement lui-même. Je montre ici comment l'intensification de l'épidémie du sida a contribué à une manière décisive d'influer sur la construction du sens, et ainsi de l'action, du mouvement *Balokole* (« les *Savedees* ») en Ouganda. En théorie, cet article a pour objectif de contribuer à combler la lacune dans l'analyse des mouvements sociaux en Afrique, en particulier en abordant la spécificité de la participation des croyants aux activités de l'Église et à des organisations religieuses évangéliques en illustrant la manière dont l'identité collective des « *born-again* » (chrétiens nés de nouveau) et leur mobilisation dans la lutte contre le sida sont réciproquement liées. La connexion identité/participation éclaircit à quel point le sentiment d'appartenance à un groupe comportant de fortes connexions et partiellement fermé, celui des chrétiens « sauvés », est crucial au moment de pousser les *Balokole* à agir.

Abstract

Based on fieldwork data collected since 2005 in Uganda, the paper explores the connections between young Pentecostals' involvement in HIV prevention programs, with a particular attention to the "abstinence campaign", and the process of identity construction within the movement itself. I show how the rise of the AIDS epidemic contributed in a decisive way to shaping the construction of meaning, and thus the action, of the *Balokole* ("the Savedees") movement in Uganda. Theoretically, the article aims at contributing to fill the gap in the analysis of social movements in Africa, especially addressing the specificity of believers' participation in church activities and in evangelical faith-based organizations (FBOs) by exemplifying how the collective identity of the born-again and their mobilization to fight AIDS are reciprocally related. The identity/participation connection clarifies how the feeling of belonging to a strongly connected and partially closed group, that of the "saved" Christians, is pivotal in pushing the *Balokole* to become active.

I. Introduction

Based on fieldwork data collected since 2005 in Uganda, this paper explores the connections between young Pentecostals' involvement in HIV-prevention programs, with a particular attention to the "abstinence campaign", and the process of identity construction within the movement itself. For this purpose, I analyze the significant space acquired by the Pentecostal movement (locally referred to as the *Balokole* movement)[1] in the public sphere in Uganda during the last decade, with a growing engagement both in society and in politics. This occurred especially through the moralizing attitude of Pentecostals, which contributed to focus HIV education for young people mainly on abstinence, with the support, and under the influence, of the main international source of funds in the struggle against AIDS: the PEPFAR Program.[2]

The article aims to show how the presence of the AIDS epidemic contributed to give shape to the collective identity of Pentecostals in Uganda who, due to the particular historical conditions, in the middle of the 1980s were still a marginal presence in the country.[3] The parallel history of Pentecostalism and HIV/AIDS in Uganda is of particular interest as it shows how an external, unpredictable circumstance (the rising of the AIDS epidemic) can contribute in a decisive way to shaping the construction of meaning, and thus the action, of a social movement. With reference to literature concerning the formation of identities in social movements, the paper demonstrates the way Pentecostals' engagement in HIV/AIDS programs – and mainly in the "abstinence campaign" – has contributed to defining the collective identity of the young people involved to the movement, and to the building of moral borders between the *Balokole* and the others, with a stress on the common belonging to a new group, based not on biological birth, but on spiritual rebirth.

In parallel with these processes, the movement itself has been influential in reconfiguring the social representation of the epidemic, which has been read through the lens of the "sinful behavior" and "satanic action" perspective.

Theoretically, the paper aims at contributing to fill the gap in the analysis of social movements in Africa, especially addressing the specificity of believers' participation in church activities and in evangelical faith-based organizations (FBOs).[4] It has been argued that these organizations are particularly effective in engaging their members in activities, and that it is through this involvement that Pentecostal churches are able to flourish as institutions (Robbins 2010). The paper exemplifies how the collective identity of the *Balokole* and their mobilization to fight AIDS are reciprocally related. The identity/ participation connection clarifies how the feeling of belonging to a strongly connected and partially closed group, that of the "saved" Christians, is pivotal in pushing the *Balokole* to activate.

This paper is divided into six sections. After the introduction, in the second section, I trace the methodology utilized for the present study. In the third section, I discuss some theoretical aspects concerning the formation of collective identities in social movements.

The fourth section provides the context within which the growth of Pentecostalism as a movement in Uganda took place. I highlight the presence of pre-existing factors – mainly the religious heritage of the East African Revival (EAR) – that contributed to direct the process of identity building and the forms of mobilization. I also discuss the growing social and political engagement of the movement during the last decade, especially in relation with HIV/AIDS programs and policies.

The fifth section shows how participating in these programs is crucial for the definition of young believers' identities as part of the *Balokole* group: through interviews with activists and pastors, the section examines the expectations and motivations that these young people have when they decide to actively take part in church activities. The development of a dualistic worldview that separates the saved from the non-saved is also part of this process of identification and mobilization. In the conclusion, I discuss some practical effects of the process of identity building and of mobilization in HIV/AIDS prevention and care in evangelical FBOs.

II. Methodology

Data presented in this paper were collected during three separate periods, as part of my doctoral research in anthropology (for ten months in total, during 2005–2007), and in 2010 (for two months). During this last period, I specifically focused on the topic this paper deals with, conducting 15 in-depth, open-ended interviews with young activists (9 males, and 6 females, from 22 to 30 years old) in Pentecostal organizations. The majority of them were volunteering both in the *Living Hope Ministry* at Watoto Church (a program caring for over 2100 abandoned or widowed HIV+ women in Kampala and Gulu), or at the *Campus Alliance to Wipeout AIDS* (CAWA) at the Makerere Community Church (MCC); four of them were not engaged directly in organizations, but were members of cells at Watoto Church or at Makerere Full Gospel Church (FGC) and were engaged in AIDS-related activities such as the "adoption" (with material and spiritual support) of people living with HIV/AIDS (PLWHA), or community-based programs of prevention organized by these churches. The interviews were focused especially on their participation in church activities concerning HIV prevention, and on how this involvement reinforces their feeling of belonging to the congregation. Besides this, throughout the years I observed and participated in a number of initiatives of prevention and care programs carried out by Pentecostal groups in schools, at Makerere University campus, and throughout the town in Kampala. During my stay in the field, I was a member of three different cell groups (to which I make reference in this work) at Watoto Church, Makerere Full Gospel Church, and Makerere Community Church, and I participated in several camps organized by these churches.

The three churches that I consider in this article are among the biggest and most influential in the Ugandan Pentecostal movement; Watoto Church and the FGC are two of the most established Pentecostal churches in Kampala, each with hundreds of cell groups (small groups of 10 to 15 people meeting weekly) in town. The MCC (now called One Love Church) has a smaller congregation of about 1000 believers, but is particularly active within the campus and popular among university students for its initiatives (marches in town, rallies, and Saturday nights at the swimming pool of Makerere University, with music, dances, and praying). The three churches are predominantly English-speaking, are located near the campus of Makerere, the main Ugandan university, and hold a number of social activities, including HIV/AIDS educational initiatives, and prevention and care programs. Because of the use of English and the level of complexity in the content of the preaching, these congregations are composed mainly of middle-class people and university students.

The research has been almost totally carried out in the urban setting of Kampala, the capital city of Uganda; therefore, it cannot be considered representative of the Ugandan context in general. The engagement in the public sphere, with the mobilization of young believers in prevention programs, which I consider in this article as both driving the creation of a collective identity among young born-agains and resulting from that identity, is in fact mostly a specific urban phenomenon.

III. Social movements and the formation of a collective identity

Literature on social movements has been increasingly focused on the concept of "collective identity" since the 1980s, as a reaction to previous collective behaviorist theories that explained participation in terms of irrationality and crowd contagion.[5] With the reference to identity, scholars of social movements have been able to better analyze the emergence of collective actors, their motivation for mobilization, the strategic choices made by these actors, and the cultural effects of their actions (Escobar 1992; Johnston and Klandermans 1995).

Collective identity has been variously defined as a shared sense of "we-ness" (Snow 2001) and as "an individual's cognitive, moral, and emotional connection with a broader community, category, practice, or institution" (Polletta and Jasper 2001, 284). Definitions of collective identity usually contain references to "belonging", "solidarity", and "commitment" (Hunt and Benford 2004); as a result of these characteristics, identity is seen as a basis for action (Melucci 1995). The most cited, and probably the most influential definition, is the one provided by Alberto Melucci, according to which

> collective identity [is] the process of "constructing" an action system. Collective identity is an interactive and shared definition produced by a number of individuals (or groups at a more complex level) concerning the orientations of their action and the field of opportunities and constraints in which such action is to take place. (Melucci 1996, 70).

This paper utilizes Melucci's definition to illustrate the specific case of the formation of a collective identity among young Ugandan Pentecostals, stressing the interactive components of this process, in which elements from both the top and the grassroots levels of the movement interact to create the "action system" for the group activities.

The three concepts of recruitment, participation, and building a collective identity are strictly connected in social movement studies; this correlation was already present in the literature in the 1970s, but became more evident and structured during the last ten years, when collective identity came to be seen not only as a precondition for mobilization but also both as a part and a result of the process of mobilization itself (Kurzman 2008, 9). This implies that collective identity is continuously negotiated within the movement: it is not fixed once and for all, but constructed and reconstructed through the actors' participation in the movement, and in a strategic way, in order to respond to external stimuli. Individuals join a social movement in search of a collective identity (Jasper 1997); at the same time, participating in the movement they contribute to group identity formation (Melucci 1988, 343).

In the case of Ugandan Pentecostalism, the exogenous factors that have been driving the process of identity negotiation are the presence of the AIDS epidemic and the availability of donor funding, mainly PEPFAR funds; this led the movement to focus particularly on abstinence as a strategy, and to build its identity around the ideas of "sexual purity" and "moral revolution". The decisions which actors make in this case study revolve around decisions on how to address HIV, after considering structural constraints and opportunities.

Collective identity thus shows its "fluid and relational" nature (Polletta and Jasper 2001, 298). However, relations are not only with the other members of the movement, but with the exterior as well. The identification of one or more adversaries is necessary in order for mobilization to occur (Melucci 1996, 292); as I will show in the paper, *Balokole* individuate different categories of "others", whose common feature is the fact of being outside the spiritual and moral boundaries of the group of the "saved ones". This operation traces social barriers, and provides categories through which people make sense of the social world.

Finally, "frames" and "framing processes" play a central role in the building of a collective identity. The concept of "frame" was introduced by Erving Goffman (1974), and then formulated more rigorously by David Snow and his colleagues as "interpretive schemata" developed by collectivities in order to understand the world (Snow et al. 1986). According to this theory, "frame alignment" is necessary in order to have a successful mobilization (Snow and Benford 1988); this means that frames need to resonate with already existing cultural repertoires (Williams 2002), so that the movement's ideology can be easily recognized and understood by the audience.

In the specific case of Ugandan Pentecostalism, frames come mostly from the global dimension of the movement (music, "prosperity Gospel", demonization, etc.) but are re-elaborated in order to make them more understandable at the local level. Moreover, some of the elements composing the frames through which Ugandan believers interpret events and the local reality were already present in the country before the advent of Pentecostalism; particularly significant for the influence they have on this interpretation are the presence of the AIDS epidemic, and a peculiar concept of salvation inherited from the EAR. Together with the moralizing attitude that is a trait of the movement, these factors led the framing process to assume a strong moral connotation, organized around the concepts of "purity"[6] and "salvation". For this reason, in the next section I analyze the roots of the Pentecostal movement in Uganda, and its growing political role, as well as the phases of the AIDS epidemic, marked by different political responses.

IV. The *Balokole* movement

A. *The roots of Pentecostalism in Uganda: finding identity in heterogeneity*

There are some concerns in qualifying Pentecostalism in Uganda (as probably anywhere else) as one homogeneous social movement with a collective identity; while often presented by pastors and believers as a unified religious group, the movement defies being considered monolithic, and instead shows a plurality of multi-faceted expressions, teachings and beliefs. There is no unified theology, and no single historical foundation.

It is possible to identify at least three different sources for the expansion of Pentecostalism in Uganda, thus providing a good example of what Paul Gifford calls the "complex provenance" of the elements marking the movement in Africa (Gifford 2001). The first source was North American, with missionaries from the US and Canada, during the 1960s; the second was indigenous, while the third was formed by missions from other African countries where the movement was already well established.[7] The overlapping of the different Pentecostal "waves" in a short period[8] produced the coexistence of churches focused on the so-called "Prosperity Gospel" (i.e., the Miracle Center) – where the preaching centers on material prosperity – with other, more "traditional" forms of Pentecostalism (i.e., Watoto Church), where the idea of prosperity, though not absent, is expressed in a different idiom, emphasizing spiritual richness instead of material prosperity.

Language use during services may be seen as a further element of heterogeneity; while some congregations are "English speaking" from their statement,[9] others use a mix of English and Luganda, often with simultaneous translation (although these congregations are turning more and more to English only). Other churches, usually those located in the poorest areas of the town, utilize only (or mainly) Luganda.

Despite these differences, at least a part of the movement finds a feeling of shared identity in the common belonging to the community of the "saved" (*Balokole*), and in the mobilization around HIV/AIDS.

B. *The idea of salvation from the East African Revival to contemporary Pentecostalism*

The roots of the word *Balokole*, today used to identify born-again Christians in Uganda, can be traced back to the EAR, one of the movements of awakening which marked the history of African Christianity.[10] The origin of the EAR is usually found in the "Christmas convention" held at the missionary station of Gahini (Rwanda) in 1933, when a group of missionaries and believers started confessing their sins in public. The movement grew fast, and spread in Uganda, starting from the contiguous region of Kigezi (with its core in Kabale, where in 1935 the real Revival started, after the prelude in Gahini) to the near kingdoms of Ankole and Toro (Stenning 1965; Kassimir 1998), to Buganda, where it was introduced by some young students of the Bishop Tucker Memorial College (Ward 1989).

During the 1950s the EAR became more integrated into the Church of Uganda, losing part of its reformist energy. In spite of this, its legacy is still visible inside the Anglican Church, where the *Balokole* are growing again in number in the footsteps of the Pentecostal boom, and inside the Pentecostal movement itself, which in its Ugandan version caught more than one legacy of the East African Revival, not least the stress on the idea of "salvation" as a dimension to achieve through personal repentance and confession within a regular fellowship of small groups of people.

From this perspective, the use of the local term *Balokole* to identify Ugandan born-again Christians is even more significant: the idea is that, starting with the EAR, there is a group of Ugandan Christians who, having become born-again and having taken up a certain way of life, can call themselves "saved". It should be noted that, in the context of the AIDS epidemic, this word assumes a different and more extensive meaning, including both a spiritual and a physical dimension. Being a *Mulokole*, a saved person, does not only mean receiving the baptism of the Holy Spirit (spiritual salvation), but also having a strict morality based on the "AB" (Abstain, Be Faithful) model of HIV prevention, which is supposed to take the individual far from sinful and "dangerous" behaviors.

The historical background of the Pentecostal movement in Uganda thus shows that some of the ideas that one can commonly hear during a Sunday sermon (i.e., the idea of a "holistic" – spiritual and physical – salvation) did not come with the first Pentecostal missions in the 1960s or after 1986 when the movement grew rapidly. Using social movement terminology, when Pentecostalism came to Uganda there was not a need for a completely new frame, but rather for a process of "frame amplification", "the clarification and invigoration of an interpretive frame that bears on a particular issue, problem, or set of events" (Snow et al. 1986, 469). This amplification happened especially with the growing engagement of Pentecostal congregations in the public and political sphere.

C. *Pentecostals and politics in Uganda*

Religious groups play an important public role in Uganda, competing, appropriating and contesting public spaces. While classic Christian denominations (Catholic and Anglican) had long been highly influential in the political arena, the entry of Pentecostals into this scenario began only after 2000.

Mainstream religions played a central role in Ugandan politics since the early colonial era (Hansen 1984), and after the independence in 1962 the Anglican Church of Uganda and the Catholic Church profoundly influenced the new political scenario, establishing strong links with the two main parties; the Uganda People's Congress (UPC) had an Anglican base, while the Democratic Party (DP) had a Catholic base (Welbourn 1965). This dualism was even reinforced under the regimes of Idi Amin (1971–1979) and Milton Obote (1966–1971, 1980–1985), but the context changed when the National Resistance Movement (NRM) led by the current President Yoweri Museveni came to power in 1986, opening the space for new political influence from other religious groups (Gifford 1998). Ugandan Pentecostalism was a young and relatively underdeveloped movement at the time, marked mainly by an "other-worldly" attitude; indeed, it did not immediately enter the political arena, but its influence grew little by little, and increasingly during the last decade, to the extent that according to Maxwell (2006) Pentecostalism in Uganda might already be considered as mainstream as the two major Christian churches.

Ugandan Pentecostals began to engage in social programs during the 1990s, but the real growth of these activities occurred after the turn of the millennium, for two main reasons: first, because of a theological shift from an "other-worldly" to a "this worldly" perspective; and second, because of the availability of new resources (notably the PEPFAR funds) for the action of religious organizations in the social service delivery field.[11]

Regarding the first point, it is important to stress that Pentecostalism provides a particular religious "frame" for the interpretation of reality. Pentecostal theology in fact contains a theory to explain the origin of social problems; immorality, and the consequent spread of diseases and corruption, are seen as the result of the satanic presence in the world. As Smilde (1998, 294) writes, "[t]his theory, in turn, frames their [the Pentecostals'] sense of agency, their sense of how they can change current conditions". That is, social and political mobilization can be seen as a way to contrast the satanic presence in society, whose main evidences, according to the worldview expressed by most of the *Balokole*, are corruption in politics, the spread of AIDS (viewed as a consequence of sexual immorality), and homosexuality. From this perspective an "other-worldly" religious action, exclusively directed to the spiritual salvation of believers, cannot be sufficient to guarantee the victory of Jesus over Satan. A direct engagement – a stronger presence in the social arena – is needed in order to provide safety for the whole society; individual salvation cannot in fact easily be realized within a corrupt society. Salvation becomes real and finds its full realization only in the broader context of the common good. As a result, many Ugandan Pentecostals believe that engaging in the political sphere, even though risky, is necessary not to leave the nation "in the hands of Satan".[12]

As Terence Ranger has pointed out, the increasing importance assumed by the evangelicals in African politics is much connected to this theological shift towards a more "this-worldly" perspective, where the "earthly kingdom" becomes an essential element in the preaching and in the activities of the churches (Ranger 2008, 8). The idea of the separation of the "two kingdoms", which was at the center of classic Pentecostal theology, could not find many followers in the African context; so the question was not "*whether* evangelical Christianity has been, is, and will be intensely 'political', but *how*" (Ranger 2008, 5; original emphasis).

Due to the focus on the moralization of politics, and on the struggle against AIDS as the instrument to promote a "new" and "saved" generation for the country, entering the political arena for the *Balokole* movement meant especially focusing on AIDS policies and related activities.

D.   The AIDS epidemic in Uganda and political responses

Considering the link between the AIDS epidemic and the development of the Pentecostal movement in Uganda, it is essential to stress the superimposition of the two stories. The growth of Pentecostalism in the country occurred after 1986, thus taking place almost at the same time as the creation of policies to counteract the spreading of the virus. The movement began to engage more deeply in social programs after 2000, with a focus on HIV-prevention programs that promote abstinence, in conjunction with the development of new health policies and the arrival of PEPFAR funds.

Three distinct phases can be identified in the history of the HIV/AIDS epidemic in Uganda: the first (1982–1992) saw the rapid spread of the epidemic through the country, starting from the South West. During the second (1992–2001) there was a significant decline in infection rates (from 18% nationally, with peaks of 30% in some districts, to 6.1% in 2001). During this second phase, Uganda came to be seen as a country that is successful in fighting HIV/AIDS (Iliffe 2006), and thus as a model for other African countries. The third and ongoing phase (2002–present) is marked by the stabilization of the HIV rate at around 6 to 7%, but with a tendency to a new increase (UAC 2006; UNAIDS 2010).

The three phases of the epidemic are marked by different political interventions. National HIV and AIDS programs started in 1987 when Museveni declared the struggle against the epidemic as one of the government's priorities. Strong information campaigns about the virus were launched, but at the time almost no references were made to the use of condoms (Allen and Heald 2004). During the 1990s, the "ABC model" (Abstain, Be faithful, use Condoms) appeared and became a core concept in the struggle against the virus. The distribution of condoms grew considerably, in spite of the moralizing message preached by church leaders, especially those of the fast-growing Pentecostal movement, who insisted on changing individual "sinful" behavior to control the spread of HIV.

National HIV/AIDS-prevention strategies changed again during the third phase, putting more stress on abstinence and being faithful. In November 2004, Uganda drafted the "Uganda National Abstinence and Being Faithful Policy and Strategy on Prevention of Transmission on HIV", which received criticism from a number of international observers, including Human Rights Watch (HRW 2005).

There is a timely coincidence between this shift in HIV prevention policies and the start of PEPFAR. The program was first introduced in Uganda in 2004, with an initial allocation of 90 million dollars (SIECUS 2008); according to the PEPFAR agenda, at the time, one third of the sum for prevention had to be spent on abstinence-only and fidelity programs. With 1.216 billion dollars donated from 2004 to 2009, PEPFAR was by far the main source of money for treatment and prevention programs in the struggle against HIV/AIDS in Uganda. During the same period, in Uganda, "AB" programs received nearly one-third of the prevention budget and, according to the SIECUS report, programs promoting abstinence and fidelity were "the predominant intervention used with the general population. Programs addressing correct and consistent condom use are most often used with specific target population that the PEPFAR guidance identifies as being most at-risk" (SIECUS 2008, 9). While the use of condoms in the fight against AIDS had long been a "contested terrain" (Schoepf 2003), it is in this more recent phase that "abstinence" became prominent. Led by the government, and strongly supported by religious movements, notably by a number of Pentecostal congregations, Uganda's HIV/AIDS prevention programs began to put more and more emphasis on the "Abstinence" and "Be Faithful" messages, rather than the use of condoms (Epstein 2007).

The Ugandan government policy emphasis on A and B seems to have had some effect on sexual behavior and the attention to and knowledge about condoms among Ugandans. Recent surveys confirm that in the period under consideration, condom use has in fact significantly declined both in premarital sex among youth (from an overall of 54% in 2004/5 to 44% in 2011) (UAIS 2012, 111) and more drastically in sexual intercourse in multiple relationships (UAC 2012, 42). The overall distribution of condoms has declined from around 118 million in 2007/8 to less than 69 million in 2010/11 (UAC 2012, 43).

The *Uganda AIDS Indicator Survey* also shows that knowledge of means of HIV transmission is high among the Ugandan population, and higher for "abstinence" (89%)

and "being faithful" than for the "C" factor, "use condoms" (82%), and that according to the respondents young people (aged 12–14) should be taught about abstaining from sex until marriage (more than 94% of positive answers) much more than to use condoms (around 65%) in order to protect themselves from AIDS (UAIS 2012, 80).

These data are even more significant considering that the number of new infections increased by 11.4%, from 115.775 in 2007/8 to 128.980 in 2010/11, and that 65% of these occurred among married people (UAC 2011). As Josh Kron (2012) wrote in the *New York Times*, "over roughly the same period, the United States, through its AIDS prevention strategy known as PEPFAR, spent $1.7 billion in Uganda to fight AIDS [...] the results raise questions about the effectiveness of the United States' AIDS-prevention strategy here". The increase of infections led to a reconsideration of AIDS prevention strategies in the *National HIV/AIDS Strategic Plan 2011/12–2014/15* (UAC 2011), where more emphasis is placed on the recognition that key target population groups have changed, now being especially married people, who may not be helped by the earlier HIV prevention strategies, and that more efforts should be made at the political level in addressing the structural, contextual and social factors driving the epidemic. The country is thus probably entering a new phase in the political response to HIV/AIDS.

In the following sections, I will provide evidence of the nature of changed identities among *Balokole*, and show the forms of mobilization against AIDS that emerge from this process. I will also show that, at the same time, mobilization against AIDS influences identities.

V. The "abstinence campaign" and the construction of a collective *Balokole* identity

A. Some factors of identification for Ugandan Pentecostals

Opening the fourth section, I discussed the presence of significant differences within the *Balokole* movement; in spite of this, it is possible to point out some elements which provide a collective identity beyond these diversities.

Starting from the global level, the universalism of the Pentecostal message, with the emphasis on being part of a unique "body of Christ" that includes all born-again Christians, creates a sense of belonging to a worldwide group that transcends social, economic and ethnic divisions. Although perceived by the believers as an important aspect for the construction of a global identity, the reference to the "body of Christ" is too broad to be sufficient to mobilize people.

At the local level, other factors contribute to the formation of the collective identity of Pentecostals in Kampala, not just as born-again Christians, but as *Balokole*. Firstly, the use of the term *Balokole*, which includes born-again Christians belonging to all the different Pentecostal congregations, and to the Church of Uganda, creates a certain unity beyond the various divisions. Secondly, the differences in the use of language during services do not prevent the formation of a collective identity. When asked about this significant diversity, pastors and members of the churches usually told me that the language is one, regardless of whether Luganda, English or another language is used: that is, the language that unifies people is the language of the Bible. Others reinforced this argument with reference to *glossolalia* (speaking in tongues) as a way to transcend linguistic differences not only in Uganda, but globally.

Thirdly, and most important for the present discourse, the development of churches' activities targeting HIV/AIDS creates a sense of shared identity within the movement, especially among those young believers who actively participate in these campaigns. During my fieldwork, I was often struck by the sense of "we-ness" emerging from the discourses of my informants, both in formal interviews and in informal contexts; it was very common for them to refer to a collective "we", meaning "the *Balokole*": "we are the new generation", "we are changing the country", and other such expressions were repeatedly (and proudly) affirmed in conversations. These conversations, and the observations I made during cell meetings, abstinence training and teaching at schools, and other occasions such as camps (see below) and pro-abstinence marches and rallies, led me to infer that activities related to the prevention of the spread of HIV/AIDS play an important part in this identity-building process.

The number of young people involved is considerable; one of the main activities is preaching abstinence in the schools: more than 100 university students have been involved as volunteers in CAWA at the MCC, and over 300 youth workers trained in the abstinence program of *True Love Waits* (TLW), one of the oldest faith-based prevention programs in the country. Pastor Andrew Mwenge, former Director of TLW, said

> We started in 1994 – we developed our own material, and we started going to schools. I don't know in how many schools I've been, over a thousand, for sure. The schools gave us three to four hours, and we engaged the students through dialogues to reflect on their dreams for life, and on how sexuality fits into their total life. At the end of this presentation everybody leaves the room and then those who want to do the commitment come back into the room and sign a commitment card. They take one card, and we keep one card. We have over half a million of those cards, through the years.[13]

Apart from abstinence-related activities, young believers participate in several other programs concerning HIV/AIDS; to provide an example, the cell group I frequented at Watoto Church during my fieldwork was taking care of an HIV+ woman; members of the cell went to visit her every week, bringing some food or other goods, and spending around one hour talking and praying with her. When the woman died in 2007, the cell group started helping another woman, but this time the members collected a sum with which she started a small business in town, so that they went to see her at the shop and talked and prayed with her, but she did not feel dependent on the cell.[14] As a member of the cell explained after one of the visits:

> coming here, helping people, makes us feel [like] real Christians. We feel we are doing something great to change the lives of these people, and to change Uganda. We are the cycle breakers, because we don't just talk about love and transformation: we practice love and transformation, every day. This is what we really are.[15]

These activities thus seem to provide a basis for the self-definition of the identity of the *Balokole* as those who are charged with changing the country, and as agents for the renewal of society. The fact of being active in society to transform it, to make Uganda a "saved country", was often at the core of the discourses of the young Pentecostals I talked with in Kampala. The general feeling was well summarized in one pastor's preaching at Makerere Full Gospel Church: "If everyone wins a soul, together we will win thousands" (Fred Wantaate, Pastor, Makerere Full Gospel Church, 17 December 2006).

In recent years some of the most active Pentecostal groups have been partially changing their attitudes towards HIV prevention, putting more emphasis on "Be[ing] faithful", considering the actual trends in the epidemic. Yet the "abstinence campaign" – which attracted much of the Pentecostals' efforts during the period 2004 to 2010 – still significantly contributes to the process of formation of a collective identity, especially for young, well-educated, urban *Balokole*, who are led to focus their energies into religiously-motivated action. This sense of identity rests on concepts such as "salvation" and "purity" and, as I will show later, on the intra- and intergenerational contrast to groups of "non-saved" others. The religious language contributes to generating a frame in which the epidemic is interpreted as the result of a supposed immorality of the previous generations. The insistence on the idea of "renovation" ("new generation", "rebirth") is significant in this regard. Within this view, the present is the age of the struggle to set Uganda free from the influence of satanic spirits, and the future the golden age for a finally Christian and saved country, free from the AIDS scourge, in opposition with the past, which is represented as a dark age. The Pentecostal theme of the "break with the past" (Meyer 1998; Van Dijk 1998) also assumes in this context the meaning of breaking with "risky behaviors", with an equation between being spiritually "saved" and physically "safe".

Young Pentecostals' mobilization thus occurs around the need to face the "epidemic of immorality" (as one of my informants labeled the Ugandan situation), and to build a new Christian generation in order to save Uganda. The first and most important strategy to achieve this goal, according to the *Balokole* ideology, is to learn how to "resist temptations", and to spread this message to all young, unmarried, people (personal communication, December 2009).

B. "Saving the new generation"

The progressive transition of Pentecostal churches into FBOs, with a particular focus on HIV/AIDS-related programs (prevention with a stress on the "AB" policy, care, and assistance to orphans and widows, etc.), has been the most relevant transformation that has occurred within the Pentecostal movement in Uganda during the last decade (Gusman 2009). These macro-level changes have influenced identity construction at a grassroots level, particularly among young Pentecostal activists, whose engagement in prevention and education programs about sexuality and HIV/AIDS has become a crucial element in the definition of their identity as believers. What is their motivation for devoting so much of their everyday time to church-related activities? What are their expectations? How do they perceive and represent their role in society, and the impact they are able to have on other people's lives?

To understand the motivations of the actors involved in these programs, I argue that the particular religious frame in which this discourse is located is crucial. This frame focuses on morality and the need to change the country through the transformation of individual lives; spreading the Gospel and teaching the "AB" model are the two sides of this action of moralization. One recurrent argument in believers' discourses and in preaching is that one cannot be spiritually saved if he/she is not morally (and sexually) pure. This frame is highly effective in motivating people to participate, as it contextualizes mobilization to impact other people's lives as part of the mission of the "good Christian", or the "true *Mulokole*". Going around schools preaching the "abstinence-only" model to students; volunteering in programs of care for AIDS orphans or PLWHA; organizing events to promote the "AB"; all of these activities, and other similar ones, are considered to be part of the call that each born-again receives from God. This action of care and prevention is thus perceived as a service not only to the person, or to society, but to God himself. The following quote from Sam, a young team pastor at Makerere Full Gospel Church, illustrates this sense of duty:

> Reaching out to those who are in need is a service; as a Christian you have a mandate to share your wealth, your gifts. You are required to do that. It's not only pastors' work; this is something you have to do as a Christian – it's not even volunteering, it's a command, the command to share, to be there for one another, to pray. People are doing so not because Full Gospel Church says so, but because the Bible says so.[16]

In particular, for young activists involved in the "abstinence campaign" promoted by a number of FBOs and Pentecostal churches in Kampala, "love" seems to be the key word, the main factor for explaining their motivation to mobilize. G., a young female activist at CAWA, has already visited more than 70 schools in Kampala and the surrounding area, volunteering in the abstinence campaign; she explains:

> I do this out of love −[it] is the love for people, for reaching out [to] the lost souls. It's also the love for God, and the love Pastor [Ssempa] shows for us, that motivate me. I can't stay close[d away] in my room when I know that someone in the next room is suffering.

Personal experiences are often told with details of past direct contact with suffering caused by the epidemic, usually with the death of relatives. G. continues:

> My auntie died of AIDS; it was 1996 [and] there were no treatments at that time. She was the person who brought me up. I saw her body perishing; when you see these things, then you develop fear, for yourself and for your beloved ones.[17]

"Fear" was a recurring word in the discourses of my informants while talking about their involvement in prevention and education programs about HIV. This fear is related both to the direct experience of having seen someone dying from AIDS and to a past lifestyle that could have led to the believer contracting the virus. This discontinuity in sexual and other behaviors considered as both immoral and risky is, again, supported by the idea of the "break with the past". Experiences with AIDS thus become a further element in the feeling of a shared identity of the young *Balokole* as "saved": becoming a born-again, getting saved, one feels renewed. Conversion stories people told me were usually stories in which the old self, a sinful self, died after the individual received the baptism of the Holy Spirit. Becoming a born-again and entering a new group, the one of the "saved people" (*Balokole*), drives young believers to embrace the "abstinence" perspective. The story A., another of the CAWA ambassadors at the Makerere Community Church, told me is exemplary of the confusion and fear that many students experience when they arrive in Kampala to study at Makerere University; at the same time, it illustrates how feeling that one is part of a group is considered a key factor in the decision to change one's life and to mobilize in the abstinence campaign.

> When I joined MUK [Makerere University], my first year was a year of sin, I [drank] myself away, my life was just like that, going from nightclub to nightclub, involved in sexual activities with a number of girlfriends [. . . I was] just a dysfunctional person. But after that year I was tired of the life I was living [. . .] I was tired of smoking, tired of drugs, tired of womanizing, I was afraid that I even acquired HIV [. . .] so I was living in fear, but then I was also living in desperation and I needed a message of hope.

This was the moment when he came to know about the MCC, through the evangelizing activities that church members carry out on campus:

> Among my peers no one could give me that message of hope, so when these two guys came and knocked at my door, I opened and they came in and told me about hope, they told me about a Jesus who can forgive, a Jesus who can restore. The next day was a Sunday, that's when I joined [the] MCC, and I found a group of very happy young people, they were praising God, they were dancing. So I joined them, I also jumped around, I sang around, and eventually before I could realize, I was already one of them. Soon after, I joined CAWA and began to go to schools, and tell young people that there was a treasure inside of them, and that they didn't need to give their life away to everyone, sleeping with every man, every woman there, I told them that there was a specific person waiting for them, who was also saving her life somewhere.[18]

Mobilization thus comes from a sense of being part of a group ("I was already one of them") in which one feels "safe"; indeed, the existence of a collective identity is central to attracting and mobilizing people, but at the same time this identity is constructed through mobilization. By going to schools, sharing their experiences with younger students, and talking about their choice of abstaining from sex until marriage (although this decision in some cases, as in A.'s story, follows a period of sexual activity), young activists strengthen their feeling of "we-ness", of being part of the "new generation" of Christians who are in charge of bringing about a moral revolution in Uganda. Through this identity creation, they believe they are transforming Uganda into a Christian country, free from sin and thus free from AIDS.

Saving the young generation, both spiritually and physically, by preventing people from contracting HIV, is perceived as a mission, and preaching abstinence as a way to thank God for the gift of salvation. A. concluded our conversation with these words:

> This program touches the best nature of my life; because I believe, if I had not been reached by those two boys who came as agents of transformation, right now I would be having HIV/AIDS, because the speed at which I was walking, man, it was so quick. So I believe therefore it is my mandate to also reach others, before AIDS reaches them. So even if I get whatever it comes my way, I am committed, I'm fully committed to reach[ing] out to the generation.

Religious motivations, and the feeling of a shared identity built through the reference to abstinence and moral transformation, are central factors in the mobilization of young Pentecostals in Kampala. On the other hand, it should be noted that by participating in the movement, they are also looking for their place within society: as Catrine Christiansen has remarked, young people have a weak social positioning in Uganda; church contexts thus also become a space in which to give public expression to their criticism, by proposing a "break" with the past, and a transformation in morality (Christiansen 2011). Finally, the engagement in social programs could also turn, in some cases, into a job opportunity. It is not uncommon that, after a period of "volunteering" with a program, some of the persons involved are able to get a job, either with the church/organization with which they were volunteering or with other related organizations they came into contact with during their volunteer activity. Material incentives should not be overestimated, and most of the volunteers will never receive direct material benefits from their participation in these activities. Yet, for some of the people involved, volunteering is also a training to develop an expertise in order to get "a proper job and a real salary", as a young woman at Makerere Full Gospel Church told me (personal communication, July 2006).

C. Collective identity and the formation of moral borders

The construction of a collective identity is crucial in the recruitment phase, but also in the development of the movement, as it sustains solidarity and commitment. Going back to Melucci's definition (Melucci 1996), it is worth focusing especially on two elements: identity as the construction of an "action system", and as an "interactive definition". To link this definition to the case of the *Balokole* mobilization around AIDS campaigns, it is necessary to ask the question concerning "who" is constructing the action system. In other words, is the collective identity of the *Balokole* movement constructed through top-down or bottom-up processes?

Religious leaders are largely responsible for the framing process, with their loud and persistent preaching on morality, sexuality, and the need for the country to undergo a moral revolution. This is a top-down process, in which the mediatization of the message plays an important role: pastors often organize this moralizing frame using influences from the international context, like for example the availability of funds for specific campaigns, or imitating North American pastors' way of preaching. The massive use of media (TV, radio, the Internet, etc.) facilitates a process of "frame alignment", as it conveys similar themes all around the world, and enables religious leaders to spread their message broadly and intensively (Meyer and Moors 2006). Many of my informants listened to and watched evangelical TV and radio channels almost exclusively.

Nevertheless, the sense of being part of a collective "we", while punctually constructed during Sunday services and other communitarian occasions in which the whole congregation comes together, needs to be continuously reaffirmed in the relationships with other members of the group. The organization of the "cell-groups" is central in this regard, as these small assemblies are the place where people exchange ideas, ask for and provide financial, spiritual, and psychological help, and discuss personal topics such as love relationships or diseases. One pastor at Watoto Church thus explained the importance of being a cell-based church during an interview:

> [it] all started from the Bible; Jesus Christ gave his time to only twelve disciples. If a person can only impact twelve people, then a big church like this one can't serve its members effectively, if it's not organized in cell-groups. So, if you want to be part of the church, you need to be part of a cell.[19]

Cell-meetings take place every week at one of the members' homes, and last one hour or more. They usually start with singing some hymns, then one of the members takes the role of leader of the meeting, and coordinates the discussion around one or two topics proposed by the church (although it is also possible to propose other topics, if something urgent has to be discussed within the group). All the members are invited to participate actively in the discussion and to share ideas, personal testimonies, and experiences about the topics. At the end of the meeting, the leader collects requests for prayers: members ask for prayers for personal reasons (such as the need for money, a job, or improved health), on behalf of relatives or friends who are in need, for the Church, and for the whole society.

The meeting often ends with a shared meal, where the conversation continues in a more informal way, focusing mainly on individual or familial problems, or on the organization of future initiatives. Cells are in fact also the basis for action, as they are responsible for some important church activities. For example, each cell group at the Watoto Church adopts an HIV-positive person or the person's affected family, providing spiritual sustenance and some material support.

Other important moments in the construction of the identity are the camps taking place during the year. All the most important congregations in Kampala organize these events; in this context, members of the church are living together for several days, sharing meals and activities, and receiving specific teachings from pastors or assistants. Young people are strongly encouraged to take part in camps as part of their Christian training and education. It is worth noting that these are usually gendered places for the construction of identity, as male and female camps are separated, and the teachings offered are addressing specific questions related to the way in which a male/female has to behave, especially regarding sex and marriage.

The use of the camps for mobilization resounds with David Snow's assertion that the growth of a movement relies on the ability to create highly interconnected networks, but that at the same time networks "do not tell us what transpires when constituents and bystanders or adherents get together" (Snow 1986 et al., 468). Being part of a congregation with thousands of members means it is impossible to know and interact with everyone; indeed, a considerable portion of the time devoted to church activities is spent in small encounters, where significant interactional processes take place. Local meetings show different dynamics in comparison with congregational gatherings; while in the latter, context hierarchical divisions are more evident, in the former, differences are nuanced, and social relationships are re-patterned in the language of the Christian brotherhood (Maxwell 2000, 269). This micro level is at least as important as the macro level in the construction of a collective identity, because it carries, confirms and reinforces the messages of the church through the interaction with a restricted group of followers.

Through this particular structure, the value frame is constructed around the keywords of "purity", "safeness", "re-birth", "resisting temptations", "abstinence", and "faithfulness". What happens if the construction of a shared meaning – which is central to the formation of a collective identity able to motivate people to action – is based on this strict morality? I suggest that this results in the formation of a series of oppositions by which the *Balokole* set themselves as apart from the world as a separate group.

The centrality of being saved implies that the "others" are not. Who are these others?

(a) The first opposition is against the previous generations, and finds an expression in the notion of a "Joseph Generation"; the reference is to the biblical character of Joseph, who is considered as an example to follow for the *Balokole*, as he became a leader in Egypt after resisting the courtship of his Egyptian master's wife (Gusman 2009). This discourse assumes that a new, morally pure young generation will be able to transform Ugandan society, reversing the moral corruption of the parental generation, charged with being responsible for the spread of HIV/AIDS in the country. This creates conflicts inside the familial context (Gusman 2012).

(b) Secondly, the *Balokole* oppose "tradition", especially traditional religions, because they believe that the spirits on which these religions were based are satanic. The opposition against both previous generations and traditional religions are towards the past; the idea of the past as a dark period, and of the need to close with it, find support in the rhetoric of the "complete break with the past", which is one the main points of Pentecostal theology (Meyer 1998; Van Dijk 1998).

(c) Thirdly, young believers oppose their own – unsaved – peers, whom they consider sexually promiscuous and "serious sinners", because they frequent clubs and drink alcohol. The fracture is thus not only with the past, but also with the present, resulting in the building of strong moral borders between the *Balokole* and all the "others".

The common element among the three groups of "others" is the assumed proximity to satanic forces, such as alcohol, traditional religious beliefs, and sexual relations before and outside of marriage. The strict set of beliefs and values the group takes as constituent of its collective identity creates separation from everyone who is not "saved", because he or she is potentially "contaminating". The collective identity of the *Balokole* group is thus built on a strongly oppositional logic: to avoid the dangerous contact with "the world", many *Balokole* spend most of their time with other *Balokole*.

The group of the "saved" is thus conceived as a separate entity. As O., a young born-again woman, told me: "I have now a new family, new friends, a new job. I contribute to my church, giving the tithe. I belong to a new clan. Here, we are all of the same clan, the clan of Jesus Christ".[20]

On the one side, this is an open group, where ethnic, social and economic differences are (or should be) erased; on the other, it is an exclusive group, as one can only access it through spiritual conversion and through adhering to the moralistic behavior which the movement demands. This creates a sort of obligation to act with the other members, a loyalty to the group that cannot be betrayed (Polletta and Jasper 2001). This loyalty is particularly evident in the case of Ugandan Pentecostals, as the "brotherhood in Christ" is stressed to the point that the *Balokole* feel as though they are part of a "new clan". This clan is not based on their biological birth, but on their religious rebirth.

This construction of a common interpretation of the world outside as dangerous and contaminating is at least in part a reaction to the presence of AIDS in the country. The epidemic is seen by the *Balokole* as the most evident proof of the sinfulness of the "others", and abstinence as the only solution for young people to be saved and safe. Mobilization is thus pushed by a religious–moralistic frame, and motivated by the need to remove sinfulness from society, thus helping people to be saved (at both a spiritual and a physical level).

VI. Conclusion

This paper has illustrated how Pentecostals' mobilization in Kampala, both at a political and social level, has been driven by the incumbent presence of the AIDS epidemic in the country, and interpreted within a moralistic religious frame in which the spread of the virus is due to "immorality", whose final responsibility has to be found in the satanic forces menacing the social order.

The reinforcement of the identity of the *Balokole* as "saved", and the mobilization against AIDS that accompanied it, coincided with the introduction of PEPFAR into Uganda: PEPFAR's focus on abstinence created opportunities for Pentecostal churches to engage in prevention programs. Thus, external (PEPFAR funds) and unpredictable (the virus) circumstances provided a larger context for the formation of a collective identity for the *Balokole* group, and in the following mobilization in activities related to AIDS prevention and education. Taken together, these elements generate a significant mobilization around HIV/AIDS-prevention programs in some of the most important Pentecostal congregations in Kampala; young believers are particularly energetic in their carrying out of these activities, and the religious frame provided by the Pentecostal ideology proves especially effective in motivating people to action. This ability to engage people in volunteer work, together with some of the results of this mobilization – especially the grassroots initiatives such as the adoption of an HIV-positive person by cell groups at the Watoto Church – raises questions about the role of the Pentecostal movement in the struggle against AIDS, and more generally in the public sphere in Uganda and in other African countries. Finally, through the stress on concepts such as "purity", "contamination" and "immorality", attributed to the fathers' generation, and often to all the non-Christians (and thus non-saved), the *Balokole* group create a dualistic worldview in which their identity is constructed through the opposition against different groups of "others" and the building of strong moral and social barriers. This strategy may result in an increasing of the stigma against those who are HIV positive, both within and outside the group; *Balokole* who contract the virus after conversion are in fact often expelled from the congregation. Thus, paradoxically, while talking (and acting) consistently about AIDS, Pentecostals are also creating, at the same time, silence around the virus. This may cause a tendency to increase secrecy about "risky behaviors" such as infidelity (Parikh 2007), and generate a perception of the social risk as higher than the biomedical risk.

Notes

1. The term *Balokole* literally means "the saved ones", and was introduced during the 1930s with the East African Revival; although employed to translate the English word "Pentecostals", it identifies also the "saved" Anglicans, in continuity with the origin of the word, which was born against an Anglican background. So, today the word indicates all the saved people, with the

exception of the charismatic groups inside the Catholic Church which, even though agreeing with the idea of salvation through the action of Christ and the Holy Spirit, do not refer to themselves as *Balokole*.

2. The President's Emergency Plan For AIDS Relief (PEPFAR) is a five-year program for a total expenditure of 15 billion dollars approved by the US Congress in 2003, and then renewed for another five-year period in 2008. Of the total sum, 55% had to be used for treatment, 15% for palliative care, 10% for orphans and vulnerable children, and 20% for prevention. The original 2003 act required that at least 33% (1 billion dollars) of the money for prevention had to be spent on abstinence and fidelity ("be faithful") programs (*United States Leadership Against HIV/AIDS, Tuberculosis and Malaria Act of 2003*). The 2008 reauthorized program increased the sum for abstinence and fidelity promotion to 50% of the total, although countries can assign a reduced amount to this sum if they provide explanation for their decision (*United States Global Leadership Against HIV/AIDS, Tuberculosis and Malaria Reauthorization Act of 2008*).

3. The history of Ugandan Pentecostalism is recent, if compared with other African countries. Due to the persecution which Pentecostals suffered under the governments of Obote and Idi Amin, the growth of the movement was extremely limited until 1986, the year when Yoweri Museveni took control of the country.

4. A decade ago, Erica Bornstein noticed how FBOs were still largely left outside the analysis of the role that non-governmental organizations (NGOs) have in Africa (Bornstein 2002). Actually, the whole field of study of social movements in the continent is still underdeveloped, but studies are emerging to fill this gap (see Ellis and van Kessel 2009).

5. For a critical overview of the use of "collective identity" in social movements theory, see Polletta and Jasper (2001) and Snow and McAdam (2000). For a critique of the possible limits of this approach, see McDonald (2002).

6. Purity includes both "abstaining" from premarital sex, and "being faithful" to the husband/wife.

7. The first Pentecostal churches were founded by missionaries from North America; the Canadian pastor Hugh Layzeel established the Full Gospel Church of Uganda in 1960, and two years later Arthur Dodzeit – a missionary from the US – started the Elim Church. The second source originated when a group of young Anglicans separated from the Church of Uganda in 1971 to start the Deliverance Church, led by Pastor Stephen Mungoma. The third source has to be traced back to a Ghanaian missionary, John Obiri Yeboah, who made his work evangelization during the late 1970s, introducing into Uganda the focus on miracles (Musana 2006).

8. For an explanation of the three "waves" of Pentecostal Churches with reference to their history in Africa, see Meyer (2004).

9. The Watoto Church, "Statement of Faith".

10. The EAR was not the first revival inside the Anglican Church of Uganda; some of the members of the Church Mission Society, which brought Anglicanism to Uganda, did not appreciate the political connections the COU had established with the British Protectorate. Wanting to reaffirm the primacy of the spiritual work of the mission, they started the so-called Pilkington Revival in 1893. Nevertheless, the impact of the EAR on the local society and on the COU was much bigger than earlier movements, mainly because the EAR didn't present itself as schismatic, but as an attempt to reform the COU from inside.

11. It should be noted that this kind of engagement is predominantly urban and mostly involves young and educated members of some of the main congregations. In the rural settings the situation is different, as Pentecostal Churches influence village politics through the interaction with customary institutions such as the village council and the clan committees (Jones 2005).

12. One of the most influential pastors in Kampala told me during an interview in this regard that "politics is a dangerous thing, because power and money are strictly related to corruption. It is not easy for a born-again to move in[to] this setting; but it is necessary. If we want to have an impact on Uganda, we have to participate in political decisions. If we want to change this country, we need to take the risk". Martin Ssempa (Pastor, Makerere Community Church). Interview by author. Kampala, 28 June 2005.

13. Andrew Mwenga (Pastor, Kampala Baptist Church, former Director of *True Love Waits Uganda*). Interviewed by the author. Kampala, 19 July, 2010.

14. The Watoto Church has more than 2000 cells around Kampala, and almost two thirds of them are taking care of an HIV+ person, mostly women.
15. R., male, 24 (member of a cell, Watoto Church). Interviewed by the author. Kampala, 10 January 2007.
16. Sam (Pastor, Makerere Full Gospel Church). Interviewed by the author. Kampala, 16 July 2010.
17. G., female, 23 (activist, Makerere Community Church, and CAWA). Interviewed by the author. Kampala, 28 July 2010.
18. A., male, 28 (activist, Makerere Community Church, and CAWA). Interviewed by the author. Kampala, 12 July 2010.
19. Bob (Pastor, Watoto Church). Interviewed by the author. Kampala, 15 December 2006.
20. O., female, 25 (member of a cell, Makerere Full Gospel Church). Interviewed by the author. Kampala, 23 July 2005.

Bibliography

Allen, Tim, and Suzette Heald. 2004. "HIV/AIDS policy in Africa: what has worked in Uganda and what has failed in Botswana?" *Journal of International Development* 16 (8): 1141–1154.

Bornstein, Erica. 2002. "Developing faith: Theologies of economic development in Zimbabwe." *Journal of Religion in Africa* 32 (1): 4–31.

Christiansen, Catrine. 2011. "Youth religiosity and moral critique: God, government and generations in a time of AIDS in Uganda." *Africa Development* 36: 127–145.

Ellis, Stephen, and Ineke van Kessel. 2009. *Movers and shakers. Social movements in Africa.* Leiden-Boston: Brill.

Epstein, Helen. 2007. *The invisible cure. Africa, the west and the fight against AIDS.* New York, NY: Farrar, Straus and Giroux.

Escobar, Arturo. 1992. "Culture, practice and politics: anthropology and the study of social movements." *Critique of Anthropology* 12 (4): 395–432.

Gifford, Paul. 1998. *African Christianity. Its public role.* London: Hurst & Company.

Gifford, Paul. 2001. "The complex provenance of some elements of African Pentecostal theology." In *Between Babel and Pentecost. Transnational Pentecostalism in Africa and Latin America,* edited by A. Corten, and R. Marshall, 62–79. Bloomington: Indiana University Press.

Goffman, Erving. 1974. *Frame analysis.* Cambridge: Harvard University Press.

Gusman, Alessandro. 2009. "HIV/AIDS, Pentecostal churches, and the "Joseph Generation" in Uganda." *Africa Today* 56 (1): 66–86.

Gusman, Alessandro. 2012. "Pentecôtisme ougandais entre individualisme et la formation de la 'new generation'." In *Afrique: d'une génération à l'autre,* edited by MN Leblanc, and M Gomez-Perez. Paris: Khartala.

Hansen, Holger Bernt. 1984. *Mission, church and state in a colonial setting: Uganda 1890–1925.* London: Heinemann.

Human Rights Watch. 2005. "The less they know, the better: Abstinence-only HIV/AIDS programs in Uganda." *HRW* 17: 4.

Hunt, Scott A., and Robert D. Benford. 2004. "Collective identity, solidarity, and commitment." In *The Blackwell companion to social movements,* edited by D. Snow, S. Soule, and H. Kriesi, 433–457. Oxford: Blackwell.

Iliffe, John. 2006. *The African AIDS epidemic: A history.* Oxford: James Currey.

Jasper, James. 1997. *The art of moral protest: Culture, biography, and creativity in social movements.* Chicago: University of Chicago Press.

Johnston, Hank, and Bert Klandermans. 1995. *Social movements and culture.* Minneapolis: University of Minnesota Press.

Jones, Ben. 2005. "The church in the village, the village in the church. Pentecostalism in Teso, Uganda." *Cahiers d'études africaines* 45 (178): 497–517.

Kassimir, Ronald. 1998. "The social power of religious organisation and civil society: The Catholic church in Uganda." In *Civil society and democracy in Africa – critical perspectives*, edited by N. Kasfir, 54–83. London: Frank Cass.

Kron, Josh. 2012. In "Uganda, an AIDS success story comes undone." *NY Times*, August 3, p. A5.

Kurzman, Charles. 2008. "Introduction: Meaning-making in social movements." *Anthropological Quarterly* 81 (1): 5–15.

Maxwell, David. 2000. "'Catch the Cockerel Before Dawn': Pentecostalism and politics in post-colonial Zimbabwe." *Africa* 70 (2): 249–277.

Maxwell, David. 2006. "Post-colonial Christianity in Africa." In *The Cambridge history of Christianity*, edited by H. McLeod. Vol. 9, 401–421. Cambridge: Cambridge University Press.

McDonald, Kevin. 2002. "From solidarity to fluidarity: Social movements beyond 'collective identity'–the case of globalization conflicts." *Social Movement Studies* 1 (2): 109–128.

Melucci, Alberto. 1988. "Getting involved: Identity and mobilization in social movements." *International Social Movements Research* 1: 329–348.

Melucci, Alberto. 1995. "The process of collective identity." In *Social movements and culture*, edited by H. Johnston, and B. Klandermans, 41–63. Minneapolis: University of Minnesota Press.

Melucci, Alberto. 1996. *Challenging codes. Collective action in the information age*. Cambridge: Cambridge University Press.

Meyer, Birgit. 1998. "'Make a Complete Break with the Past': Memory and post-colonial modernity in Ghanaian Pentecostalist discourse." *Journal of Religion in Africa* 28: 316–349.

Meyer, Birgit. 2004. "Christianity in Africa: From African independent to Pentecostal-Charismatic churches." *Annual Review of Anthropology* 33 (1): 447–474.

Meyer, Birgit, and Annelise Moors, eds. 2006. *Religion, media and the public sphere*. Bloomington: Indiana University Press.

Musana, Paddy. 2006. "Pentecostal/Charismatic Christianity as a new factor in the national politics of Uganda." Paper presented at the 5th international cultural studies workshop in Uganda, Department of Women and Gender Studies, Makerere University, August 7–9, 2006.

Parikh, Shanti. 2007. "The political economy of marriage and HIV: The ABC approach, "Safe" infidelity, and managing moral risk in Uganda." *American Journal of Public Health* 97 (7): 1198–1208.

Polletta, Francesca, and James Jasper. 2001. "Collective identity and social movements." *Annual Review of Sociology* 27 (1): 283–305.

Ranger, Terence, ed. 2008. *Evangelical Christianity and democracy in Africa*. Oxford: Oxford University Press.

Robbins, Joel. 2008. "Pentecostal networks and the spirit of globalization." In *Contemporary religiosities. Emergent socialities and the post-nation state*, edited by B. Kapferer, K. Telle, and A. Eriksen, 55–66. New York-Oxford: Berghahn Books.

Schoepf, Brooke G. 2003. "Uganda: Lessons for AIDS control in Africa." *Review of African Political Economy* 30: 553–572.

SIECUS. 2008. *2008 PEPFAR Country Profile Updates*. Uganda. Accessed 6 June 2013. http://www.siecus.org/index.cfm?fuseaction=page.viewPage&pageID=968&nodeID=1

Smilde, David A. 1998. "'Letting God Govern': Supernatural agency in the Venezuelan Pentecostal approach to social change." *Sociology of Religion* 59 (3): 287–303.

Snow, David. 2001. "Collective identity and expressive forms." In *International encyclopaedia of the social and behavioural sciences*, edited by NJ Smelser, and PB Baltes, 196–254. London: Elsevier Science.

Snow, David, and Robert D. Benford. 1988. "Ideology, frame resonance, and participant mobilization." *International Social Movement Research* 1: 197–217.

Snow, David, and Doug McAdam. 2000. "Identity work processes in the context of social movements: Clarifying the identity/movement nexus." In *Self, identity, and social movements*, edited by S. Stryker, TJ Owens, and RW White, 41–67. Minneapolis: University of Minnesota Press.

Snow, David, E. Burke Rochford Jr, Steven K. Worden, and Robert D. Benford. 1986. "Frame alignment processes, micromobilization, and movement participation." *American Sociological Review* 51 (4): 464–481.

Stenning, Derrick. 1965. "Salvation in Ankole." In *African systems of thought*, edited by M. Fortes, and G. Dieterlen, 258–275. Oxford: Oxford University Press.

UAC. 2006. *The Uganda HIV/AIDS status report July 2004–December 2005*. Uganda AIDS Commission, Republic of Uganda.

UAC. 2012. *National HIV & AIDS strategic plan 2011/12-2014/15*. Uganda AIDS Commission, Republic of Uganda.

UAC. 2012. *Global AIDS response progress report. Country progress report Uganda*. Uganda AIDS Commission, Republic of Uganda.

UAIS. 2012. *Uganda AIDS indicator survey 2011*. Ministry of Health, Republic of Uganda.

UNAIDS. 2008. *Report on the global AIDS epidemic*. Accessed 2 June 2013. http://www.unaids.org/globalreport/documents/20081123_GlobalReport_full_en.pdf

Van Dijk, Rijk. 1998. "Pentecostalism, cultural memory and the state. Contested representations of time in postcolonial Malawi." In *Memory and the Postcolony*, edited by R. Werbner, 155–181. London: Zed Books.

Ward, Kevin. 1989. "Obedient rebels: The relationship between the early 'Balokole' and the church of Uganda: The Mukono crisis, 1941." *Journal of Religion in Africa* 19: 194–227.

Welbourn, Fred B. 1965. *Religion and politics in Uganda, 1952–1962*. Nairobi: East African Publishing House.

Williams, Rhys H. 2002. "From the 'Beloved Community' to 'Family Values': Religious language, symbolic repertories, and democratic culture." In *Social movements. Identity, culture, and the state*, edited by D.S. Meyer, N. Whittier, and B. Robnett, 247–265. Oxford: Oxford University Press.

Yao migrant communities, identity construction and social mobilisation against HIV and AIDS through circumcision schools in Zimbabwe

Anusa Daimon

Centre for Africa Studies, University of the Free State, Bloemfontein, South Africa

Résumé

Cet article examine la pratique de la circoncision masculine au sein du peuple migrant des Yaos, au Zimbabwe, dans le but de mettre en évidence l'importance de la circoncision comme une plateforme pour la mobilisation sociale contre le VIH et le sida. Cet article traite des avantages que présente cette pratique sur le plan de la santé et de la nouvelle forme d'identité qu'elle crée pour la lutte contre le sida. Il examine donc le rôle du rite dans la création d'une identité yao collective qui facilite la mobilisation contre la pandémie au sein de la communauté. Cette mobilisation est un processus complexe et sujet à controverse, qui fait intervenir divers niveaux de négociation, de reconstruction et de reconfiguration de l'identité yao et de la pratique de la circoncision (l'acte chirurgical et les enseignements l'entourant), tant à l'intérieur qu'à l'extérieur du groupe. Cet article soutient que la pratique peut être considérée comme une forme de mouvement social africain qui est largement impulsé par une identité collective complexe mais consciente, et qui est aussi provoqué par l'intérêt des bailleurs à l'échelle mondiale concernant le débat portant sur la circoncision et le sida.

Abstract

This article examines the practice of male circumcision among the migrant Yao people in Zimbabwe with the goal of showing circumcision's importance as a platform for social mobilisation against HIV and AIDS. The work looks at how the practice has health benefits and creates a new form of identity to fight AIDS. It therefore examines the role of the rite in the creation of a collective Yao identity that facilitates mobilisation against the pandemic within the community. This mobilisation is a complex and contentious process, which involves various levels of negotiation, reconstruction and reconfiguration of Yao identity and the circumcision practice (the surgical act and teachings about it), both within and outside the group. The article argues that the practice can be viewed as a form of an African social movement that is largely driven by a complex but self-conscious collective identity and is also induced by the global donor interest in the circumcision–AIDS debate.

I. Introduction

The study examines the practice of male circumcision among the Yao people of Malawian descent in relation to the HIV and AIDS epidemic in Zimbabwe. It looks at how the Yao rite of male circumcision creates health benefits and new identities that facilitate mobilisation to fight AIDS. The practice can be framed as a form of African social activism, since it mobilises individuals to act in response to both their marginalised position in society and, more recently, the fear of AIDS. The practice is largely driven by a complex and self-conscious collective/group identity, but it is also informed by donors' interest in combating the pandemic. This has led to an intricate reconstruction and renegotiation of an important and popular Yao identity in the context of AIDS in Zimbabwe.

The disease has greatly affected the globe, with sub-Saharan Africa and southern Africa in particular being the most affected. The 2010 Report of the Joint United Nations Programme on HIV/AIDS (UNAIDS) on the Global AIDS Epidemic notes that sub-Saharan Africa is more heavily affected by HIV and AIDS than any other region of the world, with an estimated 22.9 million people living with HIV in the region – around two thirds of the global total. In 2010, around 1.2 million people died from AIDS in sub-Saharan Africa and 1.9 million people became infected with HIV. Southern Africa is still the most severely affected region, with an estimated 11.3 million people living with HIV in the region in 2009, nearly one third (31%) more than the 8.6 million a decade earlier. Globally, 34% of people living with HIV, 31% of new HIV infections, and 34% of all AIDS-related deaths in 2009 occurred in the ten countries of southern Africa (UNAIDS 2010, 28).

About 1.2 million people are living with HIV and AIDS in Zimbabwe (Leach-Lemens 2010; UNAIDS 2010). The first reported case of AIDS in Zimbabwe occurred in 1985. By the end of the 1980s, around 10% of the adult population was thought to be infected with HIV. This figure rose dramatically in the first half of the 1990s, peaking and stabilising at 29% between 1995 and 2000. Since then the HIV prevalence rate has declined and, according to government figures, the adult prevalence rate was 24.6% in 2003 and has fallen to about 14.3% in 2010 (Barnett and Whiteside 2003; Chikova 2010; Leach-Lemens 2010).

In the face of the epidemic, Zimbabweans have employed various strategies to curb the spread of HIV, including increasing condom distribution, encouraging abstinence, and free HIV testing and counselling. Recently, AIDS experts have looked to some traditional African cultural practices such as male circumcision to fight the disease. First viewed by the colonialists and later by many indigenous Zimbabweans to be a primitive and dangerous practice, the circumcision rite has become a central part of the campaign against the epidemic. Male circumcision involves the surgical removal of the foreskin of the penis to expose the head (glans) which, after the procedure, begins to keratinise (or toughen) and eventually become more durable (Barnett and Whiteside 2003; Chimedza 2006; Loygren 2005). Stefan Loygren observes that male circumcision in Africa is performed at birth or during initiation ceremonies in early puberty and about 60–70% of African men are circumcised, mostly according to ethnic and religious affiliation (Loygren 2005).

Traditionally, the Yao have viewed male circumcision as a platform for religious and cultural expression. They have used the practice to initiate their youth into adulthood, combining the surgical act with teachings about their culture (Sanderson 1920, 1955; Kubik 1978). The practice has also been important in symbolising and marking their identity as a minority migrant community in Zimbabwe. However, the practice has attained new dimensions as the state and the donor community have become more interested in the HIV-prevention aspects of circumcision. The article therefore examines how the Yao community has transformed from an ethnically defined formation into a social movement precisely through the political and medical repositioning of their male circumcision in the broader context of HIV prevention and the development discourses surrounding it.

Research into these dynamics was derived principally from my ethnography conducted among the Yao communities in Zimbabwe's Mashonaland West province between 2008 and 2010. I visited commercial farms and mines where most of the Yao live, such as the Dalny Mine in Chakari near Kadoma, the Muriel Mine and the Ayrshire Mine near Chinhoyi, and the Riverside, Inchefu and Ayrshire farms near Banket. Much of the ethnography targeted the Yao circumcision doctors, elders, and initiates, as well as medical practitioners and non-governmental organisation (NGO) personnel. Respondents were selected through snowball sampling techniques and the data was gathered through oral interviews, focused group discussions, and participant observations at the Yao initiation schools and public hospitals. The study also discovered and used "archives in the bush" (Zeitlyn 2005), such as signs, billboards, symbols, inscriptions and graffiti that provided unique community perceptions about circumcision and AIDS.

II. Identity creation for mobilisation: a theoretical overview

In a bid to show the importance of Yao circumcision in identity construction and mobilisation against AIDS in Zimbabwe, the study engages various themes on social movements, especially identity creation (Melucci 1996), resistance (Scott 1990) and globalisation (Keck and Sikkink 1998), in order to analyse the Yao practices. Alberto Melucci dwells on the concept of collective identity construction by discussing the ways that identity construction can be a contentious and complex process. He observes that collective identity is a crucial concept of contemporary social movements and at the core of this identity are cultural processes through which people seek to make sense or meaning of a situation (Melucci 1996, 70). As a process, collective identity entails a network of active relationships between actors who interact, communicate, influence each other, negotiate and make decisions concerning the symbolic orientations and meanings of their actions and the field of opportunities and constraints for mobilisation (Melucci 1996). Melucci's ideas can be used to better understand how the Yao circumcision rite creates an identity rooted in the meanings of their ritual. For example, Melucci's point about symbolic orientations links to the symbolic aspects of the removal of the foreskin and blood spilling which occur during circumcision and which are important markers of Yao identity, as I will demonstrate further below.

Likewise, the Yao circumcision practice can be analysed in relation to the theme of domination and resistance, specifically how actions of marginalised groups may challenge old forms of social domination in complex societies. Scott (1990) probes the public display of power and the hidden discourses of the marginalised, emphasising how the covert non-violent forms of resistance entail a cultural struggle or artful form of resistance against power structures. He observes that when the culture of the weak is left unconquered or non-colonised, the marginalised tend to clothe their resistance in "ritualisms" of subordination which serve to disguise their purpose and help them remain ambiguous enough for "retreat" (Scott 1990, 96). Scott's idea about the non-colonised culture of the weak is applicable to the Yao, because they have maintained their practice of circumcision in spite of their marginalisation in Zimbabwe. Over the years Malawian migrants have been confined to the margins of Zimbabwean society by dominant groups and power hierarchies. The state and the dominant autochthonous Shona and Ndebele people have categorised Yao migrants as non-citizens and foreigners due to their Malawian ancestry (Daimon 2007). In light of the Yao's marginal position in society, Yao circumcision as a ritual can be viewed as an indirect cultural form of resistance, or what Scott (1990) terms "hidden transcripts", whose covert social mobilisation occurs in circumcision schools and rituals which provide the means to express their emotions and make them collective. This cultural resistance creates a new identity or reinvigorates old identities that can be used to fight or mobilise against AIDS by the Yao community. As shall be demonstrated later, the Yao rite does not legitimise the powerful or dominant local groups but instead empowers the Yao who have in turn become important actors in the HIV and AIDS discourse in Zimbabwe. With the AIDS–circumcision links and state and donor funding, the Yao have evolved from a position of weakness to that of dominance and popularity, a scenario that Scott does not fully envision in his analysis of domination and resistance.

Finally, Yao mobilisation against the disease is set within a global context, which provides opportunities for local groups to access funds and gain technical support from external actors. Keck and Sikkink (1998) note that social movements are situated within a global context. Social movements in Africa may be driven by outside stimuli in the form of aid money from donors whose policy goals overlap with the practices or interests of local groups (Ellis and van Kessel 2009). In the case of the Yao's circumcision efforts, these are placed in a global arena where world health institutions like the World Health Organization (WHO) and UNAIDS have paid great attention to male circumcision and to groups like the Yao that practise it. Local actors (such as the Yao) have been drawn into networks of globalisation where health agencies become interested in studying them extensively and donor money is being pumped into their initiation schools across Zimbabwe. This has led to an interactive relationship between the circumcision rite and donor attention. The implications and impact of being drawn into such global networks on Yao collective identity and the practice itself are debatable and have created divisions within the Yao communities, as shall be shown later in the paper.

III.   The Yao and the importance of male circumcision

A.   *The Yao community in Zimbabwe*

The Yao people are part of the broad Malawian migrant population that is composed of various ethnic groups that include the Chewa, Manganja, Tumbuka, Ngoni, Nsenga, Chikunda, Zimba, and Yao (Mitchell 1951). These groups migrated to Zimbabwe between 1900 and 1970 during the Southern African labour migration period when Malawi acted as a labour reservoir for Zimbabwean and South African colonial economic enterprises (Daimon 2007; Mudenge 1988; Pikirayi 2001). These immigrants became an integral part of Zimbabwe's labour history. Most found employment and continue to live on commercial farms, estates and mines across Zimbabwe. Others worked in urban areas and lived under the colonial hostel system in black townships (Raftopoulos and Phimister 1997; van Onselen 1976). It was in these locales that the colonial government categorised Malawian migrants as "native aliens" and stereotyped them as excellent garden boys, housemaids, miners and farm workers (Ranger 1985). This stereotyping started the marginalisation of the migrants, and most of their descendants have inherited these colonial occupations in post-colonial Zimbabwe. Many continue to work in mines, and on estates and farms. Overall, these Malawian migrants are a minority group that constitutes about ten per cent of the fourteen million Zimbabwean population and the Yao occupy about two per cent of this Malawian migrant population.

However, the Yao are distinct from the other clusters of Malawian migrants such as the Chewa, Manganja, Tumbuka and Ngoni. The Yao were Muslim traders who originated from the East African coast (Tanzania in particular), while the other groups originally came from the Congo basin and settled in Malawi around the early fourteenth century (Thorold 1995). It would be portions of these Malawian groups that would later migrate as labourers during the twentieth century to settle in Zimbabwe and provide cheap labour for mines and farms. In Zimbabwe, not all Malawian migrants are Yao and not all Muslims are of Yao origin or Malawian origin. Likewise, Zimbabwe has a significant Muslim population. In the 1990s it was around 150,000 (Nkrumah 1991), but has doubled in the new millennium. Arab settlers account for a quarter of this population and the remainder consists of Muslim Africans – mainly the Yao. More broadly, there are many non-Muslim African groups such as the Remba, Xhosa, Mfengu and Shangaan that conduct male circumcision rituals but they are mainly found in South Africa, Lesotho, Swaziland and Botswana (Mandivenga 1989; Nkrumah 1991). Therefore, the Yao are the only African community in Zimbabwe that is both Muslim and practises circumcision. However, it should be noted that in the context of HIV and AIDS, their circumcision rite, not their religion, has been crucial in the articulation of their identity and in the current mobilisation against the epidemic in Zimbabwe.

B.   Yao circumcision and identity construction in Zimbabwe

Traditionally, the Yao have used their circumcision schools as platforms to mobilise and carve their identity as foreigners in Zimbabwe. However, this process of creating a collective Yao identity through circumcision has been complex and contentious. It has involved the definition of their identity both from within and beyond their community. Melucci (1996, 73) states that collective identity defines the capacity for autonomous action; a differentiation of the actor from others and this ability to distinguish from others must be recognised by these "others". The Yao have used circumcision (both its ritual and the physical outcome) as a means to distinguish themselves from other non-Yao, particularly the indigenous Zimbabwean groups of the Shona and Ndebele. This type of "othering" by the Yao has two components.

The first component is the actual surgical act of cutting the foreskin, experiencing pain and spilling blood. This rite has been the most important marker of Yao identity because of its pain and blood-spilling symbolism, which leads to the formation and maintenance of a unified identity among any Yao who has undergone the process. This shared experience of pain, loss, and the required stoicism that accompanies the surgery has the capacity to create a bond that helps Yao men to mobilise against various constraints. Ali Manangwa, who was circumcised at Riverside Farm near Banket in 2000, illustrates the aspects of this symbolism. He states that during the cutting of the foreskin, the initiate is not expected to wail, cry out in pain or flinch in pain so that his manhood is not stigmatised.[1] Nyathi (2008) observes that the blood spilled by the initiate is viewed as a sacrifice that connects the circumcised person to the land. Musa Chetambara, who is a Yao circumcision doctor in Zimbabwe, explains that blood spilling represents one's connections with the soil or the spiritual land of the Yao ancestors. He notes that mixing the initiates' blood with soil is a necessary recipe for a successful initiation and transformation into manhood because soil/land is a life-giver that acts as a platform for fertility and fecundity, and so this sacrifice guarantees success in reproductive life as the process ensures a symbiotic connection with nature and the spiritual realm.[2] The emotion and symbolism involved in this process binds the initiates together and bolsters the creation of a collective Yao identity. In this way, Yao circumcision appeals to Yao members to be part of the common group which is distinct from both the majority Zimbabweans (Shona and Ndebele) and the minority migrants who do not practise circumcision.

A second aspect of this "othering" is the way that the Yao then perceive and define themselves in terms of the practice and exclude non-Yao, partly because they have not undergone the ritual. While the local Shona and Ndebele (as outsiders or others) have

127

defined and seen circumcision as pagan and primitive, the Yao (as insiders) have celebrated it as a rite of passage or an intrinsic part of becoming an adult. The Yao hold numerous negative perceptions about the uncircumcised. Austin Kalonje, who was circumcised in 2003, asserted:

> We are circumcised because it is necessary. If I had not been circumcised I would not be a man, I would have no children and thus I would be nothing ... I would not marry a Yao girl because no girl would look at me, after all I would only be a child who does not know anything about adulthood.[3]

Musa Chetambara, the circumcision doctor, reiterates:

> An uncircumcised man cannot inherit his father's possessions or estate, nor can he establish a family. He cannot officiate in ritual ceremonies because he is seen as a child who has not yet transformed into adulthood. No Yao girl will sleep with an uncircumcised man because other girls would laugh at her and mock her [about] why she likes sleeping with children.[4]

Funani (1990) also adds that a Yao who is not circumcised is described quite simply as a boy, an *inja* (dog) and an *ingami* (unclean thing). This indicates that if one is not circumcised he is perceived to be someone without the requisite identity to fit into the social hierarchy of the Yao community. Melucci (1996) asserts that it is important for social-movement participants to be accepted before they can be mobilised for collective action. A man who is not circumcised will therefore not be able to participate in the community's collective action and make decisions within the Yao community. Such a person is basically voiceless and is not part of the Yao social mobilisation against challenges like AIDS and marginalisation in Zimbabwe.

Before the AIDS links, the Yao had employed their practice as a local social movement characterised by covert cultural forms of resistance against colonial and missionary condemnation. Starting from the 1910s, there were many reports by colonial native commissioners and missionaries castigating the practice, especially the numerous deaths of initiates.[5] Despite numerous spirited attempts to stop Yao male circumcision by native commissioners and missionaries, the Yao resolutely continued with the rite by conducting it deep in the forests or sometimes indoors. In post-colonial Zimbabwe, the Yao continued to use their rite to resist domination and marginalisation by indigenous Zimbabweans. This was typical of Scott's (1990) observations on cultural artful forms that act as hidden transcripts or discourses of resistance against power structures, where the weak hide their resistance in "ritualisms" of subordination. The local Shona and Ndebele scoffed at Yao foreign ancestry and their ritual, to the extent of taking away or burning down territorial spaces where the Yao conducted the practice.[6] In spite of this, the Yao found solace in persisting with the practice and this resistance was further consolidated by the discovery of the links between circumcision and HIV/AIDS and the resultant global donor interest, which in the process has made the Yao principal actors in the context of the epidemic in Zimbabwe.

IV. Circumcision, HIV prevention and donor interest

The Yao practice of circumcision is situated within a context in which there have been important recent scientific findings on HIV prevention and circumcision. The idea that male circumcision may protect against HIV infection was first introduced and developed in North America in 1986 by Professor Valiere Alcena. The theory was then promoted by Fink (1986) who maintained that removal of the penis foreskin and subsequent keratinisation of the penis glans reduced the chance of HIV penetration. Further research has demonstrated that the underside of the foreskin is mucosal and has a heavy concentration of macrophages, dendritic and Langerhan cells, which are the primary entry points for HIV infection (Ford 2006; Morris 1999). The Langerhan cells are rich in white blood cells and are vulnerable target cells for HIV, while the rest of the skin on the penis is highly impenetrable. Because the foreskin is not a strong piece of tissue, it is vulnerable to traumatic epithelial disruptions during intercourse, which can allow HIV to enter the bloodstream (Ford 2006; Morris 1999).

In recent years, there has been even greater support for male circumcision as a way to reduce HIV transmission. A 2002 study in South Africa among HIV-negative men aged 18 to 24 found strong evidence for this link. Half of the men in the study were randomly assigned to be circumcised, while the other half remained uncircumcised. The researchers found that for every ten uncircumcised men in the study who contracted HIV, only about three circumcised men did (Auvert 2005; Connolly and Simbayi 2008; Loygren 2005). In another study in Kenya and Uganda, men who were initially not infected with HIV were given safe sex instructions, and then were regularly checked for infection. The circumcised men were found to have a reduction of 53% in contracting new cases of HIV in Kenya and 48% in Uganda (Ford 2006).

Observational studies in sub-Saharan Africa have shown that circumcised men have a lower risk of acquiring HIV infection than uncircumcised men. Infection rates are much lower in Ghana (2.38%) and Kenya (11.64%), where circumcision is entrenched, than in Namibia (19.94%) and Botswana (25.1%) where circumcision is less prevalent (Barnett and Whiteside 2003; Loygren 2005; Whiteside and Loewenson 1997). The startling disparity between HIV prevalence in West Africa (where circumcision is prevalent) and southern Africa (where it is not) has led researchers to conclude that it is circumcision as an ingrained cultural and traditional practice that has kept HIV at bay.[7]

While evidence on male circumcision is still somewhat inconclusive and sceptics do exist (Bonner 2001), the fact that the WHO has recommended circumcision to reduce HIV infection means that the practice has validity within the global health community. Even though no statistical data exist yet, it can be argued that the Yao in Zimbabwe have helped to curtail the spread of sexually transmitted diseases (STDs) including HIV and AIDS through their circumcision practice. These observations have led to donor interest in the Yao male circumcision rite.

V.   Yao circumcision and mobilisation against HIV and AIDS

A.   Collaboration with the state and donors

As argued above, Yao male circumcision has evolved into a local social movement around which the Yao have constructed and negotiated their collective identity and mobilised against challenges in Zimbabwe. It is these same characteristics that are being reinvented in the fight against HIV and AIDS in a new donor-funded context. While the knowledge that circumcision reduces HIV infection gained much prominence in Zimbabwe after 2007, it was only in 2009 that state- and donor-funded public campaigns to promote circumcision expanded, initially through both print and electronic media (TV commercials, newspaper adverts and billboards) and later through collaborative state and donor public outreach programmes. Before this, many Yao people were not aware that their ancient cultural practice had health benefits, or that they practised a rite that further "othered" or "set them further apart" in the fight against AIDS. Musa Chetambara noted that "we just conducted circumcision as per cultural custom and did not know its health benefits against the pandemic until now and this makes our rite more important and attractive to our Yao community and the Zimbabwean society as a whole".[8]

The sudden state and donor interest in circumcision and AIDS has seen many advocacy networks and organisations being at the forefront of this drive to promote circumcision in Zimbabwe, and these have been funded mainly by the US Agency for International Development (USAID), the Global Fund, and Population Services International (PSI). The networks include the New Start Centre (NSC), which is responsible for HIV tests and counselling, and the Zimbabwe AIDS Network. The government, through its Ministry of Health, has also promoted circumcision awareness campaigns and introduced an AIDS levy or tax on its citizens that is administered by the National AIDS Council (NAC) to prevent the spread of the disease and provide HIV-positive people with medication. Dr Blessing Mutede, who is the NAC public health officer, stated that the AIDS levy is pegged at two per cent of one's salary (Yikoniko 2012). In her 31 July 2011 *Sunday Mail* article entitled "Circumcised men are 'smart'", Fortunate Gova reported that free male circumcision is currently available at Harare Central Hospital, Bulawayo Eye Clinic, Manyame Air Base Hospital, Mutare Provincial Hospital, Concession Hospital, and Mt Darwin's Karanda Mission Hospital. Mobile male circumcision services are also available nationwide, especially during public outreach campaigns. For example, every summer, a one-month-long Summer Smart Male Circumcision Campaign, which is part of the Voluntary Medical Male Circumcision Programme, is held countrywide to encourage men to get circumcised and be smart (Gova 2011).

This interest in circumcision to prevent HIV infection has led to the promotion of Yao circumcision by the Zimbabwean state and citizens, and donors. Many are now promoting and assisting Yao mobilisation efforts through public health campaigns, advertisements and even through persuasion. For example, in 2010, state- and donor-sponsored calendars, T-shirts and caps were produced and freely distributed across the whole country, publicising and citing the benefits of male circumcision in fighting HIV. The country's major roads and towns are also dotted with big billboards promoting male circumcision (see Figure 1 below). On 24 June 2012, the promotion was further bolstered by 44 Zimbabwean legislators or members of parliament who got circumcised under the Zimbabwe Parliamentarians against HIV and AIDS programme (ZIPAH), a voluntary organisation made up of members of parliament that is aimed at promoting awareness and fighting the stigma associated with HIV and AIDS (Chipunza 2012). The initiative, dubbed "Parliamentarians making the smart choice", seeks to send a message to male constituents in order to encourage them to follow suit. Population Services International Zimbabwe country director Ms Louisa Norman hailed the legislators for taking such an important step in promoting male circumcision by saying that "[t]hese are leaders setting an example for their communities, their constituencies and the country as a whole" (Chipunza 2012).

Although clinical circumcision is now at the core of these public campaigns, the state and donor community are also not discouraging people from the traditional ritualised Yao circumcision. Members of the Yao community, especially the traditional circumcisers, are also being approached by the state health and donor agencies for professional training. The NAC and the NSC have collaborated with the Yao to facilitate the training of their circumcision doctors so as to professionalise their occupation. About ten individuals have benefited from this exercise so far.[9] The NAC and NSC are providing medical doctors to facilitate clinical circumcision of Yao youths/initiates in public hospitals, before the Yao elders take the initiates to the circumcision schools for the duration of the initiation rite.

Figure 1. State and donor efforts in promoting male circumcision in Zimbabwe 2010. Note: Zimbabwe calendar produced by PSI, NAC, USAID and the Ministry of Health and Child Welfare (taken from *The Sunday Mail*, 15 July 2012).

In January 2010, the NSC in conjunction with Harare Central Hospital circumcised about 50 Yao initiates during the school holidays.[10] The state and donors have intensified their clinical circumcision of the Yao and other interested Zimbabweans such that about 70,000 men have been circumcised since the launch of the campaign in 2009 (Yikoniko 2012). The Head of the HIV and TB unit at the Ministry of Health and Child Welfare, Dr Owen Mugurungi, stated that the Zimbabwe campaign is targeting 1.2 million boys and men to be circumcised by 2015 (Yikoniko 2012).

These campaigns have also publicised hitherto unknown hygienic benefits of circumcision to the Zimbabwean populace, a process which has further reinforced the Yao rite and identity. Musa Chetambara asserted that a circumcised person is more clean and hygienic than an uncircumcised one because of the absence of the foreskin under which bacteria accumulates.[11] Funani (1990) substantiates this by noting that various medical practitioners have asserted that removing the foreskin to expose the glans penis prevents the accumulation, from a number of glands, of an odoriferous cheese-like substance called smegma, which can cause discomfort and infection. This benefit has always appealed to initiates and the Yao have emphasised it in their mobilisation against AIDS, both among the Yao and the wider population. For example, the Yao circumcision doctors have been part of the Summer Smart Male Circumcision Campaign and radio and television adverts and jingles where they stress the improved personal hygiene benefits of circumcision (Gova 2011).

Yao attitudes have also experienced a drastic change in the wake of the discovery of the link between HIV prevention and male circumcision. Before the discovery, the Yao rarely discussed their circumcision in public, because society would laugh and mock them. Young graduate initiates always had a tough time concealing their penises from curious friends when bathing, swimming or urinating in public. Austin Kalonje recalls that he resorted to bathing at midnight at boarding school when everyone was asleep so as to avoid prying eyes of fellows who were curious to know about his experiences at a Yao circumcision school in 2003.[12] With the AIDS links and benefits, Yao attitudes towards privacy have changed. In fact the Yao have gained some newfound respect since male circumcision has become fashionable and is being marketed as the smart thing to do; it has become an integral part of the imagery of a "real modern man". Ishmael Mwanyalu observes that "circumcision has become an intrinsic part of the real modern man and now most Yao are keen and free to talk about their status and experiences in public".[13] This has been bolstered by the "smart" campaigns among other outreach programmes that encourage circumcision (Gova 2011).

The Yao have also used their Islamic connections to capture donor interest from the Arab or Muslim world and in the process, consolidate their Yao identity in Zimbabwe. Much of the funding to fight AIDS has come from Middle East nations, especially the United Arab Emirates and Iran, and has been channelled through their Cultural Consulate Sections in their embassies in Zimbabwe. Some of the money is given to the main Muslim Teaching School known as Iqra Daarul Ilm, located in Harare, Zimbabwe's capital city, where many aspiring Yao youths are trained to become proper Islamic sheikhs and circumcision doctors.[14]

All of this external attention to Yao circumcision has had a contentious impact on the Yao community and on the practice itself. In some cases, the attention has led to the reconfiguration of the practice to satisfy donor needs. For example, with the increasing Islamic funding, some Yao circumcision practitioners and doctors such as Jafari Kawinga from the Dalny Mine in Chakari have broadly accommodated Islamic teachings within their rituals.[15] However, these external connections have led to generational debates within the Yao communities. Most Yao elders have been against external interference into their rite. Musa Chetambara, the circumcision doctor, has always been very sceptical about state and donor interest in their practice, arguing that it gives outsiders the chance to contaminate their cultural rite and identity.[16] Yao youth such as John Amidu and Austin Kalonje, on the other hand, find the attention very beneficial to the Yao community in the long run. They argue that this outside interest improves and refines their practice in fighting AIDS and helps to publicise and promote Yao identity in Zimbabwe through the many campaigns.[17] All of these debates show that identity formation is dynamic and is not a smooth, static process but highly debatable. This is also part of the contention found in social movements. Nonetheless, all of these developments have also triggered the Yao to redesign their initiation institutions, as well as the nature of their teachings within their circumcision schools.

B.   Circumcision schools as focal points for mobilisation against HIV and AIDS

Much of the Yao mobilisation against AIDS has been carried out within their circumcision or initiation schools, which have acted as "weapons of the weak" in which "hidden transcripts" of resistance against AIDS and domination have been carried out and acted. The circumcision school which is known as the *ndagala* is always located in the forest for privacy purposes. The secluded bush camp has a long but narrow shelter built of grass and twigs to serve as the sleeping quarters for the initiates.[18] Yao boys usually go to the circumcision school beginning at the age of eight and the school lasts for about a month. The school is held during the winter months of June to September so that the initiates' wounds will not fester as they might in hotter temperatures. Furthermore, this period is devoid of the discomfort of rains, which could disturb the smooth running of the initiation school. Systematic indoctrination about Yao culture and identity is accomplished through various activities, songs and sacred teachings on sex, sexuality, health, hygiene, death, marriage, and procreation. These curricula are meant to inculcate a sense of belonging to a common and collective Yao identity.

AIDS education within the Yao circumcision schools began to creep into their curricula from the late 1990s, when the disease had become more severe in Zimbabwe. At that time, the Yao were not aware of the potential health benefits of circumcision in the fight against AIDS. According to Ali Manangwa, "AIDS education was limited to the obvious and general risks posed by the disease and emphasis was on the fact that it was not curable".[19] Another graduate, Austin Kalonje, adds that AIDS was not treated with the respect it deserved. In fact, demonstrations about how to use protection, especially condoms, were regarded by the circumcision doctors and guardians as unnecessary.[20] While not helpful for AIDS awareness, this practice may have been rooted in the contentious desire by Yao elders to maintain the purity of the practice and preserve the Yao identity. The circumcision doctors Chetambara and Kawinga noted that, at that time, they wanted to maintain the traditions of their rite as much as possible, without interference or contamination from modernity, so that the Yao identity would be preserved.[21]

Nonetheless, the recent state and donor interest in circumcision has led to the reconfiguration of the Yao rite as it responds to outside factors like science and HIV itself. One of the early changes was to address contentious health and hygiene concerns over the surgical act itself. As late as 2003, some Yao circumcision schools continued to use a single tool for group circumcisions. Fearing for their hygiene and HIV infection, some potential Yao initiates were sceptical about using a single knife or razor blade for all members during traditional circumcision. Because of the high prevalence of HIV infection and persuasion from parents and the initiates themselves, each initiate began to be allocated his own razor blade for the act. Many Yao elders, and especially the doctors, were at first reluctant to change but they were compelled to do so over time because of the risks posed by the disease and other hygienic concerns. Chetambara and Kawinga were at the forefront in resisting the change in pursuit of identity preservation, and many Yao initiates avoided their circumcision schools until they reformed and embraced the change in 2003.[22]

Another change in the initiation schools' curricula was teaching initiates why and how to use condoms, urging other protective methods such as abstinence, and discussing the need to limit exposure to multiple partners. Initiates are also discouraged from practising dry sex, which is believed to increase the risk of HIV infection.[23] The circumcision school acts as a medium that teaches the youth social principles on marriage, particularly monogamy and endogamy, which helps in the mobilisation of AIDS prevention, as the initiates are urged to uphold and respect their Yao marriage institutions. The AIDS lessons also focus on the possible dangers or limits of circumcision today. It has been observed that circumcision usually alters sexual behaviour, as circumcised men have a greater tendency to engage in riskier "more highly elaborated" sexual practices (Gova 2011; Yikoniko 2012). Such behaviour includes less frequent use of condoms, anal sex, or sex with multiple partners. Initiates are usually made aware of such dangers and are always encouraged to use protective methods. All of this sex education within the initiation schools prepares the Yao youth for the dangers posed by the pandemic.

The experiences and teachings within the circumcision schools provide a fertile platform for the initiates and their guardians or leaders to bond and create a collective identity that allows them to share knowledge and mobilise against HIV. In most cases, the knowledge learnt is usually shared and spread outside by enthusiastic initiates through practice and interaction with friends, colleagues, girlfriends, or spouses. For example, borrowing from the Summer Smart campaign, some Yao graduate initiates in Mashonaland West province have established an organisation known as the Yao Boys Association, aimed at encouraging other non-Yao boys to get circumcised and become real and smart adults. Austin Kalonje, who is the president of the organisation, said that their aim is to spread the message about the merits of circumcision and in the process make local people appreciate the Yao circumcision rite and Yao identity.[24] In a way this has led to the expansion or spread of Yao social mobilisation against AIDS outside of the circle of initiates, leading to a unique but unheralded social movement that is contributing to the HIV and AIDS fight. While statistical data on Yao HIV prevalence rates is not available, going by the general scientific observations and state/donor campaigns, it can be asserted that the Yao circumcision schools are acting as cultural "weapons of the weak" or "hidden transcripts" through which the Yao community has been fighting the epidemic in Zimbabwe.

VI. Conclusion

The study has examined the practice of male circumcision among the Yao, showing its importance as a platform for social mobilisation or activism against AIDS. It has revealed that this mobilisation is a complex process involving continuous reconfiguration of the rite and the reconstruction and repositioning of Yao collective identity in relation to the sudden state and donor interest in the practice. As a traditional rite, Yao circumcision has been central to defining their identity in Zimbabwe and they have used its appeal to collectively bond and mobilise around a common cause. The practice has since the colonial times separated the Yao from fellow migrants, other Muslims and indigenous Zimbabweans. They have also used it as an alternative form of resistance to the dominant hegemonies in Zimbabwe. With the emergence of the circumcision–AIDS links, the study has shown that the ethnically defined Yao formation has transformed into a social movement through the repositioning of their circumcision in the context of HIV prevention. Yao identity has been reinforced and their ritual has been reconfigured to fit into the new global context of mobilisation through advocacy networks and donor aid. The realisation that their practice has health benefits has brought a new sense of respect for the Yao people, and in the process they have become important actors by collaborating with the state and donor agencies to mobilise against AIDS. They have made the surgical act less risky and incorporated AIDS curricula into their circumcision schools. New forms of Yao identity have emerged as the Zimbabwean state has promoted the cultural rite and the image of a Yao man as the real modern and smart man through mobile campaigns, print and electronic adverts, and jingles. Ironically, what was once viewed as a primitive cultural ritual has become one of the World Health Organization's trump cards in the fight against the deadly disease. This has brought the Yao into a broader social movement, characterised by global donor interest. The potential impact of these new global connections on Yao identity is still unclear and debatable and it is part of the contention found in social movements worldwide. All of this demands further research, including how and if the education that individuals receive in the initiation schools actually works.

Notes

1. Interview with Ali Manangwa (Yao graduate), by author. Riverside Farm, Banket, 16 May 2010.
2. Interview with Musa Chetambara (circumcision doctor), by author. Inchefu Farm, Raffingora, 13 May 2010.

3. Interview with Austin Kalonje (Yao graduate), by author. Ayrshire Mine, Banket, 15 May 2010.
4. Interview with Musa Chetambara (circumcision doctor), by author. Inchefu Farm, Raffingora, 13 May 2010.
5. From the 1910s deaths caused by incorrect circumcision methods, mistakes like cutting/slitting the glans penis together with the foreskin or the failure of wounds to heal leading to sepsis were reported. For example, in 1913, three circumcision-related deaths were reported by the Native Commissioner of the Hartley district, E. G. Howman. Another death caused by *septic nephritis*, which is often associated with circumcision, was also reported in 1914 by Native Commissioner L. C. Meredith in Hartley (National Archives of Zimbabwe 1913, 1914).
6. Most of the informants testified about the xenophobic tendencies of indigenous Zimbabweans towards migrants, especially Malawian descendants, who are treated as foreigners or "aliens".
7. However it should be noted that there are other factors that limit HIV prevalence in West Africa, such as less migration by individuals, polygamy, early marriage for women in Muslim societies, and relatively low levels of alcohol use. Likewise, in West Africa, the less virulent HIV 2 strain is more prevalent than HIV 1, the strain responsible for the global pandemic.
8. Interview with Musa Chetambara (circumcision doctor), by author. Inchefu Farm, Raffingora, 13 May 2010.
9. Interview with Jafari Kawinga (circumcision doctor), by author. Dalny Mine, Chakari, 20 May 2010; interview with Musa Chetambara (circumcision doctor), by author. Inchefu Farm, Raffingora, 13 May 2010.
10. The author visited the New Start Centre and interacted with the Yao coordinators and initiates who were first tested for HIV and then circumcised, and later transported to the initiation camp on the outskirts of the city of Harare.
11. Interview with Musa Chetambara (circumcision doctor), by author. Inchefu Farm, Raffingora, 13 May 2010.
12. Interview with Austin Kalonje (Yao graduate), by author. Ayrshire Mine, Banket, 15 May 2010.
13. Interview with Ishmael Mwanyalu (Yao graduate), by author. Inchefu Farm, Raffingora, 13 May 2010.
14. The Muslim school is found in a residential suburb called Waterfalls and was established in the early 1980s. It enrols Yao youth to learn Islamic practices and the Arabic language and culture.
15. Interview with Jafari Kawinga (circumcision doctor), by author. Dalny Mine, Chakari, 20 May 2010.
16. Interview with Musa Chetambara (circumcision doctor), by author. Inchefu Farm, Raffingora, 13 May 2010.
17. Interview with Austin Kalonje (Yao graduate), by author. Ayrshire Mine, Banket, 15 May 2010; interview with John Amidu (Yao graduate), by author. Ayrshire Mine, Banket, 15 May 2010.
18. Interview with John Amidu (Yao graduate), by author. Ayrshire Mine, Banket, 15 May 2010.
19. Interview with Ali Manangwa (Yao graduate), by author. Riverside Farm, Banket, 16 May 2010.
20. Interview with Austin Kalonje (Yao graduate), by author. Ayrshire Mine, Banket, 15 May 2010.
21. Interview with Jafari Kawinga (circumcision doctor), by author. Dalny Mine, Chakari, 20 May 2010; interview with Musa Chetambara (circumcision doctor), by author. Inchefu Farm, Raffingora, 13 May 2010.
22. Interview with Jafari Kawinga (circumcision doctor), by author. Dalny Mine, Chakari, 20 May 2010; interview with Musa Chetambara (circumcision doctor), by author. Inchefu Farm, Raffingora, 13 May 2010.
23. Dry sex is a popular and pervasive practice in sub-Saharan Africa which involves the drying and/or tightening of the vagina by various methods of douching and/or application of leaves and powders to absorb the vaginal lubrication, purportedly to increase the man's sexual pleasure. This practice dramatically increases HIV infection risk because it may itself cause abrasion and lacerations of the vagina, thus creating entry points for the HIV virus.
24. Interview with Austin Kalonje (Yao graduate), by author. Ayrshire Mine Banket, 15 May 2010.

Bibliography

Auvert, Betran, Dirk Taljaard, Emmanuel Lagarde, Joe Sobngwi-Tambekou, Remi Sitta and Adrian Puren. 2005. "Randomized, Controlled Intervention Trial of Male Circumcision for Reduction of HIV Infection Risk: The ANRS 1265 Trial." *PLoS Med* 2 (11): 1112–1122.

Barnett, Tony, and Alan Whiteside. 2003. *AIDS in the 21st Century: Disease and Globalization*. Basingstoke and New York: Palgrave Macmillan.

Bonner, Kate. 2001. "Male Circumcision as an HIV Control Strategy: Not a 'Natural Condom'." *Reproductive Health Matters* 9 (18): 143–155.

Chikova, Larisa. 2010. "Celebrating Circumcision." *The Sunday Mail*, 6 June.

Chimedza, Paul. 2006. "Can Circumcision Help Prevent HIV Infection?" *The Sunday Mail*, 2 April.

Chipunza, Paidamoyo. 2012. "Forty MPs Circumcised." *The Herald*, 25 June.

Connolly, Catherine, and Leickness Simbayi. 2008. "Male Circumcision and Its Relationship to HIV Infection in South Africa: Results of a National Survey in 2002." *South African Medical Journal* 98 (10): 789–794.

Daimon, Anusa. 2007. "Kukalamba: Trials and Tribulations of Aged Former Malawian Migrant Workers in Squalid Residential Zones: The Case of Epworth Suburb in Harare." Conference paper presented at the Nordic Africa Institute conference on ageing in African cities: Revisiting the issues, responses and outcomes. Zomba, Malawi. 29 November–1 December.

Ellis, Stephen, and Ineke van Kessel. 2009. "Introduction: African Social Movements or Social Movements in Africa?" In *Movers and Shakers: Social Movements in Africa*, edited by Stephen Ellis, and Ineke van Kessel, 1–16. Leiden: Brill Publishers.

Fink, Aaron. 1986. "A Possible Explanation for Heterosexual Male Infection with AIDS." *New England Journal of Medicine* 315 (18): 1167.

Ford, Matt. 2006. "Circumcision Significantly Reduces HIV and AIDS Risk." *Ars Technica*, 12 July. http://arstechnica.com/science/news/2006/12/6287.ars

Funani, Lumka. 1990. *Circumcision Among the Ama-Xhosa: A Medical Investigation*. Braamfontein: Skotaville.

Gova, Fortunate. 2011. "Circumcised Men are 'Smart'." *The Sunday Mail*, 31 July.

Keck, Margaret, and Kathryn Sikkink. 1998. *Activists Beyond Borders: Advocacy Networks in International Politics*. Ithaca and London: Cornell University Press.

Kubik, Gerhard. 1978. "Boys Circumcision School of the Yao – A Cinematographic Documentation at Chief Makanjila's Village in Malawi, 1967." *Review of Ethnology* 6: 1–7.

Leach-Lemens, Carole. 2010. "Zimbabwe HIV Prevalence Rate Declining." *The Sunday Mail*, 13 June.

Loygren, Stefan. 2005. "Circumcision Can Reduce AIDS Risk Study Says." *National Geographic News*, 27 July.

Mandivenga, Ephraim. 1989. "The History and 'Re-conversion' of the VaRemba of Zimbabwe." *Journal of Religion in Africa* 19 (2): 98–124.

Melucci, Alberto. 1996. *Challenging Codes: Collective Action in the Information Age*. Cambridge: Cambridge University Press.

Mitchell, Clyde. 1951. "The Yao of Southern Nyasaland." In *Seven Tribes of British Central Africa*, edited by Eric Colson, and Mark Gluckman, 292–353. London: Oxford University Press.

Morris, Brian. 1999. *In Favour of Circumcision*. Sydney: University of New South Wales Press.

Mudenge, Stanley. 1988. *A Political History of Munhumutapa*. Harare: Zimbabwe Publishing House.

National Archives of Zimbabwe. 1913. "Native Commissioner Hartley." Annual Report for Year Ended December 1913. S2184. Harare, Zimbabwe.

National Archives of Zimbabwe. 1914. "Native Commissioner Gatooma and Hartley, L.C. Meredith." Annual Report for Year Ended December 1914. S2184. Harare, Zimbabwe.

Nkrumah, Gorkeh Gamal. 1991. "Islam in Southern Africa." *Review of African Political Economy* 18 (52): 94–97.

Nyathi, Pathisa. 2008. *Zimbabwe's Cultural Heritage*. Bulawayo: Amabooks.

Pikirayi, Innocent. 2001. *The Zimbabwe Culture: Origins and Decline of Southern Zambezian States*. New York: Altamina Press.

Raftopoulos, Brian, and Ian Phimister. 1997. *Keep on Knocking: A History of Labour and the Labour Movement in Zimbabwe 1900–97*. Harare: Baobab Books.

Ranger, Terence. 1985. *The Invention of Tribalism in Zimbabwe*. Gweru: Mambo Press.

Sanderson, Meredith. 1920. "Relationships Among the Wayao." *The Journal of the Royal Anthropological Institute of Great Britain and Ireland* 50: 369–376.

Sanderson, Meredith. 1955. "Inyago: The Picture-Models of the Yao Initiation Ceremonies." *The Nyasaland Journal* 8 (2): 36–57.

Scott, James. 1990. *Domination and the Arts of Resistance*. London: Yale University Press.

Thorold, Alan. 1995. "The Yao Muslims: Religion and Social Change in Southern Malawi." PhD thesis, University of Cambridge.

UNAIDS. 2010. *Global Report: UNAIDS Report on the Global AIDS Epidemic*. http://www.unaids. org/globalreport/global_report.htm

van Onselen, Charles. 1976. *Chibaro: African Mine Labour in Southern Rhodesia 1900–1933*. Johannesburg: Ravan Press.

Whiteside, Alan, and Rene Loewenson. 1997. *Social and Economic Issues of HIV and AIDS in Southern Africa: A Review of Current Research*. Harare: Southern Africa HIV and AIDS Information Dissemination Service.

Yikoniko, Shamiso. 2012. "Circumcised Men Not Spared from HIV Infection." *The Sunday Mail*, 8 July.

Zeitlyn, David. 2005. "The Documentary Impulse: Archives in the Bush." *History in Africa* 32 (1): 415–434.

Index

139

For Product Safety Concerns and Information please contact our EU representative GPSR@taylorandfrancis.com Taylor & Francis Verlag GmbH, Kaufingerstraße 24, 80331 München, Germany

Batch number: 08158490

Printed by Printforce, the Netherlands